PRAYERS THAT AVAIL MUCH

25TH ANNIVERSARY COMMEMORATIVE EDITION

Three Bestselling Volumes
Complete in One Book

James 5:16

by

Germaine Copeland
Word Ministries, Inc.

And this is the confidence that we have in him, that, if we ask any thing according to his will, he heareth us: and if we know that he hear us, whatsoever we ask, we know that we have the petitions that we desired of him.

1 John 5:14,15

Harrison House
Tulsa, Oklahoma

Presented to

_____

By

_____

Date

_____

Occasion

_____

CONTENTS

C. PRAYERS FOR THE NEEDS AND CONCERNS OF THE INDIVIDUAL

D. PRAYERS FOR THE NEEDS AND CONCERNS OF THE SINGLE, DIVORCED, AND WIDOWED

E. PRAYERS FOR THE NEEDS AND CONCERNS OF MARRIAGE PARTNERS AND HEADS OF HOUSEHOLDS

F. PRAYERS FOR CHILDREN

Part II: Group Prayers

A. AN INTERCESSORY PRAYER GROUP

A WORD TO THE READER

Dear Friend,

It was twenty-five years ago when Harrison House agreed to publish *Prayers That Avail Much*. The original book was a compilation of prayers that I wrote for my marriage and family situations, and included prayers composed by members of a prayer group that I was conducting. The "little yellow book" turned up in unusual places bringing hope, salvation, healing and deliverance to people who were looking for answers.

Several books of Scriptural prayers have been written over the years. Thousands have learned to go before the Throne of Grace with confidence and boldness. They learned to offer their petitions to the Father with Thansgiving, and the testimonies we receive continue to come in.

A special thanks to over four million readers who buy and give these books to others because these prayers are practical and workable. I am grateful to our publisher, the churches and bookstores who continue to believe in the value of these books, which are proven, effective spiritual tools for prayer. Today they are also available in several languages.

This classic book of Scriptural prayers is designed to enhance your ability to pray effectively for specific needs. Whether you are a seasoned prayer or a novice, never forget the power of prayer. It is the very foundation that enables you to go from faith to faith and glory to glory.

Sincerely in His Love,

Germaine Copeland
President of Word Ministries, Inc.
The Home of *Prayers That Avail Much* Family of Books

HOW TO PRAY
PRAYERS THAT AVAIL MUCH®

The prayers in this book are to be used by you for yourself and for others. They are a matter of the heart. Deliberately pray and meditate on each prayer. Allow the Holy Spirit to make the Word a reality in your heart. Your spirit will become alive to God's Word, and you will begin to think like God thinks and talk like He talks. You will find yourself poring over His Word, hungering for more and more. The Father rewards those who diligently seek Him (Heb. 11:6).

Research and contemplate the spiritual significance of each verse listed with the prayers. These are by no means the only Scriptures on certain subjects, but they are a beginning.

These prayers are a guide for you to have a more intimate relationship with your Heavenly Father. The study of His Word transforms your mind and lifestyle. Then others will know that it is possible to change, and you will give hope to those who come to you seeking advice. When you admonish someone with the Word, you are offering spiritual guidance and consolation.

Walk in God's counsel, and prize His wisdom (Ps. 1; Prov. 4:7,8). People are looking for something on which they can depend. When someone in need comes to you, you can point him to that portion in God's Word that is the answer to his problem. You become victorious, trustworthy, and the one with the answer, for your heart is fixed and established on His Word (Ps. 112).

Once you begin delving into God's Word, you must commit to ordering your conversation aright (Ps. 50:23). That is being a doer of the Word. Faith always has a good report. You cannot pray effectively for yourself, for someone else, or about something and then talk negatively about the matter (Matt. 12:34-37). This is being double minded, and a double-minded man receives *nothing* from God (James 1:6-8).

In Ephesians 4:29, 30 AMP it is written:

> **Let no foul or polluting language, nor evil word, nor unwholesome or worthless talk [ever] come out of your mouth; but only such [speech] as is good and beneficial to the spiritual progress of others, as is fitting to the need and the occasion, that it may be a blessing and give grace (God's favor) to those who hear it.**

> **And do not grieve the Holy Spirit of God, (do not offend, or vex, or sadden Him) by Whom you were sealed (marked, branded as God's own, secured) for the day of redemption — of final deliverance through Christ from evil and the consequences of sin.**

Reflect on these words and give them time to keep your perspective in line with God's will. Our Father has much, so very much, to say about that little member, the tongue (James 3). Give the devil no opportunity by getting into worry, unforgiveness, strife, and criticism. Put a stop to idle and foolish talking (Eph. 4:27; 5:4). You are to be a blessing to others (Gal. 6:10).

Talk the answer, not the problem. The answer is in God's Word. You must have knowledge of that Word — revelation knowledge (1 Cor. 2:7-16). The Holy Spirit, your Teacher, will reveal the things that have been freely given to us by God (John 14:26).

As an intercessor, unite with others in prayer. United prayer is a mighty weapon that the Body of Christ is to use.

Have the faith of God, and approach Him confidently. When you pray according to His will, He hears you. Then you know you have what you ask of Him (1 John 5:14,15 NIV). "Do not throw away your confidence; it will be richly rewarded" (Heb. 10:35 NIV). Allow your spirit to pray by the Holy Spirit. Praise God for the victory now before any manifestation. *Walk by faith and not by sight* (2 Cor. 5:7).

When your faith comes under pressure, don't be moved. As Satan attempts to challenge you, resist him steadfastly in the faith — letting patience have her perfect work (James 1:4). Take the Sword of the Spirit and the shield of faith and quench his every fiery dart (Eph. 6:16,17). The entire substitutionary work of Christ was for you. Satan is now a defeated foe because Jesus conquered him (Col. 2:14,15). Satan is overcome by the blood of the Lamb and the word of our testimony (Rev. 12:11). "Fight the good fight of faith" (1 Tim. 6:12). Withstand the adversary and be firm in faith against his onset — rooted, established, strong, and determined (1 Pet. 5:9). Speak God's Word boldly and courageously.

Your desire should be to please and to bless the Father. As you pray according to His Word, He joyfully hears that you — His child — are living and walking in the truth (3 John 4).

How exciting to know that the prayers of the saints are forever in the throne room (Rev. 5:8). Hallelujah!

Praise God for His Word and the limitlessness of prayer in the name of Jesus. It belongs to every child of God. Therefore, run with patience the race that is set before you, looking unto Jesus, the Author and Finisher of your faith (Heb. 12:1,2). God's Word is able to build you up and give you your rightful inheritance among all God's set-apart ones (Acts 20:32).

Commit yourself to pray, and to pray correctly, by approaching the throne with your mouth filled with His Word!

EFFECTUAL PRAYER

The earnest (heartfelt, continued) prayer of a righteous man makes tremendous power available — dynamic in its working.

James 5:16 AMP

Prayer is fellowshiping with the Father — a vital, personal contact with God, Who is more than enough. We are to be in constant communion with Him:

For the eyes of the Lord are upon the righteous — those who are upright and in right standing with God — and His ears are attentive (open) to their prayer....

1 Peter 3:12 AMP

Prayer is not to be a religious form with no power. It is to be effective and accurate and bring *results*. God watches over His Word to perform it (Jer. 1:12).

Prayer that brings results must be based on God's Word.

For the Word that God speaks is alive and full of power — making it active, operative, energizing and effective; it is sharper than any two-edged sword, penetrating to the dividing line of the breath of life (soul) and [the immortal] spirit, and of joints and marrow [that is, of the deepest parts of our nature] exposing and sifting and analyzing and judging the very thoughts and purposes of the heart.

Hebrews 4:12 AMP

Prayer is this "1iving" Word in our mouths. Our mouths must speak forth faith, for faith is what pleases God (Heb. 11:6). We hold His Word up to Him in prayer, and our Father sees Himself in His Word.

God's Word is our contact with Him. We put Him in remembrance of His Word (Isa. 43:26), asking Him for what we need in the name of our Lord Jesus. The woman in Mark 5:25-34 placed a demand on the power of God when she said, "If I can but touch the hem of his garment, I will be healed." By faith she touched His clothes and was healed. We remind Him that He supplies all of our needs according to His riches in glory by Christ Jesus (Phil. 4:19). That Word does not return to Him void — without producing any effect, useless — but it *shall* accomplish that which He pleases and purposes, and it shall prosper in the thing for which He sent it (Isa. 55:11). Hallelujah!

God did *not* leave us without His thoughts and His ways for we have His Word — His bond. God instructs us to call Him, and He will answer and show us great and mighty things (Jer. 33:3). Prayer is to be exciting — not drudgery.

It takes someone to pray. God moves as we pray in faith — believing. He says that His eyes run to and fro throughout the whole earth to show Himself strong in behalf of those whose hearts are blameless toward Him (2 Chron. 16:9). We are blameless (Eph. 1:4). We are His very own children (Eph. 1:5). We are His righteousness in Christ Jesus (2 Cor. 5:21). He tells us to come boldly to the throne of grace and *obtain* mercy and find grace to help in time of need — appropriate and well-timed help (Heb. 4:16). Praise the Lord!

The prayer armor is for every believer, every member of the Body of Christ, who will put it on and walk in it, for the weapons of our warfare are *not carnal* but mighty through God for the pulling down of the strongholds of the enemy (Satan, the god of this world, and all his demonic forces). Spiritual warfare takes place in prayer (2 Cor. 10:4; Eph. 6:12,18).

There are many different kinds of prayer, such as the prayer of thanksgiving and praise, the prayer of dedication and worship, and the prayer that changes *things* (not God). All prayer involves a time of fellowshiping with the Father.

In Ephesians 6, we are instructed to take the Sword of the Spirit, which is the Word of God, and "pray at all times — on every occasion, in every season — in the Spirit, with all [manner of] prayer and entreaty" (Eph. 6:18 AMP).

In 1 Timothy 2 we are admonished and urged that "petitions, prayers, intercessions and thanksgivings be offered on behalf of all men" (1 Tim. 2:1 AMP). *Prayer is our responsibility.*

Prayer must be the foundation of every Christian endeavor. Any failure is a prayer failure. We are *not* to be ignorant concerning God's Word. God desires for His people to be successful, to be filled with a full, deep, and clear knowledge of His will (His Word) and to bear fruit in every good work (Col. 1:9-13). We then bring honor and glory to Him (John 15:8). He desires that we know how to pray, for "the prayer of the upright is his delight" (Prov. 15:8).

Our Father has not left us helpless. Not only has He given us His Word, but also He has given us the Holy Spirit to help our infirmities when we know not how to pray as we ought (Rom. 8:26). Praise God! Our Father has provided His people with every possible avenue to ensure their complete and total victory in this life in the name of our Lord Jesus (1 John 5:3-5).

We pray to the Father, in the name of Jesus, through the Holy Spirit, according to the Word!

Using God's Word on purpose, specifically, in prayer is one means of prayer, and it is a most effective and accurate means. Jesus said, "The words (truths) that I have been speaking to you are spirit and life" (John 6:63 AMP).

When Jesus faced Satan in the wilderness, He said, "It is written...it is written...it is written." We are to live, be upheld, and be sustained by every word that proceeds from the mouth of God (Matt. 4:4).

James, by the Spirit, admonishes that we do not have because we do not ask. We ask and receive not because we ask amiss (James 4:2,3). We must heed that admonishment now, for we are to become experts in prayer, rightly dividing the Word of Truth (2 Tim. 2:15).

Using the Word in prayer is *not* taking it out of context, for His Word in us is the key to answered prayer — to prayer that brings results. He is able to do exceedingly abundantly above all we ask or think, according to the power that works in us (Eph. 3:20). The power lies within God's Word. It is anointed by the Holy Spirit. The Spirit of God does not lead us apart from the Word, for the Word is of the Spirit of God. We apply that Word personally to ourselves and to others — not adding to or taking from it — in the name of Jesus. We apply the Word to the *now* — to those things, circumstances and situations facing each of us *now*.

Paul was very specific and definite in his praying. The first chapters of Ephesians, Philippians, Colossians, and 2 Thessalonians are examples of how Paul prayed for believers. There are numerous others. *Search them out.* Paul wrote under the inspiration of the Holy Spirit. We can use these Spirit-given prayers today!

In 2 Corinthians 1:11, 2 Corinthians 9:14, and Philippians 1:4, we see examples of how believers prayed one for another — putting others first in their prayer life with *joy.* Our faith does work by love (Gal. 5:6). We grow spiritually as we reach out to help others — praying for and with them and holding out to them the Word of Life (Phil. 2:16).

Man is a spirit, he has a soul, and he lives in a body (1 Thess. 5:23). In order to operate successfully, each of these three parts must be fed properly. The soul, or intellect, feeds on intellectual food to produce intellectual strength. The body feeds on physical food to produce physical strength. The spirit — the heart or inward man — is the real you, the part that has been reborn in Christ Jesus. It must feed on spiritual food, which is God's Word, in order to produce and develop faith. As we feast upon God's Word, our minds become renewed with His Word, and we have a fresh mental and spiritual attitude (Eph. 4:23,24).

Likewise, we are to present our bodies a living sacrifice, holy, acceptable unto God (Rom. 12:1) and not let that body dominate us but bring it into subjection to the spirit man (1 Cor. 9:27). God's Word is healing and health to all our flesh (Prov. 4:22). Therefore, God's Word affects each part of us — spirit, soul, and body. We become vitally united to the Father, to Jesus, and to the Holy Spirit — one with Them (John 16:13-15; John 17:21; Col. 2:10).

Purpose to hear, accept, and welcome the Word, and it will take root within your spirit and save your soul. Believe the Word, speak the Word, and act on the Word — it is a creative force. The Word is a double-edged sword. Often it places a demand on you to change attitudes and behaviors toward the person for whom you are praying.

Be doers of the Word and not hearers only, deceiving your own selves (James 1:22). Faith without works or corresponding action is *dead* (James 2:17). Don't be mental assenters — those who agree that the Bible is true but never act on it. *Real faith is acting on God's Word now.* We cannot build faith without practicing the Word. We cannot develop an effective prayer life that is anything but empty words unless God's Word actually has a part in our lives. We are to hold fast to our *confession* of the Word's truthfulness. Our Lord Jesus is the High Priest of our confession (Heb. 3:1), and He is the Guarantee of a better agreement — a more excellent and advantageous covenant (Heb. 7:22).

Prayer does not cause faith to work, but faith causes prayer to work. Therefore, any prayer problem is a lack of knowledge or a problem of doubt — doubting the integrity of the Word and the ability of God to stand behind His promises or the statements of fact in the Word.

You can spend fruitless hours in prayer if your heart is not prepared beforehand. Preparation of the heart, the spirit, comes from meditation in the Father's Word, meditation on who you are in Christ, what He is to you, and what the Holy Spirit can mean to you as you become God-inside minded. Just as God told Joshua (Josh. 1:8), as you meditate on the Word day and night and do according to all that is written, then shall you make your way prosperous and have good success. Attend to God's Word, submit to His sayings, keep them in the center of your heart, and put away contrary talk (Prov. 4:20-24).

The Holy Spirit is a divine helper, and He will direct your prayer and help you pray when you don't know how. When you use God's Word in prayer, this is *not* something you just rush through, uttering once. Do *not* be mistaken. There is nothing "magical" nor "manipulative" about it — no set pattern or device in order to satisfy what you want or think out of your flesh. Instead, you are holding God's Word before Him. Jesus said for you to ask the Father in His name.

We expect His divine intervention while we choose not to look at the things that are seen but at the things that are unseen, for the things that are seen are subject to change (2 Cor. 4:18).

Prayer based upon the Word rises above the senses, contacts the Author of the Word, and sets His spiritual laws into motion. It is not just saying prayers that gets results, but it is spending time with the Father, learning His wisdom, drawing on His strength, being filled with His quietness, and basking in His love that bring results to our prayers. Praise the Lord!

The prayers in this book are designed to teach and train you in the art of prayer. As you pray them, you will be reinforcing the prayer armor, which we have been instructed to put on in Ephesians 6:11. The fabric from which the armor is made is the Word of God. We are to live by every word that proceeds from the mouth of God. We desire the whole counsel of God because we know it changes us. By receiving that counsel, you will be "...transformed (changed) by the [entire] renewal of your mind — by its new ideals and its new attitude — so that you may prove [for yourselves] what is the good and acceptable and perfect will of God, even the thing which is good and acceptable and perfect [in His sight for you]" (Rom. 12:2 AMP).

The Personal Prayers (Part I) may be used as intercessory prayer by simply praying them in the third person, changing the pronouns *I* or *we* to the name of the person for whom you are interceding and then adjusting the verbs accordingly. The Holy Spirit is your Helper. Remember that you cannot control another's will, but your prayers prepare the way for the individual to hear truth and understand truth.

An often-asked question is this: "How many times should I pray the same prayer?"

The answer is simple: You pray until you know that the answer is fixed in your heart. After that, you need to repeat the prayer whenever adverse circumstances or long delays cause you to be tempted to doubt that your prayer has been heard and your request granted.

The Word of God is your weapon against the temptation to lose heart and grow weary in your prayer life. When that Word of promise becomes fixed in your heart, you will find yourself praising, giving glory to God for the answer, even when the only evidence you have of that answer is your own faith. Reaffirming your faith enforces the triumphant victory of our Lord Jesus Christ.

Another question often asked is this: "When we repeat prayers more than once, aren't we praying 'vain repetitions'?"

Obviously, such people are referring to the admonition of Jesus when He told His disciples: "And when you pray do not (multiply words, repeating the same ones over and over, and) heap up phrases as the Gentiles do, for they think they will be heard for their much speaking" (Matt. 6:7 AMP). Praying the Word of God is not praying the kind of prayer that the "heathen" pray. You will note in 1 Kings 18:25-29 the manner of prayer that was offered to the gods who could not hear. That is not the way you and I pray. The words that we speak are not vain, but they are spirit and life and mighty through God to the pulling down of strongholds. We have a God Whose eyes are over the righteous and Whose ears are open to us: When we pray, He hears us.

You are the righteousness of God in Christ Jesus, and your prayers will avail much. They will bring salvation to the sinner, deliverance to the oppressed, healing to the sick, and prosperity to the poor. They will usher in the next move of God on the earth. In addition to affecting outward circumstances and other people, your prayers will also affect you.

In the very process of praying, your life will be changed as you go from faith to faith and from glory to glory.

As a Christian, your first priority is to love the Lord your God with your entire being and your neighbor as yourself. You are called to be an intercessor, a man or woman of prayer. You are to seek the face of the Lord as you inquire, listen, meditate, and consider in the temple of the Lord.

As one of "God's set-apart ones," the will of the Lord for your life is the same as it is for the life of every other true believer: "Seek ye first the kingdom of God, and his righteousness; and all these things shall be added unto you" (Matt. 6:33).

PERSONAL CONFESSIONS

Jesus is Lord over my spirit, my soul, and my body (Phil. 2:9-11).

Jesus has been made unto me wisdom, righteousness, sanctification, and redemption. I can do all things through Christ Who strengthens me (1 Cor. 1:30; Phil. 4:13).

The Lord is my Shepherd. I do not want. My God supplies all my need according to His riches in glory in Christ Jesus (Ps. 23; Phil. 4:19).

I do not fret or have anxiety about anything. I do not have a care (Phil. 4:6; 1 Pet. 5:6,7).

I am the Body of Christ. I am redeemed from the curse, because Jesus bore my sicknesses and carried my diseases in His own body. By His stripes I am healed. I forbid any sickness or disease to operate in my body. Every organ, every tissue of my body functions in the perfection in which God created it to function. I honor God and bring glory to Him in my body (Gal. 3:13; Matt. 8:17; 1 Pet. 2:24; 1 Cor. 6:20).

I have the mind of Christ and hold the thoughts, feelings, and purposes of His heart (1 Cor. 2:16).

I am a believer and not a doubter. I hold fast to my confession of faith. I decide to walk by faith and practice faith. My faith comes by hearing, and hearing by the Word of God. Jesus is the Author and the Developer of my faith (Heb. 4:14; Heb. 11:6; Rom. 10:17; Heb. 12:2).

PERSONAL CONFESSIONS

The love of God has been shed abroad in my heart by the Holy Spirit, and His love abides in me richly. I keep myself in the Kingdom of light, in love, in the Word; and the wicked one touches me not (Rom. 5:5; 1 John 4:16; 1 John 5:18).

I tread upon serpents and scorpions and over all the power of the enemy. I take my shield of faith and quench his every fiery dart. Greater is He that is in me than he that is in the world (Ps. 91:13; Eph. 6:16; 1 John 4:4).

I am delivered from this present evil world. I am seated with Christ in heavenly places. I reside in the Kingdom of God's dear Son. The law of the Spirit of life in Christ Jesus has made me free from the law of sin and death (Gal. 1:4; Eph. 2:6; Col. 1:13; Rom. 8:2).

I fear *not*, for God has given me a spirit of power, of love, and of a sound mind. God is on my side (2 Tim. 1:7; Rom. 8:31).

I hear the voice of the Good Shepherd. I hear my Father's voice, and the voice of a stranger I will not follow. I roll my works upon the Lord. I commit and trust them wholly to Him. He will cause my thoughts to become agreeable to His will, and so shall my plans be established and succeed (John 10:27; Prov. 16:3).

I am a world overcomer because I am born of God. I represent the Father and Jesus well. I am a useful member in the Body of Christ. I am His workmanship recreated in Christ Jesus. My Father God is all the while effectually at work in me both to will and do His good pleasure (1 John 5:4,5; Eph. 2:10; Phil. 2:13).

I let the Word dwell in me richly. He Who began a good work in me will continue until the day of Christ (Col. 3:16; Phil. 1:6).

Personal Prayers

PART ONE

To Receive Jesus as Savior and Lord

Father, it is written in Your Word that if I confess with my mouth that Jesus is Lord and believe in my heart that You have raised Him from the dead, I shall be saved. Therefore, Father, I confess that Jesus is my Lord. I make Him Lord of my life right now. I believe in my heart that You raised Jesus from the dead. I renounce my past life with Satan and close the door to any of his devices.

I thank You for forgiving me of all my sin. Jesus is my Lord, and I am a new creation. Old things have passed away; now all things become new in Jesus' name. Amen.

Scripture References

John 3:16	John 14:6
John 6:37	Romans 10:9,10
John 10:10	Romans 10:13
Romans 3:23	Ephesians 2:1-10
2 Corinthians 5:19	2 Corinthians 5:17
John 16:8,9	John 1:12
Romans 5:8	2 Corinthians 5:21

To Pray

Father, in the name of Jesus, I thank You for calling me to be a fellow workman — a joint promoter and a laborer together — with You. I commit to pray and not to give up.

Jesus, You are the Son of God, and I will never stop trusting You. You are my High Priest, and You understand my weaknesses. So I come boldly to the throne of my gracious God. There I receive mercy and find grace to help when I need it.

There are times I do not know what I ought to pray for. Holy Spirit, I submit to Your leadership and thank You for interceding for us with groans that words cannot express. You search hearts and know the mind of the spirit, because You intercede for the saints in accordance with God's will.

Therefore, I am assured and know that (with God being a partner in my labor) all things work together and are [fitting into a plan] for my good, because I love God and am called according to [His] design and purpose.

I resist the temptation to be anxious about anything, but in every circumstance and in everything by prayer and petition [definite requests] with thanksgiving continue to make my wants (and the wants of others) known to God. Whatever I ask for in prayer, I believe that it is granted to me, and I will receive it.

TO PRAY

You made Christ, Who never sinned, to be the offering for our sin, so that we could be made right with You through Christ. Now my earnest (heartfelt, continued) prayer makes tremendous power available — dynamic in its working. Father, I live in You — abide vitally united to You — and Your words remain in me and continue to live in my heart. Therefore, I ask whatever I will, and it shall be done for me. When I produce much fruit it brings great glory to my Father — the Father of my Lord Jesus Christ. Amen.

Scripture References

1 Corinthians 3:9 NIV

Luke 18:1 NIV

Romans 8:26,27 NIV

Romans 8:28 AMP

Philippians 4:6 AMP

Mark 11:24 AMP

2 Corinthians 5:21 NLT

James 5:16 AMP

John 15:7,8 AMP

*T*o Be God-Inside Minded

I am a spirit learning to live in a natural world. I have a soul, and I live in a physical body. I am in the world, but I am not of the world. God of peace, I ask You to sanctify me in every way, and may my whole spirit and soul and body be kept blameless until that day when our Lord Jesus Christ comes again. Father, You called me, and You are completely dependable. You said it, and You will do this. Thank You for the Spirit Who guides me into all truth through my regenerated human spirit.

Lord, Your searchlight penetrates my human spirit, exposing every hidden motive. You actually gave me Your Spirit (not the world's spirit) so I can know the wonderful things You have given us. I am a child of God, born of the Spirit of God, filled with the Spirit of God, and led by the Spirit of God. I listen to my heart as I look to the Spirit inside me.

Thank You, Holy Spirit, for directing me and illuminating my mind. You lead me in the way I should go in all the affairs of life. You lead me by an inward witness. The eyes of my understanding are being enlightened. Wisdom is in my inward parts. God's love is perfected in me. I have an unction from the Holy One.

Father, I am becoming spirit-conscious. I listen to the voice of my spirit and obey what my spirit tells me. My spirit is controlled by the Holy Spirit and dominates me, for I walk not after the flesh, but after the spirit. I examine my leading in the light of the Word.

I trust in You, Lord, with all of my heart and lean not to my own understanding. In all of my ways I acknowledge You, and You direct my paths. I walk in the light of the Word. Holy Spirit, You are my Counselor, teaching me to educate, train, and develop my human spirit. The Word of God shall not depart out of my mouth. I meditate therein day and night. Therefore, I shall make my way prosperous, and I will have good success in life. I am a doer of the Word and put Your Word first.

Scripture References

1 Thessalonians 5:23,24	1 John 4:12
John 16:13	1 John 2:20
Proverbs 20:27 NLT	Romans 8:1
1 Corinthians 2:12 NLT	Proverbs 3:5,6
Romans 8:14,16	Psalm 119:105
John 3:6,7	John 14:26
Ephesians 5:18	Joshua 1:8
Isaiah 48:17	James 1:22
Ephesians 1:18	

*T*o Put On the Armor of God

*I*n the name of Jesus, I put on the whole armor of God, that I may be able to stand against the wiles of the devil; for I wrestle not against flesh and blood, but against principalities, powers, the rulers of the darkness of this world, and spiritual wickedness in high places.

Therefore, I take unto myself the whole armor of God, that I may be able to withstand in the evil day, and having done all, to stand. I stand, therefore, having my loins girt about with truth. Your Word, Lord, which is truth, contains all the weapons of my warfare, which are not carnal, but mighty through God to the pulling down of strongholds.

I have on the breastplate of righteousness, which is faith and love. My feet are shod with the preparation of the Gospel of peace. In Christ Jesus I have peace and pursue peace with all men. I am a minister of reconciliation, proclaiming the good news of the Gospel.

I take the shield of faith, wherewith I am able to quench all the fiery darts of the wicked; the helmet of salvation *(holding the thoughts, feelings, and purpose of God's heart);* and the sword of the Spirit, which is the Word of God. In the face of all trials, tests, temptations, and tribulation, I cut to pieces the snare of the enemy by speaking the Word of God. Greater is He that is in me than he that is in the world.

Thank You, Father, for the armor. I will pray at all times — on every occasion, in every season — in the Spirit, with all [manner of] prayer and entreaty. To that end I will keep alert and watch with strong purpose and perseverance, interceding in behalf of all the saints. My power and ability and sufficiency are from God Who has qualified me as a minister and a dispenser of a new covenant [of salvation through Christ]. Amen.

Scripture References

Ephesians 6:11-14	Psalm 34:14
John 17:17	2 Corinthians 5:18
2 Corinthians 10:4	Ephesians 6:16,17 AMP
Ephesians 6:14,15 AMP	1 John 4:4
Ephesians 2:14	2 Corinthians 3:5,6 AMP

To Rejoice in the Lord

This is the day the Lord has made. I rejoice and I am glad in it! I rejoice in You always. And again I say, I rejoice. I delight myself in You, Lord. Happy am I because God is my Lord!

Father, thank You for loving me and rejoicing over me with joy. Hallelujah! I am redeemed. I come with singing, and everlasting joy is upon my head. I obtain joy and gladness, and sorrow and sighing flee away. That spirit of rejoicing, joy, and laughter is my heritage. Where the Spirit of the Lord is, there is liberty — emancipation from bondage, freedom. I walk in that liberty.

Father, I praise You with joyful lips. I am ever filled and stimulated with the Holy Spirit. I speak out in psalms and hymns and make melody with all my heart to You, Lord. My happy heart is a good medicine and my cheerful mind works healing. The light in my eyes rejoices the hearts of others. I have a good report. My countenance radiates the joy of the Lord.

Father, I thank You that I bear much prayer fruit. I ask in Jesus' name, and I will receive, so that my joy (gladness, delight) may be full, complete, and overflowing. The joy of the Lord is my *strength*. Therefore, I count it all joy, all strength, when I encounter tests or trials of any sort because I am strong in You, Father.

I have the *victory* in the name of Jesus. Satan is under my feet. I am not moved by adverse circumstances. I have been made the righteousness of God in Christ Jesus. I dwell in the Kingdom of God and have peace and joy in the Holy Spirit! Praise the Lord!

In Jesus' name I pray, amen.

Scripture References

Psalm 118:24	Philippians 4:8
Philippians 4:4	Proverbs 15:13
Philippians 3:1	John 15:7,8
Psalm 144:15	John 16:23
Zephaniah 3:17	Nehemiah 8:10
Isaiah 51:11	James 1:2
2 Corinthians 3:17	Ephesians 6:10
James 1:25	1 John 5:4
Psalm 63:5	Ephesians 1:22
Ephesians 5:18,19	2 Corinthians 5:7
Proverbs 17:22	2 Corinthians 5:21
Proverbs 15:30	Romans 14:17

To Glorify God

In view of God's mercy, I offer my body as a living sacrifice, holy and pleasing to God — this is my spiritual act of worship. It is [not in my own strength]; for it is You, Lord, Who are all the while effectually at work in me — energizing and creating in me the power and desire — both to will and work for Your good pleasure and satisfaction and delight.

Father, I will not draw back or shrink in fear, for then Your soul would have no delight or pleasure in me. I was bought for a price — purchased with a preciousness and paid for, made Your very own. So, then, I honor You, Lord, and bring glory to You in my body.

I called on You in the day of trouble; You delivered me, and I shall honor and glorify You. I rejoice because You delivered me and drew me to Yourself out of the control and dominion of darkness (*obscurity*) and transferred me into the Kingdom of the Son of Your love. I will confess and praise You, O Lord my God, with my whole (united) heart; and I will glorify Your name forevermore.

As a bond servant of Jesus Christ, I receive and develop the talents that have been given me, for I would have You say of me, "Well done, you upright (honorable, admirable) and faithful servant!" I make use of the gifts (faculties, talents, qualities) according to the grace given me. I let my light so shine before men that they may see my moral excellence and my praiseworthy,

11

noble, and good deeds and recognize and honor and praise and glorify my Father Who is in heaven.

In the name of Jesus, I allow my life to lovingly express truth in all things — speaking truly, dealing truly, living truly. Whatever I do — no matter what it is — in word or deed, I do everything in the name of the Lord Jesus and in [dependence upon] His Person, giving praise to God the Father through Him. Whatever may be my task, I work at it heartily (from the soul), as [something done] for the Lord and not for men. To God the Father be all glory and honor and praise. Amen.

Scripture References (AMP)

Romans 12:1

Philippians 2:13

Hebrews 10:38

1 Corinthians 6:20

Psalm 50:15

Colossians 1:13

Psalm 86:12

Matthew 25:21

Romans 12:6

Matthew 5:16

Ephesians 4:15

Colossians 3:17

Colossians 3:23

To Walk in God's Wisdom and His Perfect Will

Lord and God, You are worthy to receive glory and honor and power, for You created all things, and by Your will they were created and have their being. You adopted me as Your child through Jesus Christ, in accordance with Your pleasure and will. I pray that I may be active in sharing my faith, so that I will have a full understanding of every good thing I have in Christ.

Father, I ask You to give me a complete understanding of what You want to do in my life, and I ask You to make me wise with spiritual wisdom. Then the way I live will always honor and please You, and I will continually do good, kind things for others. All the while, I will learn to know You better and better.

I roll my works upon You, Lord, and You make my thoughts agreeable to Your will, so my plans are established and succeed. You direct my steps and make them sure. I understand and firmly grasp what the will of the Lord is for I am not vague, thoughtless, or foolish. I stand firm and mature in spiritual growth, convinced and fully assured in everything willed by God.

Father, You have destined and appointed me to come progressively to know Your will — that is to perceive, to recognize more strongly and clearly, and to become better and more intimately acquainted with Your will. I thank You, Father, for the Holy Spirit Who abides permanently in me and Who guides me into all the truth — the whole, full truth — and speaks whatever He hears from the Father and announces and declares to me the things that are to come. I have the mind of Christ and hold the thoughts, feelings, and purposes of His heart.

So, Father, I have entered into that blessed rest by adhering to, trusting in, and relying on You, in the name of Jesus. Hallelujah! Amen.

Scripture References

Revelation 4:11 NIV	Colossians 4:12 AMP
Ephesians 1:5 NIV	Acts 22:14
Colossians 1:9,10 NLT	1 Corinthians 2:16 AMP
Proverbs 16:3,9 AMP	Hebrews 4:10
Ephesians 5:16 AMP	

To Walk in the Word

*F*ather, in the name of Jesus, *I commit myself to walk in the Word.* Your Word living in me produces Your life in this world. I recognize that Your Word is integrity itself — steadfast, sure, eternal — and I trust my life to its provisions.

You have sent Your Word forth into my heart. I let it dwell in me richly in all wisdom. I meditate in it day and night so that I may diligently act on it. The Incorruptible Seed, the Living Word, the Word of Truth, is abiding in my spirit. That Seed is growing mightily in me now, producing Your nature, Your life. It is my counsel, my shield, my buckler, my powerful weapon in battle. The Word is a lamp to my feet and a light to my path. It makes my way plain before me. I do not stumble, for my steps are ordered in the Word.

The Holy Spirit leads and guides me into all the truth. He gives me understanding, discernment, and comprehension so that I am preserved from the snares of the evil one.

I delight myself in You and Your Word. Because of that, You put Your desires within my heart. I commit my way unto You, and You bring it to pass. I am confident that You are at work in me now both to will and to do all Your good pleasure.

I exalt Your Word, hold it in high esteem, and give it first place. *I make my schedule around Your Word.* I make the Word the final authority to settle all questions that confront me. I choose to agree with the Word of God, and I choose to disagree with any thoughts, conditions, or circumstances contrary to Your Word. I boldly and confidently say that my heart is fixed and established on the solid foundation — the living Word of God! Amen.

Scripture References

Hebrews 4:12	1 Peter 3:12
Colossians 3:16	Colossians 4:2
Joshua 1:8	Ephesians 6:10
1 Peter 1:23	Luke 18:1
Psalm 91:4	James 5:16
Psalm 119:105	Psalm 37:4,5
Psalm 37:23	Philippians 2:13
Colossians 1:9	2 Corinthians 10:5
John 16:13	Psalm 112:7,8

To Walk in Love

Father, in Jesus' name, I thank You that the love of God has been poured forth into my heart by the Holy Spirit Who has been given to me. I keep and treasure Your Word. The love of and for You, Father, has been perfected and completed in me; and perfect love casts out all fear.

Father, I am Your child, and *I commit to walk in the God kind of love.* I endure long; I am patient and kind. I am never envious and never boil over with jealousy. I am not boastful or vainglorious, and I do not display myself haughtily. I am not rude and unmannerly, and I do not act unbecomingly. I do not insist on my own rights or my own way, for I am not self-seeking, touchy, fretful, or resentful. I take no account of an evil done to me and pay no attention to a suffered wrong. I do not rejoice at injustice and unrighteousness, but I rejoice when right and truth prevail. I bear up under anything and everything that comes. I am ever ready to believe the *best* of others. My hopes are fadeless under all circumstances. I endure everything without weakening because the love of God in me never fails.

Father, I *bless* and *pray* for those who persecute me — who are cruel in their attitude toward me. I bless them and do not curse them. Therefore, my love abounds yet more and more in knowledge and in all judgment. I approve things that are excellent. I am sincere and *without offense* till the day of Christ. I am filled with the fruits of righteousness.

Everywhere I go I commit to plant seeds of love. I thank You, Father, for preparing hearts ahead of time to receive this love. I know that these seeds will produce Your love in the hearts to whom they are given.

Father, I thank You that as I flow in Your love and wisdom, people are being blessed by my life and ministry. Father, You make me to find favor, compassion, and lovingkindness with others (*name them*).

I am rooted deep in love and founded securely on love, knowing that You are on my side and nothing is able to separate me from Your love, Father, which is in Christ Jesus my Lord. Thank You, Father, in Jesus' precious name. Amen.

Scripture References

Romans 5:5

1 John 2:5

1 John 4:18

1 Corinthians 13:4-8 AMP

Romans 12:14 AMP

Matthew 5:44

Philippians 1:9-11

John 13:34

1 Corinthians 3:6

Daniel 1:9 AMP

Ephesians 3:17 AMP

Romans 8:31,39

To Walk in Forgiveness

Father, in the name of Jesus, I make a fresh commitment to You to live in peace and harmony, not only with the other brothers and sisters of the Body of Christ, but also with my friends, associates, neighbors, and family.

Father, I repent of holding on to bad feelings toward others. I bind myself to godly repentance and loose myself from bitterness, resentment, envying, strife, and unkindness in any form. Father, I ask Your forgiveness for the sin of _____. By faith, I receive it, having assurance that I am cleansed from all unrighteousness through Jesus Christ. I ask You to forgive and release all who have wronged and hurt me. I forgive and release them. Deal with them in Your mercy and loving-kindness.

From this moment on, I purpose to walk in love, to seek peace, to live in agreement, and to conduct myself toward others in a manner that is pleasing to You. I know that I have right standing with You, and Your ears are attentive to my prayers.

It is written in Your Word that the love of God has been poured forth into my heart by the Holy Ghost Who is given to me. I believe that love flows forth into the lives of everyone I know, that we may be filled with and abound in the fruits of righteousness, which bring glory and honor unto You, Lord, in Jesus' name. So be it! Amen.

Scripture References

Romans 12:16-18	Mark 11:25
Romans 12:10	Ephesians 4:32
Philippians 2:2	1 Peter 3:8,11,12
Ephesians 4:31	Colossians 1:10
Ephesians 4:27	Romans 5:5
John 1:9	Philippians 1:9,11

*T*o Receive the Infilling of the Holy Spirit

*M*y Heavenly Father, I am Your child, for I believe in my heart that Jesus has been raised from the dead, and I have confessed Him as my Lord.

Jesus said, "How much more shall your Heavenly Father give the Holy Spirit to those who ask Him." I ask You now in the name of Jesus to fill me with the Holy Spirit. I step into the fullness and power that I desire in the name of Jesus. I confess that I am a Spirit-filled Christian. As I yield my vocal organs, I expect to speak in tongues, for the Spirit gives me utterance in the name of Jesus. Praise the Lord! Amen.

Scripture References

John 14:16,17	Acts 19:2,5,6
Luke 11:13	Romans 10:9,10
Acts 1:8	1 Corinthians14:2-15
Acts 2:4	1 Corinthians 14:18,27
Acts 2:32,33,39	Ephesians 6:18
Acts 8:12-17	Jude 1:20
Acts 10:44-46	

To Walk in Sanctification

Father, thank You for sanctifying me by the truth; Your Word is truth. Jesus, You consecrated Yourself for my sake, so I'll be truth-consecrated in my mission. In the name of Jesus, I repent and turn from my wicked ways. I wash myself, make myself clean. I cease to do evil, and I am learning to do right.

Father, You dwell in me and walk with me. So I leave the corruption and compromise; I leave it for good. You are my Father, and I will not link up with those who would pollute me, because You want me all for Yourself. I purify myself from everything that contaminates body and spirit, perfecting holiness out of reverence for God.

Father, I confess my sins. You are faithful and just to forgive me my sins and to cleanse me from all unrighteousness. Jesus has been made unto me wisdom, righteousness, sanctification, and redemption.

I submit myself to You, Lord — spirit, soul, and body. I strip myself of my old, unrenewed self and put on the new nature, changing whatever needs to be changed in my life. The desire of my heart is to be a vessel unto honor, sanctified, fitting for the Master's use, and prepared for every good work.

Thank you, Lord, that I eat the good of the land, because You have given me a willing and obedient heart. Amen.

Scripture References

John 17:17,19	Isaiah 1:16,17
2 Corinthians 6:17 MESSAGE	2 Corinthians 7:1 NIV
1 John 1:9 NKJV	1 Corinthians 1:30
Ephesians 4:22-24	2 Timothy 2:21
Isaiah 1:19	

To Bear Fruit

Lord Jesus, You chose me and appointed me to go and bear fruit — fruit that will last. Then the Father will give me whatever I ask in Your name. Father, You are the Gardener. You prune every branch that bears fruit, so it will be even more fruitful.

The Apostle Paul said to be filled with the fruit of righteousness and that he desired that fruit might abound to our account. Therefore, I commit myself to bring forth the fruit of the spirit: love, joy, peace, longsuffering, gentleness, goodness, faith, meekness, and temperance. I renounce and turn from the fruit of the flesh, because I belong to Christ and have crucified the flesh with its affections and lusts.

A seed cannot bear fruit unless it first falls into the ground and dies. I confess that I am crucified with Christ: Nevertheless I live; yet not I, but Christ lives in me. And the life that I now live in the flesh I live by the faith of the Son of God, Who loved me and gave Himself for me.

Father, I thank You that I am good ground, that I hear Your Word and understand it, and that the Word bears fruit in my life — sometimes a hundredfold, sometimes sixty, sometimes thirty. I am like a tree planted by the rivers of water that brings forth fruit in its season. My leaf shall not wither, and whatever I do shall prosper.

Father, in Jesus' name, I thank You for filling me with the knowledge of Your will in all wisdom and spiritual understanding that I may walk worthy of You, Lord, being fruitful in every good work and increasing in the knowledge of You. Amen.

Scripture References

John 15:16	Galatians 2:20
Philippians 1:11	Matthew 13:23
Philippians 4:17	Psalm 1:3
Galatians 5:22-24	Colossians 1:9,10
John 12:24	

o Help Others

ather, in the name of Jesus, I will do unto others as I would have them do unto me. I eagerly pursue and seek to acquire [this] (*agape*) love — I purpose to make it my aim, my great quest in life.

In the name of Jesus, I will esteem and look upon and be concerned for not [merely] my own interest, but also for the interest of others as they pursue success. I am strong in the Lord and in the power of His might. I will make it a practice to please (make happy) my neighbor, (*boss, co-worker, teacher, parent, child, brother, etc.*) for his good and for his true welfare, to edify him — that is, to strengthen him and build him up in all ways — spiritually, socially, and materially.

I desire to imitate my Heavenly Father, and as a child of light, I will walk in love and wisdom. Help me to encourage (admonish, exhort) others and edify them.

Father, in the name of Jesus, I love my enemies (*as well as my business associates, fellow church members, neighbors, those in authority over me*) and am kind and do good — doing favors so that someone derives benefit from them. I lend expecting and hoping for nothing in return, but considering nothing as lost and despairing of no one.

Thank You, Father, for imprinting Your laws upon my heart and inscribing them on my mind — on my inmost thoughts and understanding. According to Your Word, as I would like and desire that men would do to me, I do exactly so to them, in the name of Jesus. Amen.

Scripture References

Luke 6:31	1 Thessalonians 5:11 AMP
1 Corinthians 14:1 AMP	Luke 6:35,36 AMP
Philippians 2:4 AMP	Ephesians 5:1,2 AMP
Ephesians 6:10	Hebrews 10:16 AMP
Romans 15:2 AMP	Luke 6:31 AMP

To Watch What You Say

Father, today I make a commitment to You in the name of Jesus. I turn from speaking idle words and foolishly talking things that are contrary to my true desire to myself and toward others. Your Word says that the tongue defiles, that the tongue sets on fire the course of nature, that the tongue is set on fire of hell.

In the name of Jesus, I submit to godly wisdom that I might learn to control my tongue. I am determined that hell will not set my tongue on fire. I renounce, reject, and repent of every word that has ever proceeded out of my mouth against You, God, and Your operation. I cancel its power and dedicate my mouth to speak excellent and right things. My mouth shall utter truth.

Because I am the righteousness of God in Christ Jesus, I set the course of my life for obedience, for abundance, for wisdom, for health, and for joy. Set a guard over my mouth, O Lord; keep watch over the door of my lips. Then the words of my mouth and my deeds shall show forth Your righteousness and Your salvation all of my days. I purpose to guard my mouth and my tongue that I might keep myself from calamity.

Father, Your Words are top priority to me. They are spirit and life. I let the Word dwell in me richly in all wisdom. The ability of

God is released within me by the words of my mouth and by the Word of God. I speak Your Words out of my mouth. They are alive in me. You are alive and working in me. So, I can boldly say that my words are words of faith, words of power, words of love, and words of life. They produce good things in my life and in the lives of others because I choose Your Words for my lips, and Your will for my life, in Jesus' name. Amen.

Scripture References

Ephesians 5:4	Proverbs 21:23
2 Timothy 2:16	Ephesians 4:27
James 3:6	James 1:6
Proverbs 8:6,7	John 6:63
2 Corinthians 5:21	Colossians 3:16
Proverbs 4:23	Philemon 6

To Live Free From Worry

Father, I thank You that I have been delivered from the power of darkness and translated into the Kingdom of Your dear Son. *I commit to live free from worry in the name of Jesus,* for the law of the Spirit of life in Christ Jesus has made me *free* from the law of sin and death.

I humble myself under Your mighty hand that in due time You may exalt me. I cast the whole of my cares (*name them*) — all my anxieties, all my worries, all my concerns — once and for all on You. You care for me affectionately and care about me watchfully. You sustain me. You will never allow the consistently righteous to be moved — made to slip, fall, or fail!

Father, I delight myself in You, and You perfect that which concerns me.

I cast down imaginations (reasonings) and every high thing that exalts itself against the knowledge of You, and I bring into captivity every thought to the obedience of Christ. I lay aside every weight and the sin of worry, which does try so easily to beset me. I run with patience the race that is set before me, looking unto Jesus, the Author and Finisher of my faith.

I thank You, Father, that You are able to keep that which I have committed unto You. I think on (fix my mind on) those things that are true, honest, just, pure, lovely, of good report, virtuous, and deserving of praise. I will not let my heart be troubled. I abide in Your Word, and Your Word abides in me. Therefore, Father, I do *not* forget what manner of person I am. I look into the perfect law of liberty and continue therein, being *not* a forgetful hearer, but a *doer of the Word* and, thus, blessed in my doing!

Thank You, Father. *I am carefree.* I walk in that peace that passes all understanding, in Jesus' name! Amen.

Scripture References

Colossians 1:13	Hebrews 12:1,2
Romans 8:2	2 Timothy 1:12
1 Peter 5:6,7 AMP	Philippians 4:8
Psalm 55:22	John 14:1
Psalm 138:8	James 1:22-25
2 Corinthians 10:5	Philippians 4:6

Adoration: "Hallowed Be Thy Name"

Our Father, which art in heaven, hallowed be Thy name.

Bless the Lord, O my soul: and all that is within me, bless Your holy name. I adore You and make known to You my adoration and love this day.

I bless Your name, *Elohim*, the Creator of heaven and earth, Who was in the beginning. It is You Who made me, and You have crowned me with glory and honor. You are the God of might and strength. Hallowed be Thy name!

I bless Your name, *El-Shaddai*, the God Almighty of blessings. You are the Breasty One Who nourishes and supplies. You are all-bountiful and all-sufficient. Hallowed be Thy name!

I bless Your name, *Adonai*, my Lord and my Master. You are Jehovah — the Completely Self-Existing One, always present, revealed in Jesus, Who is the same yesterday, today, and forever. Hallowed be Thy name!

I bless Your name, *Jehovah-Jireh*, the One Who sees my needs and provides for them. Hallowed be Thy name!

I bless Your name, *Jehovah-Rapha,* my Healer and the One Who makes bitter experiences sweet. You sent Your Word and healed me. You forgave all my iniquities and You healed all my diseases. Hallowed be Thy name!

I bless Your name, *Jehovah-M'Kaddesh,* the Lord my Sanctifier. You have set me apart for Yourself. Hallowed be Thy name!

Jehovah-Nissi, You are my Victory, my Banner, and my Standard. Your banner over me is love. When the enemy comes in like a flood, You lift up a standard against him. Hallowed be Thy name!

Jehovah-Shalom, I bless Your name. You are my Peace — the peace which transcends all understanding, which garrisons and mounts guard over my heart and mind in Christ Jesus. Hallowed be Thy name!

I bless You, *Jehovah-Tsidkenu,* my Righteousness. Thank You for becoming sin for me that I might become the righteousness of God in Christ Jesus. Hallowed be Thy name!

Jehovah-Rohi, You are my Shepherd, and I shall not want for any good or beneficial thing. Hallowed be Thy name!

Hallelujah to *Jehovah-Shammah,* the One Who will never leave or forsake me. You are always there. I take comfort and am encouraged and confidently and boldly say, The Lord is my Helper; I will not be seized with alarm — I will not fear or dread or be terrified. What can man do to me? Hallowed be Thy name!

I worship and adore You, *El-Elyon,* the Most High God, Who is the First Cause of everything, the Possessor of the heavens and earth. You are the everlasting God, the great God, the living

God, the merciful God, the faithful God, the mighty God. You are Truth, Justice, Righteousness, and Perfection. You are *El-Elyon* — the Highest Sovereign of the heavens and the earth. Hallowed be Thy name!

Father, You have exalted above all else Your name and Your Word, and You have magnified Your Word above all Your name! The Word was made flesh and dwelt among us, and His name is Jesus! Hallowed be Thy name!

In Jesus' name I pray, amen.

Scripture References

Matthew 6:9	Song of Solomon 2:4
Psalm 103:1	Isaiah 59:19
Genesis 1:1,2	Judges 6:24
Psalm 8:5	Philippians 4:7 AMP
Genesis 49:24,25	Jeremiah 23:5,6
Genesis 15:1,2,8	2 Corinthians 5:21
Hebrews 13:8	Psalm 23:1
Genesis 22:14	Psalm 34:10
Psalm 147:3 AMP	Hebrews 13:5
Exodus 15:23-26 AMP	Hebrews 13:6 AMP
Psalm 107:20	Genesis 14:19,22
Psalm 103:3	Psalm 91:1
Leviticus 20:7,8	Psalm 138:2 AMP
Exodus 17:15	John 1:14
Ezekial 48:35	

Divine Intervention: "Thy Kingdom Come"

INTRODUCTION

Jesus said, "The kingdom of God is in you" (Luke 17:21). He was speaking of the spiritual kingdom. This kingdom is not meat and drink; but righteousness, and peace, and joy in the Holy Ghost (Rom. 14:17).

It is easy to get caught up in our present-day circumstances and forget that there is a plan that exceeds personal goals. In this prayer I have taken the opportunity to focus on our common goal: the time when Jesus returns to establish the visible Kingdom of God here on earth, and the government shall be upon His shoulders (Isa. 9:6). The Kingdom of God is not in word, but in power (1 Cor. 4:20).

PRAYER

Father, in Jesus' name, I pray according to Matthew 6:10, "Thy Kingdom come." I am looking for the soon coming of our Lord and Savior, Jesus Christ.

Today we are [even here and] now Your children; it is not yet disclosed (made clear) what we shall be [hereafter], *but we know that when He comes and is manifested, we shall [as God's children] resemble and be like Him, for we shall see Him just as He*

35

[really] is. You said that everyone who has this hope [resting] on Him cleanses (purifies) himself just as He is pure — chaste, undefiled, guiltless.

For the grace of God — His unmerited favor and blessing — has come forward (appeared) for the deliverance from sin and the eternal salvation for all mankind. It has trained us to reject and renounce all ungodliness (irreligion) and worldly (passionate) desires; to live discreet (temperate, self-controlled), upright, devout (spiritually whole) lives in this present world; awaiting and looking for the [fulfillment, the realization of our] blessed hope, *even the glorious appearing of our great God and Savior, Christ Jesus, the Messiah, the Anointed One.*

For the Lord Himself shall descend from heaven with a shout, with the voice of the archangel, and with the trump of God: And the dead in Christ shall rise first. Then we which are alive and remain shall be caught up together with them in the clouds to meet the Lord in the air: And so shall we ever be with the Lord.

I thank You, Father, that the Lord shall come (to earth) and all the holy ones [saints and angels] with Him; and the Lord shall be King over all the earth; in that Day He shall be one Lord, and His name one. The government shall be upon His shoulder.

Father, I thank You that we shall join the great voices in heaven saying, "The kingdoms of this world are become the kingdoms of our Lord, and of His Christ; and He shall reign for ever and ever."

Yours, O Lord, is the greatness and power and the glory and the victory and the majesty; for all that is in the heavens and the earth is Yours; Yours is the Kingdom, O Lord; and

DIVINE INTERVENTION:
"THY KINGDOM COME"

Yours it is to be exalted as Head over all. Thy Kingdom come. Hallelujah! Amen.

Scripture References

1 John 3:2,3 AMP

Titus 2:11-13 AMP

1 Thessalonians 4:16,17

Zechariah 14:5,9 AMP

Isaiah 9:6 AMP

Revelation 11:15

1 Chronicles 29:11 AMP

Submission: "Thy Will Be Done"

Father, in the name of Jesus, I pray that the will of God be done in my life as it is in heaven. For I am Your [own] handiwork (Your workmanship), recreated in Christ Jesus, [born anew] that I may do those good works that You predestined (planned beforehand) for me, (taking paths that You prepared ahead of time) that I should walk in them — living the good life that You prearranged and made ready for me to live.

Teach me to do Your will, for You are my God; let Your good Spirit lead me into a plain country and into the land of uprightness. Jesus, You gave (yielded) Yourself up [to atone] for my sins (and to save and sanctify me), in order to rescue and deliver me from this present, wicked age and world order, in accordance with the will and purpose and plan of our God and Father.

In the name of Jesus, I am not conformed to this world, but I am transformed by the renewing of my mind, that I may prove what is that good and acceptable and perfect will of God. For this is the will of God: that I should be consecrated — separated and set apart for pure and holy living; that I should abstain from all sexual vice; that I should know how to possess [control, manage] my own body (in purity, separated from things profane, and) in consecration and honor, not [to be used] in the passion of lust, like the heathen who are ignorant of the true God and have no knowledge of His will.

Father, thank You that You chose me — actually picked me out for Yourself as Your own — in Christ before the foundation of the world; that I should be holy (consecrated and set apart for You) and blameless in Your sight, even above reproach, before You in love: having predestinated me unto the adoption of a child by Jesus Christ to Yourself, according to the good pleasure of Your will.

Your will be done on earth in my life as it is in heaven. Amen and so be it!

Scripture References

Matthew 6:9,10

Romans 12:2

Ephesians 2:10 AMP

1 Thessalonians 4:4,5 AMP

Psalm 143:10 AMP

Ephesians 1:4 AMP

Galatians 1:4 AMP

Ephesians 1:5

*P*rovision: "Give Us This Day Our Daily Bread"

*I*n the name of Jesus, I confess with the Psalmist David that I have not seen the righteous forsaken, nor his seed begging bread.

Father, thank You for food, clothing, and shelter. In the name of Jesus, I am learning to stop being perpetually uneasy (anxious and worried) about my life, what I shall eat and what I shall drink, or about my body, what I shall put on. My life is greater [in quality] than food, and the body [far above and more excellent] than clothing.

The bread of idleness [gossip, discontent, and self-pity] I will not eat. It is You, Father, Who will liberally supply (fill to the full) my every need according to Your riches in glory in Christ Jesus.

In the name of Jesus, I shall not live by bread alone, but by every word that proceeds from the mouth of God. Your words were found, and I did eat them, and Your Word was to me a joy and the rejoicing of my heart.

And the Word became flesh and dwelt among us. Jesus, You are the Bread of Life that gives me life, the Living Bread.

PROVISION: "GIVE US THIS DAY OUR DAILY BREAD"

Thank You, Father, in the name of Jesus, for spiritual bread — manna from heaven. Amen.

Scripture References

Matthew 6:9-11

Psalm 37:25

Matthew 6:25 AMP

Proverbs 31:27 AMP

Philippians 4:19 AMP

Matthew 4:4

Jeremiah 15:16 AMP

John 1:14

John 6:48-51 AMP

*F*orgiveness: "Forgive Us Our Debts"

*F*ather, I forgive everyone who has trespassed against me so that You can forgive me my trespasses. [Now, having received the Holy Spirit and being led and directed by Him], if I forgive the sins of anyone, they are forgiven; if I retain the sins of anyone, they are retained.

Father, Your Word says, "Love your enemies and pray for those who persecute you" (Matt. 5:44 AMP).

I come before you in Jesus' name to lift _____ before You. I invoke blessings upon him/her and pray for his/her happiness. I implore Your blessings (favor) upon him/her.

Father, not only will I pray for _____, but I set myself to treat him/her well (do good to, act nobly toward him/her). I will be merciful, sympathetic, tender, responsive, and compassionate toward _____, even as You are, Father.

My desire is to be an imitator of You, and I can do all things through Christ Jesus Who strengthens me.

Father, I thank You that I have great peace in this situation, for I love Your law and refuse to take offense toward _____.

Jesus, I am blessed — happy [with life — joy and satisfaction in God's favor and salvation apart from outward conditions] and to be envied — because I take no offense in You and refuse to be hurt or resentful or annoyed or repelled or made to stumble, [whatever may occur].

And now, Father, I roll this work upon You — commit and trust it wholly to You; and I believe that You will cause my thoughts to become in agreement to Your will, and so my plans shall be established and succeed.

In Jesus' name, amen.

Scripture References

Matthew 6:12	Ephesians 5:1 AMP
Matthew 6:14,15	Philippians 4:13 AMP
John 20:23 AMP	Psalm 119:165 AMP
Luke 6:27 AMP	Luke 7:23 AMP
Matthew 5:44 AMP	Proverbs 16:3 AMP
Luke 6:28 AMP	

*G*uidance and Deliverance: "Lead Us Not Into Temptation"

*T*here has no temptation taken me but such as is common to man: But *God is faithful,* Who will not suffer me to be tempted above that which I am able; but will with the temptation also make a way to escape, that I may be able to bear it.

I count it all joy when I fall into various temptations; knowing this — that the trying of my faith works patience.

I will not say when I am tempted, "I am tempted from God"; for God is incapable of being tempted by [what is] evil, and He Himself tempts no one.

Thank You, Jesus, for giving Yourself for my sins, that You might deliver me from this present evil world, according to the will of God and our Father: to Whom be glory for ever and ever.

Father, in the name of Jesus, and according to the power that is at work in me, I will keep awake (give strict attention, be cautious) and watch and pray that I may not come into temptation. In Jesus' name, amen.

GUIDANCE AND DELIVERANCE:
"LEAD US NOT INTO TEMPTATION"

Scripture References

1 Corinthians 10:13	Galatians 1:4,5
James 1:2,3	Ephesians 3:20
James 1:13 AMP	Matthew 26:41 AMP

*P*raise:
"For Thine Is the Kingdom, and the Power, and the Glory"

O magnify the Lord with me, and let us exalt His name together.

As for God, His way is perfect! The Word of the Lord is tested and tried; He is a shield to all those who take refuge and put their trust in Him.

Let the words of my mouth and the meditation of my heart be acceptable in Your sight, O Lord, my firm, impenetrable Rock and my Redeemer.

Your Word has revived me and given me life.

Forever, O Lord, Your Word is settled in heaven.

Your Word is a lamp to my feet and a light to my path.

The sum of Your Word is truth, and every one of Your righteous decrees endures forever.

I will worship toward Your holy temple and praise Your name for Your loving-kindness and for Your truth and faithfulness; for

You have exalted above all else Your name and Your Word, and You have magnified Your Word above all Your name!

Let my prayer be set forth as incense before You, the lifting up of my hands as the evening sacrifice. Set a guard, O Lord, before my mouth; keep watch at the door of my lips.

He who brings an offering of praise and thanksgiving honors and glorifies Me; and he who orders his way aright — who prepares the way that I may show him — to him I will demonstrate the salvation of God.

My mouth shall be filled with Your praise and with Your honor all the day.

Because Your loving-kindness is better than life, my lips shall praise You. So will I bless You while I live; I will lift up my hands in Your name.

Your testimonies also are my delight and my counselors.

In Jesus' name I pray, amen.

Scripture References (AMP)

Psalm 34:3	Psalm 138:2
Psalm 18:30	Psalm 141:2,3
Psalm 19:14	Psalm 50:23
Psalm 119:50	Psalm 71:8
Psalm 119:89	Psalm 63:3,4
Psalm 119:105	Psalm 119:24
Psalm 119:160	

Submitting All to God

Father, You are the Supreme Authority — a God of order. You have instituted other authority structures that will support healthy relationships and maintain harmony. It is my decision to surrender my will to You, that I might find protection and dwell in the secret place of the Most High.

Father, thank You for pastors and leaders of the church — those who are submitted to You and are examples to the congregation. I submit to the church elders (the ministers and spiritual guides of the church) — [giving them due respect and yielding to their counsel].

Lord, You know just how rebellious I have been. I ask Your forgiveness for manipulating circumstances and people — for trying to manipulate You to get my own way. May Your will be done in my life, even as it is in heaven.

Father, when I feel that my life is spiraling out of control, I bind my mind to the mind of Christ, and my emotions to the control of the Holy Spirit. I loose my mind from obsessive thought patterns that try to confuse me.

Obedience is far better than sacrifice. Father, You are much more interested in my listening to You than in my offerings of material things to You. Rebellion is as bad as the sin of witchcraft, and stubbornness is as bad as worshiping idols. Forgive me for practicing witchcraft and worshiping idols.

Father, You deserve honesty from the heart; yes, utter sincerity and truthfulness. Oh, give me this wisdom. Sprinkle me with the cleansing blood, and I shall be clean again. Wash me, and I shall be whiter than snow. You have rescued me from the dominion of darkness and brought me into the Kingdom of the Son You love, in Whom I have redemption, the forgiveness of sins.

Lord, I want to follow You. I am putting aside my own desires and conveniences. I yield my desires that are not in Your plan for me. Even in the midst of my fear, I surrender and entrust my future to You. I choose to take up my cross and follow You [cleave steadfastly to You, conforming wholly to Your example in living and, if need be, in dying also]. I desire to lose my [lower life] on Your account that I might find it [the higher life].

Father, You gave Jesus to be my Example. He has returned to You, Father, and has sent the Holy Spirit to be my Helper and Guide. In this world there are temptations, trials, and tribulations; but Jesus has overcome the world, and I am of good cheer.

Jesus is my Lord. I choose to become His servant. He calls me His friend.

Lord, help me to walk through the process of surrendering my all to You. I exchange rebellion and stubbornness for a willing and obedient heart. When I refuse to listen, anoint my ears to hear; when I am blinded by my own desires, open my eyes to see.

I belong to Jesus Christ, the Anointed One, Who breaks down and destroys every yoke of bondage. In His name and in obedience to Your will, Father, I submit to the control and direction of the Holy Spirit Whom You have sent to live in me. I am Your child. All to You I surrender. I am an overcomer by the blood of the Lamb and by the word of my testimony!

In Jesus' name I pray, amen.

Scripture References

1 Corinthians 14:33	Psalm 51:6,7 TLB
1 Timothy 2:2	Colossians 1:13,14 NIV
Psalm 91:1	Matthew 10:38,39 AMP
1 Peter 5:5 AMP	John 16:33
Matthew 6:10	John 15:15
James 4:7	Revelation 12:11
1 Samuel 15:22,23 TLB	

Receiving Forgiveness

Father, Your Word declares that if I ask for forgiveness, You will forgive me and cleanse me from all unrighteousness. Help me to believe; help me to receive my forgiveness for past and present sins. Help me to forgive myself. I confess Jesus as my Lord and believe in my heart that You raised Him from the dead, and I am saved.

Father, Your Son, Jesus, said that whatever I ask for in prayer, having faith and really believing, I will receive. Lord, I believe; help my unbelief.

Father, I count myself blessed, how happy I am — I get a fresh start, my slate's wiped clean. I count myself blessed (happy, fortunate, to be envied). You, Father, are holding nothing against me, and You're not holding anything back from me.

When I keep it all inside, my bones turn to powder, and my words become daylong groans. The pressure never lets up; all the juices of my life dry up. I am letting it all out; I am saying once and for all that I am making a clean breast of my failures to You, Lord.

In the face of this feeling of guilt and unworthiness, I receive my forgiveness, and the pressure is gone — my guilt dissolved, my sin disappeared. I am blessed, for You have forgiven my transgressions — You have covered my sins. I am blessed, for You will never count my sins against me.

Father, You chose me [actually picked me out for Yourself as Your very own] in Christ before the foundation of the world, that I should be holy (consecrated and set apart for You), blameless in Your sight, even above reproach, before You in love. In Jesus I have redemption (deliverance and salvation) through His blood, the remission (forgiveness) of my offenses (shortcomings and trespasses), in accordance with the riches and the generosity of Your gracious favor.

Lord, I have received Your Son, Jesus; I believe in His name, and He has given me the right to become Your child. I acknowledge You, Lord, as my Father. Thank You for forgiving me and absolving me of all guilt. I am an overcomer by the blood of the Lamb and by the word of my testimony.

In the name of Jesus, amen.

Scripture References

1 John 1:9	Psalm 32:1-6 MESSAGE
Romans 10:9,10	Romans 4:7,8 NIV
Mark 11:23	Ephesians 1:4,7 AMP
Matthew 21:22 AMP	John 1:12 NIV
Mark 9:24	Revelation 12:11
Psalm 32:1 AMP	

Walking in Humility

Father, I clothe myself with humility [as the garb of a servant, so that its covering cannot possibly be stripped from me]. I renounce pride and arrogance. Father, You give grace to the humble. Therefore I humble myself under Your mighty hand, that in due time You may exalt me.

In the name of Jesus, I cast the whole of my care [all my anxieties, all my worries, all my concerns for my future, once and for all] on You, for You care for me affectionately and care about me watchfully. I expect a life of victory and awesome deeds because my actions are done on behalf of a spirit humbly submitted to Your truth and righteousness.

Father, in the name of Jesus, I refuse to be wise in my own eyes; but I choose to fear You and shun evil. This will bring health to my body and nourishment to my bones.

Father, I humble myself and submit to Your Word that speaks (exposes, sifts, analyzes, and judges) the very thoughts and purposes of my heart. I test my own actions, so that I might have appropriate self-esteem, without comparing myself to anyone else. The security of Your guidance will allow me to carry my own load with energy and confidence.

I listen carefully and hear what is being said to me. I incline my ear to wisdom and apply my heart to understanding and insight. Humility and fear of You bring wealth and honor and life.

Father, I hide Your Word in my heart that I might not sin against You. As one of Your chosen people, holy and dearly loved, I clothe myself with compassion, kindness, humility, gentleness, and patience. I bear with others and forgive whatever grievances I may have against anyone. I forgive as You forgave me. And over all these virtues I put on love, which binds them all together in perfect unity. I let the peace of Christ rule in my heart, and I am thankful for Your grace and the power of the Holy Spirit.

Father, may Your will be done on earth in my life as it is in heaven.

In Jesus' name, amen.

Scripture References

1 Peter 5:5-7 AMP	Proverbs 22:4 NIV
Proverbs 3:7,8 NIV	Psalm 119:11
Hebrews 4:12 AMP	Colossians 3:12-15 NIV
Galatians 6:4,5 NIV	Matthew 6:10 NIV
Proverbs 2:2 NIV	

Giving Thanks to God

INTRODUCTION

God saw you when you were in your mother's womb (Ps. 139:13-16). He knew your mother and father and the circumstances of the home where you were to grow up. He knew the schools you would attend and the neighborhood in which you would live.

God gave you the ability to survive and walked with you through good times and bad. He gave you survival techniques and guardian angels to keep and protect you (Ps. 91:11). He chose you before the foundation of the world to be holy and without blame before Him in love (Eph. 1:4).

He cried with you when you cried. He laughed with you when you laughed. He was grieved when you were misunderstood and treated unfairly. He watched and waited, looking forward to the day when you would receive Jesus as your Savior. To as many as received Him gave He the power, the right, and the authority to become the sons of God (John 1:12 AMP). He longs for your fellowship, desiring for you to know Him more and more intimately.

Your survival techniques were probably different than mine. Whatever they were, and whatever your life may have been like up to this point, the peace of God can change the regrets and the wounds of the past into thanksgiving and praise. You can experience wholeness by earnestly and sincerely praying this prayer.

I.

DAILY PRAYER OF THANKSGIVING

Father, I come to You in the name of Jesus. With the help of the Holy Spirit and by Your grace, I join with the heavenly host making a joyful noise to You and serving You with gladness! I come before Your presence with singing!

Lord, I know (perceive, recognize, and understand with approval) that You are God! It is You Who made us, not we ourselves [and we are Yours]! We are Your people and the sheep of Your pasture.

Father, I enter into Your gates with thanksgiving and present an offering of thanks. I enter into Your courts with praise! I am thankful and delight to say so. I bless and affectionately praise Your name! For You are good and Your mercy and loving-kindness are everlasting. Your faithfulness and truth endure to all generations. It is a good and delightful thing to give thanks to You, O Most High.

Lord, by Your Holy Spirit, perfect the fruit of my lips. Help me draw thanksgiving forth from my innermost resources; reach down into the most secret places of my heart that I may offer significant thanksgiving to You, Father.

Thank You for my parents who gave me life. I am grateful for the victories and achievements I have experienced in spite of my hurts — the bruises and the abuses that boxed me in when I was a small child. You used them for good even though Satan intended them for my destruction.

You prepared me to listen to the inner voice — the voice of Your Holy Spirit.

Thank You for Your grace, which is teaching me to trust myself and others. Thank You for life — life in all its abundance.

It was You Who gave me a desire to pray, and I am grateful for the prayer closet where we meet, and I thank You for Your Word. Life is exciting, and I am grateful that I am alive for such a time as this.

Thank You for past and present relationships. I learn from those who oppose me and from those who are for me. You taught me to recognize and understand my strengths and weaknesses. You gave me discernment and spiritual understanding. I enter Your gates with thanksgiving in my heart.

You are my Father. I am Your child, loved by You unconditionally. I rejoice in You, Lord, and give thanks at the remembrance of Your holiness.

I am an overcomer by the blood of the Lamb and by the word of my testimony.

In the name of Jesus, amen.

Scripture References

Psalm 100:1-5 AMP	Philippians 2:13
Psalm 92:1 AMP	Esther 4:14
Psalm 138:8	Psalm 100:4
Hebrews 13:15	Philippians 3:1
Genesis 50:20 NIV	Psalm 30:4
John 10:10	Revelation 12:11

II.
PRAYER OF THANKSGIVING FOR FOOD
EATEN WHILE TRAVELING

Father, I ask for the wisdom to order that which is healthy and nourishing to my body.

In the name of Jesus, I resist the lust of the flesh and the lust of the eye as I scan the menu. When I am in doubt about what I am to order, I will pause and ask for wisdom, which You will give generously without finding fault with me.

Should I unknowingly eat or drink any deadly thing, it will not harm me, for the Spirit of life makes me free from the law of sin and death.

Everything You have created, Father, is good, and nothing is to be thrown away or refused if it is received with thanksgiving. It is hallowed and consecrated by Your Word and by prayer.

I receive this food with thanksgiving and will eat the amount that is sufficient for me.

In the name of Jesus, amen.

Scripture References

James 1:5	Romans 8:2
1 John 2:16	1 Timothy 4:4,5 AMP
Mark 16:18	Psalm 136:1,25

Committing to a Fast

I.
BEGINNING A FAST

INTRODUCTION

There are different kinds of fasts: a total fast from foods and liquids for a short interval of time; a liquid fast, in which only water may be drunk; a juice fast, which involves drinking water and a given amount of juices at normal mealtimes; a fast from meats, in which only fruits and vegetables may be eaten.

It is important to understand the effects of fasting on the spirit, soul, and body. Before committing to a fast, I encourage you to study the Word of God and to read books that provide important nutritional and other health information. Understanding will help to avoid harm and injury — both physically and spiritually.

Do not flaunt your fast, but do talk with your family and close associates if necessary to let them know what you are doing.

(Personal note: During times of fasting I continue to prepare meals at home for my family.)

PRAYER

Father, I consecrate this fast to You and set my mind to gain understanding in these matters for which I am concerned. *(Write your concerns out and keep them before your eyes. Do not lose sight of the reason for your fast.)*

I humble myself before You, Most High God. In accordance with Daniel 10:1-3, I will eat no _____ for the period of _____.

I obey the words of Jesus by putting on festive clothing, so that no one will suspect that I am fasting.

Father, You know every secret, and I look to You for my reward. I am assured that You hear me when I pray according to Your will, and I know that I shall have the petitions that I desire of You.

Father, I delight myself in You, and You cause my desires to be agreeable with Your will.

I choose the fast You have chosen: to loose the chains of injustice and untie the cords of the yoke, to set the oppressed free and break every yoke. I share my food with the hungry and provide the poor wanderer with shelter. When I see the naked, I will clothe him, and I will not turn away from my own flesh and blood. Then my light will break forth like the dawn, and my healing will quickly appear; then my righteousness will go before me, and Your glory, Lord, will be my rear guard.

Father, thank You for cleansing me — spirit, soul, and body. All my ways seem innocent to me, but my motives are weighed by You, my Lord and my Master. I commit this fast to You, and my plans will succeed. I thank You that it is You Who give the wise answer of the tongue.

Forever, O Lord, Your Word stands firm in heaven. Your faithfulness extends to every generation, like the earth You created; it endures by Your decree, for everything serves Your plans.

In Jesus' name, amen.

Scripture References

Matthew 6:17,18 TLB   1 Thessalonians 5:23

1 John 5:14,15   Proverbs 16:2,3 NIV

Psalm 37:4   Proverbs 16:1

Proverbs 16:3 AMP   Psalm 119:89-91 TLB

Isaiah 58:6-8 TLB

II.
ENDING A FAST

INTRODUCTION

It is best to break a fast by eating fruit, broth, or a light salad, gradually adding other foods day by day depending upon the length of the fast.

PRAYER

Father, in the name of Jesus, You are my Light and my Salvation; whom shall I fear? You are the Strength of my life; of whom shall I be afraid?

Father, You have given me the desires of my heart. You have heard and answered my prayers. To You be the glory! Great things You have done!

I rest in You, awaiting the manifestation of all that I required and inquired of You.

I thank You for giving me Your strength to face each day full of sap [of spiritual vitality]. Today I break this fast as You have directed. I thank You for this food because it is consecrated by Your Word and prayer.

In Jesus' name, amen.

Scripture References

Psalm 27:1	Psalm 92:14 AMP
Psalm 37:4	1 Timothy 4:4,5 AMP
Psalm 34:4 AMP	

$\mathcal{P}$leading the Blood of Jesus

I.

MORNING PRAYER[1]

$\mathcal{F}$ather, I come in the name of Jesus to plead His blood on my life and on all that belongs to me, and on all over which You have made me a steward.

I plead the blood of Jesus on the portals of my mind, my body (the temple of the Holy Spirit), my emotions, and my will. I believe that I am protected by the blood of the Lamb which gives me access to the Holy of Holies.

I plead the blood on my children, on my grandchildren and their children, and on all those whom You have given me in this life.

Lord, You have said that the life of the flesh is in the blood. Thank You for this blood that has cleansed me from sin and sealed the New Covenant of which I am a partaker.

In Jesus' name, amen.

---

[1] Based on a prayer written by Joyce Meyer in *The Word, the Name and the Blood* (Tulsa: Harrison House, 1995).

Scripture References

Exodus 12:7,13	Leviticus 17:11
1 Corinthians 6:19	1 John 1:7
Hebrews 9:6-14	Hebrews 13:20 AMP

II.
EVENING PRAYER[2]

Father, as I lie down to sleep, I plead the blood of Jesus upon my life — within me, around me, and between me and all evil and the author of evil.

In Jesus' name, amen.

---

[2] Based on a prayer written by Mrs. C. Nuzum as recorded by Billye Brim in *The Blood and the Glory* (Tulsa: Harrison House, 1995).

Handling the Day of Trouble or Calamity

INTRODUCTION

During a time of trouble or calamity, it is sometimes difficult to remember the promises of God. The pressures of the moment may seem overwhelming. At such times, it is often helpful to read, meditate on, and pray the entire chapter of Psalm 91.

It may be that during a stressful time you will find this entire prayer too long. If so, draw from the Scriptures included in the following prayer. You may find yourself praying one paragraph or reading it aloud to yourself or to your family and friends.

I also encourage you to meditate on this prayer during good times.

At all times, remember that faith comes by hearing, and hearing by the Word of God (Rom. 10:17).

PRAYER

Father, I come to You in the name of Jesus, acknowledging You as my Refuge and High Tower. You are a refuge and a stronghold in these times of trouble (high cost, destitution, and desperation).

In the day of trouble You will hide me in Your shelter; in the secret place of Your tent will You hide me; You will set me high upon a rock. And now shall my head be lifted up above my enemies round about me; in Your tent I will offer sacrifices and shouting of joy; I will sing, yes, I will sing praises to You, O Lord. Hear, O Lord, when I cry aloud; have mercy and be gracious to me and answer me!

On the authority of Your Word, I declare that I have been made the righteousness of God in Christ Jesus. When I cry for help, You, Lord, hear me and deliver me out of all my distress and troubles. You are close to me, for I am of a broken heart, and You save such who are crushed with sorrow for sin and are humbly and thoroughly penitent. Lord, many are the evils that confront me, but You deliver me out of them all.

Thank You for being merciful and gracious to me, O God, for my soul takes refuge and finds shelter and confidence in You; yes, in the shadow of Your wings I take refuge and am confident until calamities and destructive storms are past. You perform on my behalf and reward me. You bring to pass Your purposes for me, and surely You complete them!

Father, You are my Refuge and Strength [mighty and impenetrable to temptation], a very present and well-proved help in trouble.

Lord, You have given and bequeathed to me Your peace. By Your grace, I will not let my heart be troubled, neither will I let it be afraid. With the help of the Holy Spirit, I will [stop allowing myself to be agitated and disturbed; and I refuse to permit myself to be fearful and intimidated and cowardly and unsettled].

HANDLING THE DAY OF TROUBLE
OR CALAMITY

By faith, I respond to these troubles and calamities: [I am full of joy now!] I exult and triumph in my troubles and rejoice in my sufferings, knowing that pressure and affliction and hardship produce patient and unswerving endurance. And endurance (fortitude) develops maturity of character (approved faith and tried integrity). And character [of this sort] produces [the habit of] joyful and confident hope of eternal salvation. Such hope never disappoints or deludes or shames me, for Your love has been poured out in my heart through the Holy Spirit Who has been given to me.

In Jesus' name, amen.

Scripture References

Psalm 9:9 AMP

Psalm 57:1,2 AMP

Psalm 27:5-7 AMP

Psalm 46:1 AMP

2 Corinthians 5:21

John 14:27 AMP

Psalm 34:17-20 AMP

Romans 5:3-5 AMP

*B*reaking the Curse of Abuse

INTRODUCTION

Christ redeemed us from the curse of the law by becoming a curse for us, for it is written: "Cursed is everyone who is hung on a tree."

Galatians 3:13 NIV

*O*n a Sunday morning after I had taught a lesson titled "Healing for the Emotionally Wounded," a young man wanted to speak with me. I listened intently as he told me that he had just been released from jail and was now on probation for physically abusing his family. His wife had filed for divorce, and he was living alone. It was not easy for him to confess his sin to me, and I was impressed by his humble attitude.

He said, "I am glad that this message is being given in the church and the abused can receive ministry. Is there anywhere that the abuser can go to receive spiritual help?"

He shared with me that he was attending a support group for abusers. He desired to commit to a church where he could receive forgiveness and acceptance. He knew that any lasting change would have to be from the inside out by the Spirit. I prayed with him, but it would be three years before I could write a prayer for the abuser.

As I read, studied, and sought the Lord, I discovered that the abuser is usually a person who has been abused. Often the problem is a generational curse that has been in the family of the abuser for as far back as anyone can remember. Many times the abuser declares that he will never treat his wife and children as he has been treated, but in spite of his resolve, he finds himself reacting in the same violent manner.

The generational curse is reversed as the abuser is willing to allow God to remove the character flaws that have held him in bondage.

If you are an abuser, I encourage you to pray this prayer for yourself until it becomes a reality in your life. If you know someone who is an abuser, pray this as a prayer of intercession in the third person.

PRAYER

I receive and confess that Jesus is my Lord, and I ask that Your will be done in my life.

Father, You have rescued me from the dominion of darkness and have brought me into the Kingdom of the Son of Your love. Once I was darkness, but now I am light in You; I walk as a child of light. The abuse is exposed and reproved by the light — it is made visible and clear; and where everything is visible and clear there is light.

Help me to grow in grace (undeserved favor, spiritual strength) and recognition and knowledge and understanding of my Lord and Savior, Jesus Christ, so that I may experience Your love and trust You to be a Father to me.

The history of my earthly family is filled with abusive behavior, much hatred, strife, and rage. The painful memory of past abuse *(verbal, emotional, physical, and/or sexual)* has caused me to be hostile and abusive to others.

I desire to be a doer of the Word and not a hearer only. No matter which way I turn, I can't make myself do right. I want to, but I can't. When I want to do good, I don't; and when I try not to do wrong, I do it anyway. It seems that sin still has me in its evil grasp. This pain has caused me to hurt myself and others. In my mind I want to be Your willing servant, but instead I find myself still enslaved to sin.

I confess my sin of abuse, resentment, and hostility toward others, and I ask You to forgive me. You are faithful and just to forgive my sin and cleanse me from all unrighteousness. I am tired of reliving the past in my present life, perpetuating the generational curse of anger and abuse.

Jesus was made a curse for me; therefore, Lord, I put on Your whole armor that I may be able to successfully stand against all the strategies and the tricks of the devil. I thank You that the evil power of abuse is broken, overthrown, and cast down. I submit myself to You and resist the devil. The need to hurt others no longer controls me or my family.

In Jesus' name, amen.

Scripture References

Romans 10:9

Matthew 6:10

Colossians 1:13 AMP

Ephesians 5:8,13 AMP

2 Peter 3:18 AMP

James 1:22

Romans 7:18-25 TLB

1 John 1:9

Galatians 3:13

Ephesians 6:11,12 TLB

2 Corinthians 10:5

James 4:7

Healing From Abuse

INTRODUCTION

This prayer can be applied to any form of abuse — physical, mental, emotional, or sexual. I wrote it after reading T. D. Jakes' book, *Woman, Thou Art Loosed.*[1] By praying it, I personally have experienced victory and freedom — I am no longer a victim but an overcomer.

PRAYER

Lord, You are my High Priest, and I ask You to loose me from this "infirmity." The abuse I suffered pronounced me guilty and condemned. I was bound — in an emotional prison — crippled and could in no wise lift up myself. You have called me to Yourself, and I have come.

The anointing that is upon You is present to bind up and heal the brokenness and emotional wounds of the past. You are the Truth that makes me free.

Thank You, Lord, for guiding me through the steps to emotional wholeness. You have begun a good work in me, and You will perform it until the day of Christ Jesus.

---

[1] (Shippensburg, PA: Treasure House, 1993).

Father, I desire to live according to the Spirit of life in Christ Jesus. This Spirit of life in Christ, like a strong wind, has magnificently cleared the air, freeing me from a fated lifetime of brutal tyranny at the hands of abuse.

Since I am now free, it is my desire to forget those things that lie behind and strain forward to what lies ahead. I press on toward the goal to win the [supreme and heavenly] prize to which You in Christ Jesus are calling me upward. The past will no longer control my thinking patterns or my behavior.

Praise be to You! I am a new creature in Christ Jesus. Old things have passed away; and, behold, all things have become new. I declare and decree that henceforth I will walk in newness of life.

Forgive me, Father, for self-hatred and self-condemnation. I am Your child. You sent Jesus that I might have life and have it more abundantly. Thank You for the blood of Jesus that makes me whole.

It is my desire to throw all spoiled virtue and cancerous evil in the garbage. In simple humility, I let my Gardener, You Lord, landscape me with the Word, making a salvation-garden of my life.

Father, by Your grace, I forgive my abuser/abusers and ask You to bring him/her/them to repentance.

In the name of Jesus I pray, amen.

Scripture References

Luke 13:11,12	Romans 6:4
John 14:6	1 John 3:1,2
John 8:3	2John 10:10
Philippians 1:6	1 John 1:7
Romans 8:2 MESSAGE	James 1:21 MESSAGE
Philippians 3:13,14 AMP	Matthew 5:44
2 Corinthians 5:17	2 Peter 3:9

Letting Go of the Past

Father, I realize my helplessness in saving myself, and I glory in what Christ Jesus has done for me. I let go — put aside all past sources of my confidence — counting them worth less than nothing, in order that I may experience Christ and become one with Him.

Lord, I have received Your Son, and He has given me the authority (power, privilege, and right) to become Your child.

I unfold my past and put into proper perspective those things that are behind. I have been crucified with Christ, and I no longer live, but Christ lives in me. The life I live in the body, I live by faith in the Son of God, Who loved me and gave Himself for me. I trust in You, Lord, with all of my heart and lean not on my own understanding. In all of my ways I acknowledge You, and You will make my paths straight.

I want to know Christ and the power of His resurrection and the fellowship of sharing in His sufferings, becoming like Him in His death, and so, somehow, to attain to the resurrection from the dead. So, whatever it takes, I will be one who lives in the fresh newness of life of those who are alive from the dead.

I don't mean to say that I am perfect. I haven't learned all I should, but I keep working toward that day when I will finally be all that Christ saved me for and wants me to be.

I am bringing all my energies to bear on this one thing: Regardless of my past, I look forward to what lies ahead. I strain to reach the end of the race and receive the prize for which You are calling me up to heaven because of what Christ Jesus did for me.

In His name I pray, amen.

Scripture References

Philippians 3:7-9 TLB

John 1:12 AMP

Psalm 32:5 AMP

Philippians 3:13

Galatians 2:20 NIV

Proverbs 3:5,6 NIV

Philippians 3:10,11 NIV

Romans 6:4

Philippians 3:12-14 TLB

Strength To Overcome Cares and Burdens

*W*hy are you cast down, O my inner self? And why should you moan over me and be disquieted within me?

Father, You set Yourself against the proud and haughty, but You give grace [continually] unto the humble. I submit myself therefore to You, God. In the name of Jesus, I resist the devil, and he will flee from me. I resist the cares of the world, which try to pressure me daily. Except the Lord builds the house, they labor in vain who build it.

Jesus, I come to You, for I labor and am heavy laden and overburdened, and You cause me to rest — You will ease and relieve and refresh my soul.

I take Your yoke upon me, and I learn of You; for You are gentle (meek) and humble (lowly) in heart, and I will find rest — relief, ease and refreshment and recreation and blessed quiet — for my soul. For Your yoke is wholesome (*easy*) — not harsh, hard, sharp, or pressing, but comfortable, gracious, and pleasant; and Your burden is light and easy to be borne.

I cast my burden on You, Lord, [releasing the weight of it] and You will sustain me; I thank You that You will never allow me, the [consistently] righteous, to be moved — made to slip, fall, or fail.

In the name of Jesus, I withstand the devil. I am firm in my faith [against his onset] — rooted, established, strong, immovable, and determined. I cease from [the weariness and pain] of human labor; and I am zealous and exert myself and strive diligently to enter into the rest [of God] — to know and experience it for myself.

Father, I thank You that Your presence goes with me and that You give me rest. I am still and rest in You, Lord; I wait for You and patiently stay myself upon You. I will not fret myself, nor shall I let my heart be troubled, neither shall I let it be afraid. I hope in You, God, and wait expectantly for You; for I shall yet praise You, for You are the Help of my countenance and my God.

In Jesus' name, amen.

Scripture References (AMP)

Psalm 42:11	Hebrews 4:10,11
James 4:6,7	Exodus 33:14
Psalm 127:1	Psalm 37:7
Matthew 11:28-30	John 14:27
Psalm 55:22	Psalm 42:11
1 Peter 5:9	

Renewing the Mind

Father, in Jesus' name, I thank You that I shall prosper and be in health, even as my soul prospers. I have the mind of Christ, the Messiah, and do hold the thoughts (feelings and purposes) of His heart. I trust in You, Lord, with all of my heart; I lean not unto my own understanding, but in all of my ways I acknowledge You, and You shall direct my paths.

Today I submit myself to Your Word, which exposes and sifts and analyzes and judges the very thoughts and purposes of my heart. (For the weapons of my warfare are not carnal, but mighty through You to the pulling down of strongholds — *intimidation, fears, doubts, unbelief, and failure.*) I refute arguments and theories and reasonings and every proud and lofty thing that sets itself up against the (true) knowledge of God; and I lead every thought and purpose away captive into the obedience of Christ, the Messiah, the Anointed One.

Today I shall be transformed by the renewing of my mind, that I may prove what is that good and acceptable and perfect will of God. Your Word, Lord, shall not depart out of my mouth; but I shall meditate on it day and night, that I may observe to do according to all that is written therein: for then I shall make my way prosperous, then I shall have good success.

My thoughts are the thoughts of the diligent, which tend only to plenteousness. Therefore, I am not anxious about anything, but

79

in everything by prayer and *petition, with thanksgiving, I present my requests to God. And the peace of God, which transcends all understanding, will guard my heart and my mind in Christ Jesus.

Today I fix my mind on whatever is *true,* whatever is *worthy of reverence* and is *honorable* and *seemly,* whatever is *just,* whatever is *pure,* whatever is *lovely* and *lovable,* whatever is *kind* and *winsome* and *gracious.* If there is any *virtue* and *excellence,* if there is anything *worthy of praise,* I will think on and weigh and take account of these things.

Today I roll my works upon You, Lord — I commit and trust them wholly to You; [You will cause my thoughts to become agreeable to Your will, and] so shall my plans be established and succeed.

In Jesus' name I pray, amen.

Scripture References

3 John 2	Romans 12:2
1 Corinthians 2:16 AMP	Joshua 1:8
Proverbs 3:5,6	Proverbs 21:5
Hebrews 4:12 AMP	Philippians 4:6-8 NIV
2 Corinthians 10:4	Proverbs 16:3 AMP
2 Corinthians 10:5 AMP	

---

* I encourage you to keep a prayer journal, writing down your petitions (definite requests) in prayer form.

Conquering the Thought Life

*I*n the name of Jesus, I take authority over my thought life. Even though I walk (live) in the flesh, I am not carrying on my warfare according to the flesh and using mere human weapons. For the weapons of my warfare are not physical (weapons of flesh and blood), but they are mighty before God for the overthrow and destruction of strongholds. I refute arguments and theories and reasonings and every proud and lofty thing that sets itself up against the (true) knowledge of God; and I lead every thought and purpose away captive into the obedience of Christ, the Messiah, the Anointed One.

With my soul I will bless the Lord with every thought and purpose in life. My mind will not wander out of the presence of God. My life shall glorify the Father — *spirit, soul, and body*. I take no account of the evil done to me — I pay no attention to a suffered wrong. It holds no place in my thought life. I am ever ready to believe the best of every person. I gird up the loins of my mind, and I set my mind and keep it set on what is above — the higher things — not on the things that are on the earth.

Whatever is true, whatever is worthy of reverence and is honorable and seemly, whatever is just, whatever is pure, whatever is lovely and lovable, whatever is kind and winsome and gracious, if there is any virtue and excellence, if there is anything worthy of praise, I will think on and weigh and take account of these things — I will fix my mind on them.

I have the mind of Christ, the Messiah, and do hold the thoughts (feelings and purposes) of His heart. In the name of Jesus, I will practice what I have learned and received and heard and seen in Christ and model my way of living on it, and the God of peace — of untroubled, undisturbed wellbeing — will be with me.

In Jesus' name, amen.

Scripture References (AMP)

2 Corinthians 10:3-5	Colossians 3:2
Psalm 103:1	Philippians 4:8
1 Corinthians 6:20	1 Corinthians 2:16
1 Corinthians 13:5,7	Philippians 4:9
1 Peter 1:13	

*C*asting Down Imaginations

*F*ather, though I live in the world, I do not wage war as the world does. The weapons I fight with are not the weapons of the world. On the contrary, they have divine power to demolish strongholds. I demolish arguments and every pretension that sets itself up against the knowledge of You, and I take captive every thought to make it obedient to Christ.

In the name of Jesus, I ask You, Father, to bless those who have despitefully used me. Whenever I feel afraid, I will trust in You. When I feel miserable, I will express thanksgiving; and when I feel that life is unfair, I will remember that You are more than enough.

When I feel ashamed, help me to remember that I no longer have to be afraid; I will not suffer shame. I am delivered from the fear of disgrace; I will not be humiliated. I relinquish the shame of my youth.

It is well with my soul, for You have redeemed me. You have called me by my name.

I am in Your will for my life at this time. I am being transformed through the renewing of my mind. I am able to test and approve [for myself] what Your will is — Your good and acceptable and perfect will.

You have good things reserved for my future. All my needs will be met according to Your riches in glory. I will replace worry for my family with asking You to protect and care for them.

You are love, and perfect love casts out fear.

In Jesus' name, amen.

Scripture References

2 Corinthians 10:3-5 NIV	Romans 12:2 AMP
Luke 6:28	Jeremiah 29:11 AMP
Isaiah 54:4 NIV	Philippians 4:19
Isaiah 43:1	1 Peter 5:7
Romans 12:2	1 John 4:8,18

Healing for Damaged Emotions

Father, in the name of Jesus, I come to You with a feeling of shame and emotional hurt. I confess my transgressions to You [continually unfolding the past till all is told]. You are faithful and just to forgive me and cleanse me of all unrighteousness. You are my Hiding Place, and You, Lord, preserve me from trouble. You surround me with songs and shouts of deliverance. I have chosen life. According to Your Word, You saw me while I was being formed in my mother's womb; and on the authority of Your Word, I was wonderfully made. Now I am Your handiwork, recreated in Christ Jesus.

Father, You have delivered me from the spirit of fear, and I shall not be ashamed. Neither shall I be confounded and depressed. You gave me beauty for ashes, the oil of joy for mourning, and the garment of praise for the spirit of heaviness that I might be a tree of righteousness, the planting of the Lord, that You might be glorified. I speak out in psalms, hymns, and spiritual songs, offering praise with my voice and making melody with all my heart to the Lord. Just as David did in 1 Samuel 30:6, I encourage myself in the Lord.

I believe in God Who raised from the dead Jesus, Who was betrayed and put to death because of my misdeeds and was raised to secure my acquittal, absolving me from all guilt before God. Father,

You anointed Jesus and sent Him to bind up and heal my broken heart and liberate me from the shame of my youth and the imperfections of my caretakers. In the name of Jesus, I choose to forgive all those who have wronged me in any way. You will not leave me without support as I complete the forgiveness process. I take comfort and am encouraged and confidently say, "The Lord is my Helper; I will not be seized with alarm. What can man do to me?"

My spirit is the candle of the Lord searching all the innermost parts of my being, and the Holy Spirit leads me into all truth. When reality exposes shame and emotional pain, I remember that the sufferings of this present life are not worth being compared with the glory that is about to be revealed to me and in me and for me and conferred on me! The chastisement needful to obtain my peace and wellbeing was upon Jesus, and with the stripes that wounded Him, I was healed and made whole. As Your child, Father, I have a joyful and confident hope of eternal salvation. This hope will never disappoint, delude, or shame me, for God's love has been poured out in my heart through the Holy Spirit Who has been given to me.

In His name I pray, amen.

Scripture References

Psalm 32:5-7 AMP	Romans 4:24,25
1 John 1:9	Isaiah 61:1
Deuteronomy 30:19	Mark 11:25
Psalm 139	Hebrews 13:5,6
Ephesians 2:10	Proverbs 20:27
2 Timothy 1:7	John 16:13
Isaiah 54:4	Romans 8:18
Isaiah 61:3	Isaiah 53:5
Ephesians 5:19	Romans 5:3-5

$\mathcal{V}$ictory Over Depression

$\mathcal{F}$ather, You are my Refuge and my High Tower and my Stronghold in times of trouble. I lean on and confidently put my trust in You, for You have not forsaken me. I seek You on the authority of Your Word and the right of my necessity. I praise You, the Help of my countenance and my God.

Lord, You lift up those who are bowed down. Therefore, I am strong and my heart takes courage. I establish myself on righteousness — right standing in conformity with Your will and order. I am far even from the thought of oppression or destruction, for I fear not. I am far from terror, for it shall not come near me.

Father, You have thoughts and plans for my welfare and peace. *My mind is stayed on You,* for I stop allowing myself to be agitated and disturbed and intimidated and cowardly and unsettled.

In the name of Jesus, I loose my mind from wrong thought patterns. I tear down strongholds that have protected bad perceptions about myself. I submit to You, Father, and resist fear, discouragement, self-pity, and depression. I will not give place to the devil by harboring resentment and holding onto anger. I surround myself with songs and shouts of deliverance from depression, and I will continue to be an overcomer by the word of my testimony and the blood of the Lamb.

Father, I thank You that I have been given a spirit of power and of love and of a calm and well-balanced mind. I have discipline and self-control. I have the mind of Christ and hold the thoughts, feelings, and purposes of His heart. I have a fresh mental and spiritual attitude, for I am constantly renewed in the spirit of my mind with Your Word, Father.

Therefore, I brace up and reinvigorate and cut through and make firm and straight paths for my feet — safe and upright and happy paths that go in the right direction. I arise from the depression and prostration in which circumstances have kept me. I rise to new life; I shine and am radiant with the glory of the Lord.

Thank You, Father, in Jesus' name, that I am set free from every evil work. I praise You that the joy of the Lord is my strength and stronghold! Hallelujah! Amen.

Scripture References

Psalm 9:9,10 AMP	Ephesians 4:27
Psalm 42:5,11	Luke 4:18,19
Psalm 146:8	2 Timothy 1:7 AMP
Psalm 31:22-24 AMP	1 Corinthians 2:16 AMP
Isaiah 35:3,4	Philippians 2:5
Isaiah 54:14	Ephesians 4:23,24 AMP
Isaiah 50:10	Hebrews 12:12,13 AMP
Jeremiah 29:11-13 AMP	Isaiah 60:1 AMP
Isaiah 26:3	Galations 1:4
John 14:27 AMP	Nehemiah 8:10 AMP
James 4:7	

$\mathcal{V}$ictory Over Pride

$\mathcal{F}$ather, Your Word says that You hate a proud look, that You resist the proud but give grace to the humble. I submit myself, therefore, to You, God. In the name of Jesus, I resist the devil, and he will flee from me. I renounce every manifestation of pride in my life as sin; I repent and turn from it.

As an act of faith, I clothe myself with humility and receive Your grace. I humble myself under Your mighty hand, Lord, that You may exalt me in due time. I refuse to exalt myself. I do not think of myself more highly than I ought; I do not have an exaggerated opinion of my own importance, but rate my ability with sober judgment, according to the degree of faith apportioned to me.

Proverbs 11:2 says, "When pride cometh, then cometh shame: but with the lowly is wisdom." Father, I set myself to resist pride when it comes. My desire is to be counted among the lowly, so I take on the attitude of a servant.

Father, thank You that You dwell with one who is of a contrite and humble spirit. You revive the spirit of the humble and revive the heart of the contrite one. Thank You that the reward of humility and the reverent and worshipful fear of the Lord is riches and honor and life.

In Jesus' name I pray, amen.

Scripture References

Proverbs 6:16,17   Proverbs 11:2

James 4:6,7   Matthew 23:11

Proverbs 21:4   Isaiah 57:15

1 Peter 5:5,6   Proverbs 22:4 AMP

Romans 12:3 AMP

$\mathcal{V}$ictory in a Healthy Lifestyle

$\mathcal{F}$ather, I am Your child, and Jesus is Lord over my spirit, soul, and body. I praise you because I am fearfully and wonderfully made. Your works are wonderful; I know that full well.

Lord, thank You for declaring Your plans for me — plans to prosper me and not to harm me, plans to give me hope and a future. I choose to renew my mind to Your plans for a healthy lifestyle. You have abounded toward me in all prudence and wisdom. Therefore, I give thought to my steps. Teach me knowledge and good judgment.

My body is for the Lord. So here is what I want to do with Your help, Father God. I choose to take my everyday, ordinary life — my sleeping, eating, going-to-work, and walking-around life — and place it before You as an offering. Embracing what You do for me is the best thing I can do for You.

Christ, the Messiah, will be magnified and receive glory and praise in this body of mine and will be boldly exalted in my person. Thank You, Father, in Jesus' name! Hallelujah! Amen.

Scripture References

Psalm 139:14	Psalm 119:66
Jeremiah 29:11	Romans 12:1 MESSAGE
Proverbs 14:15	Philippians 1:20 AMP

Victory Over Fear

Father, when I am afraid, I will put my confidence in You. Yes, I will trust Your promises. And since I trust You, what can mere man do to me?

You have not given me a spirit of timidity, but of power and love and discipline (sound judgment). Therefore, I am not ashamed of the testimony of my Lord. I have not received a spirit of slavery leading to fear again, but I have received a spirit of adoption as a son, by which I cry out, "Abba! Father!"

Jesus, You delivered me, who, through fear of death, had been living all my life as a slave to constant dread. I receive the gift You left me — peace of mind and heart! And the peace You give isn't fragile like the peace the world gives. I cast away troubled thoughts, and I choose not to be afraid. I believe in God; I believe also in You.

Lord, You are my Light and my Salvation; You protect me from danger — whom shall I fear? When evil men come to destroy me, they will stumble and fall! Yes, though a mighty army marches against me, my heart shall know no fear! I am confident that You will save me.

Thank You, Holy Spirit, for bringing these things to my remembrance when I am tempted to be afraid. I will trust in my God. In the name of Jesus I pray, amen.

Scripture References

Psalm 56:3-5 TLB	Hebrews 2:15 TLB
2 Timothy 1:7,8 NAS	John 14:1,17 TLB
Romans 8:15 NAS	Psalm 27:1-3 TLB

*O*vercoming a Feeling of Abandonment

INTRODUCTION

When my father and my mother forsake me, then the Lord will take me up.

Psalm 27:10

*T*his prayer was prompted by a letter I received from someone who is incarcerated. According to his letter, he grew up in a family of fighters and felt abandoned by his family and so-called friends. His pugnacious attitude controlled him, and eventually his aggressive temperament caused him to almost kill someone.

In prison he was ridiculed and harassed by inmates who encouraged him to fight. His wife divorced him, and again he was left alone. Thoughts that "no one likes me" continually tormented him, but he desired to know how to change his thinking.

A laborer of the harvest introduced him to Jesus and my book, *Prayers That Avail Much, Volume 1*.[1] He still had trouble controlling his temper even with those who might have been his friends. His letter was filled with the pain of loneliness and

---

[1] Tulsa: Harrison House, 1989.

abandonment. The following is a revised and expanded version of the original prayer I wrote, encouraging him to pray for himself.

PRAYER

Father, I have confessed Jesus as my Lord and believe in my heart that You raised Him from the dead. I ask for the power of the Holy Spirit to overcome the resentment I feel toward those who abused and abandoned me.

Now I am Your child. When other people leave me and I feel unloved, I am thankful that You will never, ever leave me alone or reject me.

Jesus gave His life for me and called me His friend. He lives in my heart, and I am on my way to heaven. That is plenty to be thankful for. So when I am lonely or discouraged, I can think of things that are pure and holy and good, even when I am apart from everyone.

Heavenly Father, I ask You to strengthen me and help me while in the presence of the dangers surrounding me. You have assigned angels who will accompany, defend, and preserve me in all my ways [of obedience and service]. I am not alone. Your Word says that there is nothing that can separate me from the love of Christ — not pain nor stress nor persecution. I will come to the top of every circumstance or trial through Jesus' love.

You are concerned with the smallest detail that concerns me, and You are my Help. I ask You for friends who will admonish and encourage me. Teach me how to trust others and be a friend who sticks closer than a brother. Help me to walk in Your love and show myself friendly.

In Jesus' name, amen.

Scripture References

Romans 10:9,10 NIV   Psalm 91:11 AMP

Hebrews 13:5 NIV   Romans 8:35,39

John 15:13-15 NIV   Psalm 138:8 AMP

1 Thessalonians 5:18 TLB   Psalm 46:1 MESSAGE

Philippians 4:8 TLB   Proverbs 18:24

Isaiah 41:10 TLB

Overcoming Discouragement

INTRODUCTION

Moses returned to the Lord and said, "O Lord, why have you brought trouble upon this people? Is this why you sent me? Ever since I went to Pharaoh to speak in your name, he has brought trouble upon this people, and you have not rescued your people at all."

Exodus 5:22,23 NIV

Here in this passage, we find Moses discouraged, complaining to God.

It is important that we approach God with integrity and in an attitude of humility. But because we fear making a negative confession, we sometimes cross the line of honesty into the line of denial and delusion.

Let's be honest. God already knows what we are feeling. He can handle our anger, complaints, and disappointments. He understands us. He is aware of our human frailties (Ps. 103:14) and can be touched with the feelings of our infirmities (Heb. 4:15).

Whether your "trouble" is a business failure, abandonment, depression, a mental disorder, a chemical imbalance, oppression, a marriage problem, a child who is in a strange land of drugs and alcohol, financial disaster, or anything else, the following prayer is for you.

Sometimes when you are in the midst of discouragement, it is difficult to remember that you have ever known any Scripture. I admonish you to read this prayer aloud until you recognize the reality of God's Word in your spirit, soul, and body. Remember, God is watching over His Word to perform it (Jer. 1:12 AMP). He will perfect that which concerns you (Ps. 138:8).

PRAYER

Lord, I do not understand why You have allowed this trouble to assail me. It was after I began to follow You in obedience that this trouble was manifested in my life. I have exhausted all my possibilities for changing my situation and circumstances and have found that I am powerless to change them. I believe; help me overcome my unbelief. All things are not possible with man, but all things are possible with You. I humble myself before You, and You will lift me up.

I have a great High Priest Who has gone through the heavens: Jesus, Your Son. And I hold firmly to the faith I profess. My High Priest is able to sympathize with my weaknesses. He was tempted in every way, just as I am — yet was without sin. I approach Your throne of grace with confidence, so that I may receive mercy and find grace to help me in my time of need.

In the face of discouragement, disappointment, and anger, I choose to believe that Your word to Moses is Your word to me. You are mighty to deliver. Because of Your mighty hand, You will drive out the forces that have set themselves up against me. You are the Lord, Yahweh, the Promise-Keeper, the Almighty One. You appeared to Abraham, to Isaac, and to Jacob and established Your covenant with them.

Father, I believe that You have heard my groaning, my cries. I will live to see Your promises of deliverance fulfilled in my life. You have not forgotten one word of Your promise; You are a Covenant-Keeper.

It is You Who will bring me out from under the yoke of bondage and free me from being a slave to _____. You have redeemed me with an outstretched arm and with mighty acts of judgment. You have taken me as Your own, and You are my God. You are a father to me. You have delivered me from the past that has held me in bondage and translated me into the Kingdom of love, peace, joy, and righteousness. I will no longer settle for the pain of the past. Where sin abounds, grace does much more abound.

Father, what You have promised, I will go and possess, in the name of Jesus. I am willing to take the chance, to take the risk, to get back into the good fight of faith. It is with patient endurance and steady and active persistence that I run the race, the appointed course that is set before me. I rebuke the spirit of fear, for I am established in righteousness. Oppression and destruction shall not come near me. Behold, they may gather together and stir up strife, but it is not from You, Father. Whoever stirs up strife against me shall fall and surrender to me. I am more than a conqueror through Him Who loves me.

In His name I pray, amen.

Scripture References

*(This prayer is based on Exodus 5:22-6:11
and includes other verses where applicable.)*

Mark 9:24 NIV

Luke 18:27

1 Peter 5:6 NIV

Hebrews 4:14-16 NIV

Exodus 6:3,4 AMP

Genesis 49:22-26 AMP

1 Kings 8:56

Deuteronomy 26:8

Colossians 1:13

Romans 5:20

1 Timothy 6:12

Hebrews 12:1 AMP

Isaiah 54:14-16

Romans 8:37

*O*vercoming Intimidation

*F*ather, I come to You in the name of Jesus, confessing that intimidation has caused me to stumble. I ask Your forgiveness for thinking of myself as inferior, for I am created in Your image, and I am Your workmanship. Jesus said that the Kingdom of God is in me. Therefore, the power that raised Jesus from the dead dwells in me and causes me to face life with hope and divine energy.

The Lord is my Light and my Salvation; whom shall I fear? The Lord is the Strength of my life; of whom shall I be afraid? Lord, You said that You would never leave me or forsake me. Therefore, I can say without any doubt or fear that You are my Helper, and I am not afraid of anything that mere man can do to me. Greater is He that is in me than he that is in the world. If God is for me, who can be against me? I am free from the fear of man and public opinion.

Father, You have not given me a spirit of timidity — of cowardice, of craven and cringing and fawning fear — but You have given me a spirit of power and of love and of a calm and well-balanced mind and discipline and self-control. I can do all things through Christ Who gives me the strength. Amen.

Scripture References

1 John 1:9	Ephesians 2:10
Luke 17:21	Ephesians 1:19,20
Colossians 1:29	Psalm 27:1
Hebrews 13:5	1 John 4:4
Romans 3:31	Proverbs 29:25
Joshua 1:5	Philippians 4:13
2 Timothy 1:7	

*O*vercoming a Sense of Hopelessness

*F*ather, as Your child I boldly come before Your throne of grace that I may receive mercy and find grace to help in this time of need.

Father, I know that Your ears are open to my prayers. I ask that You listen to my prayer, O God, and hide not Yourself from my supplication! I ask that You attend to me and answer me, for I am restless and distraught in my complaint and must moan. Fear and trembling have come upon me; horror and fright have overwhelmed me.

Oh, that I had wings like a dove! I would fly away and be at rest. Yes, I would wander far away; I would lodge in the wilderness. I would hasten to escape and to find a shelter from the stormy wind and tempest.

I am calling upon You, my God, to rescue me. You redeem my life in peace from the battle of hopelessness that is against me. I cast my burden on You, Lord, [releasing the weight of it], and You sustain me; You will never allow the [consistently] righteous to be moved (made to slip, fall, or fail).

Hopelessness lies in wait for me to swallow me up or trample me all day long. Whenever I am afraid, I will have confidence in and put my trust and reliance in You. By [Your help], God, I will praise Your Word; on You I lean, rely, and confidently put my trust; I will not fear.

You know my every sleepless night. Each tear and heartache is answered with Your promise. I am thanking You with all my heart. You pulled me from the brink of death, my feet from the cliff edge of doom. Now I stroll at leisure with You in the sunlit fields of life.

[What, what would have become of me], Lord, had I not believed that I would see Your goodness in the land of the living! I wait and hope for and expect You; I am brave and of good courage, and I let my heart be stout and enduring. Yes, I wait for and hope for and expect You.

Father, I give You all my worries and cares, for You are always thinking about me and watching everything that concerns me. I am well-balanced and careful — vigilant, watching out for attacks from Satan, my great enemy. By Your grace I am standing firm, trusting You, and I remember that other Christians all around the world are going through these sufferings too. You, God, are full of kindness through Christ and will give me Your eternal glory.

In the name of Jesus, I am an overcomer by the blood of the Lamb and by the word of my testimony. Amen.

Scripture References

Hebrews 4:16	Psalm 56:5,8 MESSAGE
Psalm 55:1 MESSAGE	Psalm 56:13 MESSAGE
Psalm 55:1,2 AMP	Psalm 27:13,14 AMP
Psalm 55:5-8 AMP	1 Peter 5:7-9 AMP, TLB
Psalm 55:16,18,22 AMP	Revelation 12:11
Psalm 56:2-4 AMP	

Overcoming a Feeling of Rejection

INTRODUCTION

Rejection seems to create an identity crisis. Rejection by those in the Body of Christ is especially cruel. It happens more often than it should. When you are thrown into an identity crisis, you have the opportunity to erase old tapes that have played in your mind for a long time and replace those self-destructive thoughts with God-thoughts.

Your Heavenly Father saw you and approved of you even while you were in your mother's womb (Ps. 139:13-16). He gave you survival tools that would bring you to the place where you are today. He is a Father Who has been waiting for you to come home to truth — the truth that will set you free (John 8:32).

Future rejection may hurt, but it will be only for a season. (1 Pet. 1:6.) The Word of God is your shield against all the fiery darts of the devil (Eph. 6:16,17).

For victory over your feeling of rejection, pray the following prayer in faith and joy.[1]

---

[1] For further support, I encourage you to read Psalm 27 and the book of Ephesians in their entirety.

PRAYER

Lord, Your Son, Jesus, is my High Priest. He understands and sympathizes with my weaknesses and this excruciating pain of rejection. In His name I approach Your throne of grace with confidence, so that I may receive mercy and find grace to help me in my time of need. I ask You to forgive my sins, and I receive Your mercy; I expect Your healing grace to dispel the rejection I am suffering because of the false accusations and demeaning actions of another.

Father, Jesus was despised and rejected — a Man of Sorrows, acquainted with bitterest grief. The grief of _____ turning against me and treating me as an outcast is consuming me, just as my rejection consumed Your Son, Who freely gave His life for me.

Forgive me for turning my back on Jesus and looking the other way — He was despised, and I didn't care. Yet it was my grief He bore, my sorrows that weighed Him down. He was wounded and bruised for my sins. He was beaten that I might have peace; He was lashed, and with His stripes I was healed.

In the face of rejection I will declare, "The Lord is my Light and my Salvation — whom shall I fear or dread? The Lord is the Refuge and Stronghold of my life — of whom shall I be afraid?" (Ps. 27:1 AMP).

I know right from wrong and cherish Your laws in my heart; I won't be afraid of people's scorn or their slanderous talk. Slanderous talk is temporal and fades away. Your Word will never pass away.

Father, I choose to look at the things that are eternal: Your justice and mercy shall last forever, and Your salvation from generation to generation. Your eyes are upon me, for I have right standing with You, and Your ears are attentive to my prayer. You spoke to me and asked, "Now who is going to hurt you if you are a zealous follower of that which is good?"

In my heart I set Christ apart as holy [and acknowledge Him] as Lord. I am always ready to give a logical defense to anyone who asks me to account for the hope that is in me, but I do it courteously and respectfully. I purpose [to see to it that] my conscience is entirely clear (unimpaired), so that, when I am falsely accused as an evildoer, those who threaten me abusively and revile my right behavior in Christ may come to be ashamed [of slandering my good life].

There is wonderful joy ahead, even though the going is rough for a while down here. These trials are only to test my faith, to see whether it is strong and pure. It is being tested as fire tests gold and purifies it — and my faith is far more precious to You, Lord, than mere gold; so if my faith remains strong after being tried in the test tube of fiery trials, it will bring me much praise and glory and honor on the day of Jesus' return.

In spite of the rejection I have experienced, I declare that everything You say about me in Your Word is true:

I am blessed with all spiritual blessings in heavenly places in Christ (Eph. 1:3).

I am chosen by You, my Father (Eph. 1:4).

I am holy and without blame (Eph. 1:4).

I am Your child according to the good pleasure of Your will (Eph. 1:5).

I am accepted in the Beloved (Eph. 1:6).

I am redeemed through the blood of Jesus (Eph. 1:7).

I am a person of wisdom and prudence (Eph. 1:8).

I am an heir (Eph. 1:11).

I have a spirit of wisdom and revelation in the knowledge of Christ (Eph. 1:17).

I am saved by Your grace (Eph. 2:5).

I am seated in heavenly places in Christ Jesus (Eph. 2:6).

I am Your workmanship (Eph. 2:10).

I am near to You by the blood of Christ (Eph. 2:13).

I am a new creation (Eph. 2:15).

I am of Your household (Eph. 2:19).

I am a citizen of heaven (Eph. 2:19).

I am a partaker of Your promises in Christ (2 Pet. 1:4).

I am strengthened with might by Your Spirit (Eph. 3:16).

I allow Christ to dwell in my heart by faith (Eph. 3:17).

I am rooted and grounded in love (Eph. 3:17).

I speak the truth in love (Eph. 4:15).

I am renewed in the spirit of my mind (Eph. 4:23).

I am Your follower (Eph. 5:1).

I walk in love (Eph. 5:2).

I am light in You (Eph. 5:8).

I walk circumspectly (Eph. 5:15).

I am filled with the Spirit (Eph. 5:18).

I am more than a conqueror (Rom. 8:37).

I am an overcomer (Rev. 12:11).

I am Your righteousness in Christ Jesus (1 Cor. 1:30).

I am healed (1 Pet. 2:24).

I am free (John 8:36).

I am salt (Matt. 5:13).

I am consecrated (1 Cor. 6:11 AMP).

I am sanctified (1 Cor. 6:11).

I am victorious (1 John 5:4).

Everything You say about me is true, Lord.

In Your name I pray, amen.

Scripture References

Hebrews 4:14-16 NIV   Isaiah 51:7,8 TLB

Isaiah 53:3-5 TLB   1 Peter 3:12-17 AMP

2 Corinthians 4:18   1 Peter 1:6,7 TLB

Overcoming Worry

Father, I depart from evil and do good. I seek, inquire for, and crave peace. I pursue (go after) it! When my ways please You, Lord, You make even my enemies to be at peace with me.

Lord, You have given to me Your peace; Your [own] peace You have bequeathed to me. It is not the peace that the world gives. I will not let my heart be troubled, neither will I let it be afraid. [I refuse to be agitated and disturbed; and I will not permit myself to be fearful and intimidated and cowardly and unsettled.]

Instead of worrying, I will pray. I will let petitions and praises shape my worries into prayers, letting You, Father, know my concerns, not forgetting to thank You for the answers. Your peace will keep my thoughts and my heart quiet and at rest as I trust in Christ Jesus, my Lord. It is wonderful what happens when Christ displaces worry at the center of my life.

Thank You for guarding me and keeping me in perfect and constant peace. My mind [both its inclination and its character] is stayed on You. I commit myself to You, lean on You, and hope confidently in You.

I let the peace (soul harmony that comes) from Christ rule (act as umpire continually) in my heart [deciding and settling with finality all questions that arise in my mind]. I am thankful (appreciative), [giving praise to You always].

In Jesus' name, amen.

Scripture References

Philippians 4:6,7   Colossians 3:15 AMP

MESSAGE, TLB   Proverbs 16:7 AMP

Psalm 34:14 AMP   John 14:27 AMP

Isaiah 26:3 AMP

*O*vercoming Hypersensitivity

INTRODUCTION

A new command I give you: Love one another. As I have loved you, so you must love one another. By this all men will know that you are my disciples, if you love one another.

John 13:34, 35 NIV

*T*he royal law of love is the counteragent for hypersensitivity.

First Corinthians 13:5 AMP reveals that love "...is not conceited (arrogant and inflated with pride); it is not rude (unmannerly) and does not act unbecomingly. Love (God's love in us) does not insist on its own rights or its own way, for it is not self-seeking; it is not touchy or fretful or resentful; it takes no account of the evil done to it [it pays no attention to a suffered wrong]."

An overly sensitive person is thin-skinned and experiences feelings of alienation, irritability, and resentment in relationships.

The hypersensitive person has usually experienced deep hurt from rejection and needs a lot of approval from others. This individual is excessively sensitive to remarks that may or may not be intended to be hurtful. It is difficult for a person of this nature to trust others, to accept constructive criticism or advice; and this weakness hinders positive relationships. When presentations or suggestions are rejected, that action is taken as a personal attack.

Hypersensitivity is an enemy that can be overcome through spiritual warfare. In waging the good warfare, we have God-given weapons to overthrow our adversary. These weapons include, among other things: the anointing that is upon Jesus to bind up and heal the brokenhearted (Luke 4:18), the sword of the Spirit, which is the Word of God (Eph. 6:17), the shield of faith (Eph. 6:16), and the help of the Holy Spirit (John 14:16 AMP), which may come through a Christian counselor, a minister, or a friend.

James instructed us, "Confess to one another therefore your faults (your slips, your false steps, your offenses, your sins); and pray [also] for one another, that you may be healed and restored [to a spiritual tone of mind and heart]. The earnest (heartfelt, continued) prayer of a righteous man makes tremendous power available [dynamic in its working]" (James 5:16 AMP). We are overcomers by the blood of the Lamb and by the word of our testimony! (Rev. 12:11).

PRAYER

Father, forgive me for my attempts to hurt and dominate others. I realize that I have released my anger inappropriately. I confess this as sin and receive Your forgiveness, knowing that You are faithful and just to forgive my sin and cleanse me from all unrighteousness. I forgive those who have wronged me, and I ask for healing of my anger and unresolved hurts.

I realize that I am responsible for my own behavior, and I am accountable to You for my thoughts, words, and actions.

Thank You for the Holy Spirit Who leads me into reality — the truth that makes me free. You have sent Your Word and healed me and delivered me from all my destructions.

Father, I am empowered through my union with You. I draw my strength from You [that strength which Your boundless might provides]. Your strength causes me to be steadfast and trustworthy, gives me the capacity for perseverance and tolerance, and enables me to resist hypersensitivity, irritability, and touchiness.

I desire to be well-balanced (temperate, sober of mind), vigilant, and cautious at all times; for I recognize that enemy — the devil — who roams around like a lion roaring, seeking someone to seize upon and devour. In the name of Jesus, I withstand him, firm in faith [against his onset — rooted, established, strong, immovable, and determined].

I am dwelling in the secret place of the Most High, and I shall remain stable and fixed under the shadow of the Almighty [Whose power no foe can withstand].

I purpose to walk in love toward my family members, my associates, and my neighbors with the help of the Holy Spirit. Whom the Son has set free is free indeed.

Thanks be to You, Lord, for You always cause me to triumph in Christ Jesus. I am an overcomer by the blood of the Lamb and by the word of my testimony.

In Jesus' name, amen.

Scripture References

1 John 1:9	Ephesians 6:10 AMP
Mark 11:24,25	1 Peter 5:8,9 AMP
Matthew 12:36	Psalm 91:1 AMP
John 16:13	John 8:36
John 8:32	2 Corinthians 2:14
Psalm 107:20	Revelation 12:11

*O*vercoming Chronic Fatigue Syndrome

INTRODUCTION

*A*ll fatigue does not fall into the category of Chronic Fatigue Syndrome. Most people at one time or another have feelings of apathy and energy loss — times when they go to bed tired and get up tired.

There are cases of fatigue that last for weeks, months, or even years. The medical profession has not determined the causes of Chronic Fatigue Syndrome and does not know its cure. In most individuals it simply runs its course.[1] Where there is no way, Jesus is the Way, the Truth, and the Life. God sent His Word to heal you and deliver you from all your destructions (Ps. 107:20).

According to those who have shared their experience with this syndrome, they have flu-like symptoms — they feel achy with a low-grade fever. One person who suffers from it and for whom we pray is considered disabled and cannot work regularly.

You and I are created triune beings — spirit, soul, and body (1 Thess. 5:23). The Apostle John wrote, "Beloved, I wish above

---

[1] Editors of *Prevention* Magazine, *Symptoms, Their Causes & Cures* (Emmaus, PA: Rodale Press, 1994), pp. 179,181.

117

all things that thou mayest prosper and be in health, even as thy soul prospereth" (3 John 2).

God's Word is medicine to our flesh (Prov. 4:20-22 AMP). If any type of medication is to bring relief and a cure, it is necessary to follow the prescribed dosage. This is true with "spiritual" medicine. It is imperative to take doses of God's Word daily through reading, meditating, and listening to healing tapes. The spirit, soul, and body are interrelated; it is the Word of God that brings the entire being into harmony.

God made us and knows us inside and out. He sent His Word to heal us and to deliver us from all our destructions (Ps. 107:20). Prayer prepares us to take action. Jesus said that if we pray in secret, our Heavenly Father will reward us openly (Matt. 6:6). Prayer includes praise, worship, and petition.

Prayer prepares us for change — it equips us for action. It puts us in tune and in harmony with the Spirit of God Who is hovering over the face of the rivers of living waters, residing within us (Gen. 1:2; John 7:38). He is waiting for us to speak, to move — to act out our faith. The ministry of the Holy Spirit is revealed in the names ascribed to Him — Comforter, Counselor, Helper, Advocate, Intercessor, Strengthener, Standby (John 16:7 AMP). He is with us and in us (John 14:17).

PRAYER

Father, in the name of Jesus, I come before Your throne of grace to receive mercy and to find grace to help in time of need. May blessing (praise, laudation, and eulogy) be to You, the God and Father of my Lord Jesus Christ (the Messiah) for You have blessed me in Christ with every spiritual (given by the Holy Spirit) blessing in the heavenly realm!

Father, Chronic Fatigue Syndrome is a curse, not a blessing. Jesus became a curse and at the same time dissolved the curse. And now, because of that, the air is cleared and I can see that Abraham's blessing is present and available for me. I am able to receive Your life, Your Spirit, just the way Abraham received it.

Christ, the Messiah, purchased my freedom with His very own blood, and the law of the Spirit of life [which is] in Christ Jesus [the law of my new being] has freed me from the law of sin and of death.

Christ lives in me. The Spirit of You Who raised up Jesus from the dead dwells in me. You, Father, are restoring to life my mortal (short-lived, perishable) body through Your Spirit Who dwells in me.

You, Sovereign Lord, have given me an instructed tongue, to know the word that sustains the weary. You waken me morning by morning, waken my ear to listen like one being taught.

I have strength for all things in Christ Who empowers me [I am ready for anything and equal to anything through Him Who infuses inner strength into me; I am self-sufficient in Christ's sufficiency].

You are my Light and my Salvation — whom shall I fear or dread? You are the Refuge and Stronghold of my life — of whom shall I be afraid? You, Lord, are my Shield, my Glory, and the Lifter of my head. With my voice I cry to You, and You hear and answer me out of Your holy hill. I lie down and sleep, I awaken again, and You sustain me.

Father, I put on Your whole armor; and, having done all, I stand, knowing that You are watching over Your Word to perform it. Your Word will not return to You void [without producing any effect, useless], but shall accomplish that which You please and purpose, and it shall prosper in the thing for which You sent it.

Lord, You used Your servant body to carry my sins to the cross so I could be rid of sin, free to live the right way. Your wounds became my healing.

I throw off the spirit of heaviness and exchange it for a garment of praise. Thank You for the superhuman energy which You so mightily enkindle and work within me.

In the name of Jesus I pray, amen.

Scripture References

Hebrews 4:16	Psalm 27:1 AMP
Ephesians 1:3 AMP	Psalm 3:3-5 AMP
Galatians 3:13,14 MESSAGE	Ephesians 6:11,13
Acts 20:28	Jeremiah 1:12 AMP
Romans 8:2,10,11 AMP	Isaiah 55:11 AMP
1 Peter 2:24 MESSAGE	Isaiah 61:3
Isaiah 50:4 NIV	Colossians 1:29 AMP
Philippians 4:13 AMP	

Health and Healing

Father, in the name of Jesus, I come before You asking You to heal me. It is written that the prayer of faith will save the sick, and the Lord will raise him up. And if I have committed sins, I will be forgiven. I let go of all unforgiveness, resentment, anger, and bad feelings toward anyone.

My body is the temple of the Holy Spirit, and I desire to be in good health. I seek truth that will make me free — both spiritual and natural (*good eating habits, medications if necessary, and appropriate rest and exercise*). You bought me at a price, and I desire to glorify You in my spirit and my body — they both belong to You.

Thank You, Father, for sending Your Word to heal me and deliver me from all my destructions. Jesus, You are the Word Who became flesh and dwelt among us. You bore my griefs (pains) and carried my sorrows (sickness). You were pierced through for my transgressions and crushed for my iniquities, the chastening for my wellbeing fell upon You, and by Your scourging I am healed.

Father, I give attention to Your words and incline my ear to Your sayings. I will not let them depart from my sight, but I will keep them in the midst of my heart, for they are life and health to my whole body.

Since the Spirit of Him Who ~~raised~~ Jesus from the dead dwells in me, He Who raised Christ from the dead will also give life to my mortal body ~~through~~ His Spirit Who dwells in me.

Thank You that I will prosper and be in ~~health~~, even as my soul prospers. Amen.

Scripture References

James 5:15 NKJV	Proverbs 4:21,22 NAS
1 Corinthians 6:19,20	Psalm 103:3-5 NAS
Psalm 107:20	Romans 8:11 NKJV
John 1:14	3 John 2
Isaiah 53:4,5 NAS	

Safety

Father, in the name of Jesus, I thank You that You watch over Your Word to perform it. I thank You that I dwell in the secret place of the Most High and that I remain stable and fixed under the shadow of the Almighty, Whose power no foe can withstand.

Father, You are my Refuge and my Fortress. *No evil shall befall me — no accident shall overtake me — nor any plague or calamity come near my home.* You give Your angels special charge over me to accompany and defend and preserve me in all my ways of obedience and service. They are encamped around about me.

Father, You are my Confidence, firm and strong. You keep my foot from being caught in a trap or hidden danger. Father, You give me safety and ease me — *Jesus is my Safety!*

Traveling — As I go, I say, "Let me pass over to the other side," and I have what I say. I walk on my way, securely and in confident trust, for my heart and mind are firmly fixed and stayed on You, and I am kept in perfect peace.

Sleeping — Father, I sing for joy upon my bed because You sustain me. In peace I lie down and sleep, for You alone, Lord, make me dwell in safety. I lie down, and I am not afraid. My sleep is sweet, for You give blessings to me in sleep. Thank You, Father, in Jesus' name. Amen.

Scripture References

Jeremiah 1:12	Proverbs 3:23 AMP
Psalm 91:1,2 AMP	Psalm 112:7
Psalm 91:10 AMP	Isaiah 26:3
Psalm 91:11 AMP	Psalm 149:5
Psalm 34:7	Psalm 3:5
Proverbs 3:26 AMP	Psalm 4:8 AMP
Isaiah 49:25	Proverbs 3:24
Mark 4:35	Psalm 127:2

*P*eaceful Sleep

*F*ather, thank You for peaceful sleep, and for Your angels that encamp around us who fear You. You deliver us and keep us safe. The angels excel in strength, do Your word, and heed the voice of Your word. You give Your angels charge over me, to keep me in all my ways.

I bring every thought, every imagination, and every dream into the captivity and obedience of Jesus Christ. Father, I thank You that, even as I sleep, my heart counsels me and reveals to me Your purpose and plan. Thank You for sweet sleep, for You promised Your beloved sweet sleep. Therefore, my heart is glad and my spirit rejoices. My body and soul rest and confidently dwell in safety. Amen.

Scripture References

Proverbs 3:24

Psalm 34:7

Psalm 103:20

Psalm 91:11

2 Corinthians 10:5

Knowing God's Will

Father, in Jesus' name, I thank You that You are instructing me in the way I should go and that You are guiding me with Your eye. I thank You for Your guidance and leading concerning Your will, Your plan, and Your purpose for my life. I do hear the voice of the Good Shepherd, for I know You and follow You. You lead me in the paths of righteousness for Your name's sake.

Thank You, Father, that my path is growing brighter and brighter until it reaches the full light of day. As I follow You, Lord, I believe my path is becoming clearer each day.

Thank You, Father, that Jesus was made unto me wisdom. Confusion is not a part of my life. I am not confused about Your will for my life. I trust in You and lean not unto my own understanding. As I acknowledge You in all of my ways, You are directing my paths. I believe that as I trust in You completely, You will show me the path of life. Amen.

Scripture References

Psalm 32:8	1 Corinthians 1:30
John 10:3,4	1 Corinthians 14:33
Psalm 23:3	Proverbs 3:5,6
Proverbs 4:18	Psalm 16:11
Ephesians 5:19	

Godly Wisdom in the Affairs of Life

Father, You said if anyone lacks wisdom, let him ask of You, Who giveth to all men liberally and upbraideth not; and it shall be given him. Therefore, I ask in faith, nothing wavering, to be filled with the knowledge of Your will in all wisdom and spiritual understanding. Today I incline my ear unto wisdom, and I apply my heart to understanding so that I might receive that which has been freely given unto me.

In the name of Jesus, I receive skill and godly wisdom and instruction. I discern and comprehend the words of understanding and insight. I receive instruction in wise dealing and the discipline of wise thoughtfulness, righteousness, justice, and integrity. Prudence, knowledge, discretion, and discernment are given to me. I increase in knowledge. As a person of understanding, I acquire skill and attain to sound counsels [so that I may be able to steer my course rightly].

Wisdom will keep, defend, and protect me; I love her and she guards me. I prize Wisdom highly and exalt her; she will bring me to honor because I embrace her. She gives to my head a wreath of gracefulness; a crown of beauty and glory will she deliver to me. Length of days is in her right hand, and in her left hand are riches and honor.

Jesus has been made unto me wisdom, and in Him are all the treasures of [divine] wisdom, [of comprehensive insight into the ways and purposes of God]; and [all the riches of spiritual] knowledge and enlightenment are stored up and lie hidden. God has hidden away sound and godly wisdom and stored it up for me, for I am the righteousness of God in Christ Jesus.

Therefore, I will walk in paths of uprightness. When I walk, my steps shall not be hampered — my path will be clear and open; and when I run, I shall not stumble. I take fast hold of instruction and do not let her go; I guard her, for she is my life. I let my eyes look right on [with fixed purpose], and my gaze is straight before me. I consider well the path of my feet, and I let all my ways be established and ordered aright.

Father, in the name of Jesus, I look carefully to how I walk! I live purposefully and worthily and accurately, not as unwise and witless, but as a wise — sensible, intelligent — person, making the very most of my time — buying up every opportunity. Amen.

Scripture References

James 1:5,6	1 Corinthians 1:30
Colossians 1:9	Colossians 2:3 AMP
Proverbs 2:2	Proverbs 2:7 AMP
Proverbs 1:2-5 AMP	2 Corinthians 5:21
Proverbs 4:6,8,9 AMP	Proverbs 4:11-13,25,26 AMP
Proverbs 3:16 AMP	Ephesians 5:15,16 AMP

Receiving a Discerning Heart

Father, I thank You for creating within me a wise and discerning heart, so that I am able to distinguish between right and wrong.

This is my prayer: that my love may abound more and more in knowledge and depth of insight, so that I may be able to discern what is best and may be pure and blameless until the day of Christ, filled with the fruit of righteousness that comes through Jesus Christ — to Your glory and praise, O Lord.

Father, I trust in You with all of my heart and lean not on my own understanding; in all of my ways I acknowledge You, and You will make my paths straight. Through Your precepts I get understanding; therefore, I hate every false way. Your Word is a lamp to my feet and a light to my path.

Joseph, in Genesis 41:39-41 NIV, was described as a discerning and wise man who was put in charge of the entire land of Egypt. As You were with Joseph, so shall You be with me. You will cause me to find favor at my place of employment, at home, or wherever I may be.

I make [special] request, [asking] that I may be filled with the full (deep and clear) knowledge of Your will in all spiritual wisdom and in understanding and discernment of spiritual things — that

I may walk (live and conduct myself) in a manner worthy of You, Lord, fully pleasing to You and desiring to please You in all things, steadily growing and increasing in and by Your knowledge [with fuller, deeper, and clearer insight, acquaintance, and recognition].

Because Jesus has been made unto me wisdom, I listen and add to my learning; I discern and get guidance, understanding Your will.

In the name of Jesus I pray, amen.

Scripture References

1 Kings 3:9 NIV	Proverbs 3:1-4
Philippians 1:9-11 NIV	Colossians 1:9,10 AMP
Proverbs 3:5 NIV	1 Corinthians 1:30
Psalm 119:104,105 AMP	Proverbs 1:5
Genesis 41:39-41 NIV	Ephesians 5:17
Joshua 1:5	

Developing Healthy Friendships

Father, help me to meet new friends — friends who will encourage me. May I find in these friendships the companionship and fellowship You have ordained for me. I know that You are my source of love, companionship, and friendship. Your love and friendship are expressed through my relationship with You and members of the Body of Christ.

According to Proverbs 27:17 CEV, as iron sharpens iron, so friends sharpen the minds of each other. As we learn from each other, may we find a worthy purpose in our relationship. Keep me well-balanced in my friendships, so that I will always please You rather than pleasing other people.

I ask for divine connections — good friendships ordained by You. Thank You for the courage and grace to let go of detrimental friendships. I ask and receive, by faith, discernment for developing healthy relationships. Your Word says that two are better than one, because if one falls, there will be someone to lift that person up.

Father, You know the hearts of people, so I won't be deceived by outward appearances. Bad friendships corrupt good morals. Thank You for quality friends who help me build a stronger character and draw me closer to You. Help me be a friend to others and to love my friends at all times. I will laugh with those

131

who laugh, I will rejoice with those who rejoice, and I will weep with those who weep. Teach me what I need to know to be a quality friend.

Develop in me a fun personality and a good sense of humor. Help me to relax around people and to be myself — the person You created me to be. Instruct my heart and mold my character, that I may be faithful and trustworthy over the friendships You are sending into my life.

Father, Your Son, Jesus, is my best Friend. He is a Friend Who sticks closer than a brother. He defined the standard when He said in John 15:13, "Greater love hath no man than this, than a man lay down his life for his friends."

Thank You, Lord, that I can entrust myself and my need for friends into Your keeping. I submit to the leadership of the Holy Spirit, in the name of Jesus. Amen.

Scripture References

Proverbs 13:20 NIV	1 Corinthians 15:33 AMP
Ephesians 5:30 NIV	James 1:17 NIV
Philippians 2:2,3 NIV	Proverbs 17:17
Proverbs 13:20 NIV	Romans 12:15
Psalm 84:11 NIV	Proverbs 18:24
Ecclesiastes 4:9,10 NIV	Psalm 37:4,5 NIV

This prayer is composed of Scriptures and writings taken from "Meeting New Friends," *Prayers That Avail Much for Teens.* (Tulsa: Harrison House, 1991), pp. 50-52.

*B*oldness

*F*ather, in the name of Jesus, I am of good courage. I pray that You grant to me that with all *boldness* I speak forth Your Word. I pray that freedom of utterance be given me that I may open my mouth to proclaim *boldly* the mystery of the good news of the Gospel — that I may declare it *boldly* as I ought to do.

Father, I believe I receive that *boldness* now in the name of Jesus. Therefore, I have *boldness* to enter into the Holy of Holies by the blood of Jesus. Because of my faith in Him, I dare to have the *boldness* (courage and confidence) of free access — an unreserved approach to You with freedom and without fear. I can draw fearlessly and confidently and *boldly* near to Your throne of grace and receive mercy and find grace to help in good time for my every need. I am *bold* to pray. I come to the throne of God with my petitions and for others who do not know how to ascend to the throne.

I will be *bold* toward Satan, demons, evil spirits, sickness, disease, and poverty, for Jesus is the Head of all rule and authority — of every angelic principality and power. Disarming those who were ranged against us, Jesus made a *bold* display and public example of them, triumphing over them. I am *bold* to declare that Satan is a defeated foe. Let God arise and His enemies be scattered.

I take comfort and am encouraged and confidently and *boldly* say, "The Lord is my Helper; I will not be seized with alarm — I will not fear or dread or be terrified. What can man do to me?" I dare to proclaim the Word toward heaven, toward hell, and toward earth. I am *bold* as a lion, for I have been made the righteousness of God in Christ Jesus. I am complete in Him! Praise the name of Jesus! Amen.

Scripture References

Psalm 27:14	Hebrews 4:16 AMP
Acts 4:29	Colossians 2:10,15 AMP
Ephesians 6:19,20 AMP	Psalm 68:1
Mark 11:23,24	Hebrews 13:6 AMP
Hebrews 10:19 AMP, kjv	Proverbs 28:1
Ephesians 3:12 AMP	2 Corinthians 5:21

*B*eing Equipped for Success

*F*ather, I thank You that the entrance of Your words gives light. I thank You that Your Word, which You speak (*and which I speak*), is alive and full of power —making it active, operative, energizing, and effective. I thank You, Father, that [You have given me a spirit] of power and of love and of a calm and well-balanced mind and discipline and self-control. I have Your power and ability and sufficiency, for You have qualified me (making me to be fit and worthy and sufficient) as a minister and dispenser of a new covenant [of salvation through Christ].

In the name of Jesus, I walk out of the realm of failure into the arena of success, giving thanks to You, Father, for You have qualified and made me fit to share the portion that is the inheritance of the saints (God's holy people) in the light.

Father, You have delivered and drawn me to Yourself out of the control and the dominion of darkness (*failure, doubt, and fear*) and have transferred me into the Kingdom of the Son of Your love, in Whom there is good success [and freedom from fears, agitating passions, and moral conflicts]. I rejoice in Jesus Who has come that I might have life and have it more abundantly.

Today I am a new creation, for I am (engrafted) in Christ, the Messiah. The old (previous moral and spiritual condition) has passed away. Behold, the fresh and new has come! I forget those things that are behind me and reach forth unto those things that are before me. I am crucified with Christ: nevertheless I live; yet not I, but Christ lives in me: And the life which I now live in the flesh I live by the faith of the Son of God, Who loved me and gave Himself for me.

Today I attend to the Word of God. I consent and submit to Your sayings, Father. Your words shall not depart from my sight; I will keep them in the midst of my heart. For they are life [*success*] to me, healing and health to all my flesh. I keep my heart with all vigilance, and, above all, that I guard; for out of it flow the springs of life.

Today I will not let mercy and kindness and truth forsake me. I bind them about my neck; I write them upon the tablet of my heart. So therefore I will find favor, good understanding and high esteem in the sight [or judgment] of God and man.

Today my delight and desire are in the law of the Lord, and on His law I habitually meditate (ponder and study) by day and by night. Therefore I am like a tree firmly planted [and tended] by the streams of water, ready to bring forth my fruit in my season; my leaf also shall not fade or wither, and everything I do shall prosper [and come to maturity].

Now thanks be to God, Who always causes me to triumph in Christ!

In His name I pray, amen.

Scripture References

Psalm 119:130

Hebrews 4:12 AMP

2 Timothy 1:7 AMP

2 Corinthians 3:5-6 AMP

Colossians 1:12,13 AMP

2 Corinthians 5:17 AMP

John 10:10

Philippians 3:13

Galatians 2:20

Proverbs 4:20-23 AMP

Proverbs 3:3,4 AMP

Psalm 1:2,3 AMP

2 Corinthians 2:14

Prayer for the Success of a Business

Father, Your Word says that I am a partaker of the inheritance and treasures of heaven. You have delivered me out of the authority of darkness and translated me into the Kingdom of Your dear Son. Father, where Your Word is there is light and, also, understanding. Your Word does not return to You void but always accomplishes what it is sent to do. I am a joint-heir with Jesus; and as Your son/daughter, I accept that the communication of my faith is effectual by the acknowledging of every good work that is in me in Christ Jesus.

Father, I commit my works (the plans and cares of my business) to You, entrust them wholly to You. Since You are effectually at work in me, You cause my thoughts to become agreeable with Your will, so that my business plans shall be established and succeed. In the name of Jesus, I submit to every kind of wisdom, practical insight, and prudence, which You have lavished upon me in accordance with the riches and generosity of Your gracious favor.

Father, I affirm that I obey Your Word by making an honest living with my own hands, so that I may be able to give to those in need. In Your strength and according to Your grace, I provide for myself and my own family. Thank You, Father, for making all grace, every favor and earthly blessing, come to me in abundance that I, having all sufficiency, may abound to every good work.

Father, thank You for the ministering spirits that You have assigned to go forth to bring in consumers. Jesus said, "You are the light of the world." In His name my light shall so shine before all men that they may see my good works glorifying You, my Heavenly Father.

Thank You for the grace to remain diligent in seeking knowledge and skill in areas where I am inexperienced. I ask You for wisdom and the ability to understand righteousness, justice, and fair dealing in every area and relationship. I affirm that I am faithful and committed to Your Word. My life and business are founded upon its principles.

Father, thank You for the success of my business!

In Your name, amen.

Scripture References

Romans 8:17	1 Timothy 5:8
Colossians 1:12	2 Corinthians 9:8
Psalm 119:130	Hebrews 1:14
Philemon 1:6	Matthew 5:14,16
Proverbs 16:3	Proverbs 22:29
Philippians 2:13	Proverbs 2:9
Ephesians 1:7,8	Proverbs 4:20-22
Ephesians 4:28	

The Setting of Proper Priorities

Father, too often I allow urgency to dictate my schedule, and I am asking You to help me establish priorities in my work. I confess my weakness* of procrastination and lack of organization. My desire is to live purposefully and worthily and accurately as a wise, sensible, intelligent person.

You have given me a seven-day week—six days to work and the seventh day to rest. I desire to make the most of the time [buying up each opportunity]. Help me plan my day, and stay focused on my assignments.

In the name of Jesus, I demolish and smash warped philosophies concerning time management, tear down barriers erected against the truth of God, and fit every loose thought, emotion and impulse into the structure of life shaped by Christ. I clear my mind of every obstruction and build a life of obedience into maturity.

Father, You are in charge of my work and my plans. I plan the way I want to live, but You alone make me able to live it. Help me to organize my efforts, schedule my activities and budget my time.

Jesus, You want me to relax. It pleases You when I am not preoccupied with getting, so I can respond to God's giving. I know

You, Father God, and how You work. I steep my life in God-reality, God-initiative and God-provisions.

By the grace given me, I will not worry about missing out, and my everyday human concerns will be met. I purpose in my heart to seek (aim at and strive after) first of all Your Kingdom, Lord, and Your righteousness [Your way of doing and being right], and then all these things taken together will be given me besides.

Father, Your Word is my compass, and it helps me see my life as complete in Christ. I cast all my cares, worries and concerns over on You, that I might be well-balanced (temperate, sober of mind), vigilant and cautious at all times.

I tune my ears to the word of wisdom and set my heart on a life of understanding. I make insight my priority.

Father, You sent Jesus that I might have life and have it more abundantly. Help me remember that my relationship with You and with others are more important than anything else. Amen.

Scripture References

Ephesians 5:15-16 AMP	Genesis 2:2 NIV
2 Corinthians 10:5-6 MESSAGE	Proverbs 16:3,9 MESSAGE
Matthew 11:29 MESSAGE, AMP	Colossians 2:10
1 Peter 5:7-8 AMP	Proverbs 2:3 MESSAGE
John 10:10	

---

* If you do not know your strengths and weaknesses, ask the Holy Spirit to reveal them to you. The Lord speaks to us: "My grace is sufficient for you, for power is perfected in weakness" (2 Cor. 12:9 NAS).

Maintaining Good Relations

*F*ather, in the name of Jesus, I will not withhold good from those to whom it is due [its rightful owners] when it is in the power of my hand to do it. I will render to all men their dues. I will [pay] taxes to whom taxes are due, revenue to whom revenue is due, respect to whom respect is due, and honor to whom honor is due.

I will not lose heart and grow weary and faint in acting nobly and doing nobly and right, for in due season I shall reap if I do not loosen and relax my courage and faint. So then, as occasion and opportunity open up to me, I will do good [morally] to all people [not only being useful or profitable to them, but also doing what is for their spiritual good and advantage]. I am mindful to be a blessing, especially to those of the household of faith [those who belong to God's family with me, the believers].

I will not contend with a man for no reason — when he has done me no wrong. If possible, as far as it depends on me, I purpose to live at peace with everyone. Amen.

Scripture References

Proverbs 3:27 AMP   Proverbs 3:30 AMP

Romans 13:7 AMP   Romans 12:18 AMP

Galatians 6:9,10 AMP

*I*mproving Communication Skills

INTRODUCTION

*L*ack of communication skills is one of the greatest hindrances to healthy relationships. Most of the time when we pray, we are seeking change. We cannot change others, but we can submit to the constant ministry of transformation by the Holy Spirit (Rom. 12:1,2).

Prayer prepares us for change. Change produces change, which may be uncomfortable. If we will move through the discomfort, God will work with us, leading us out of our self-developed defense mechanisms into a place of victory. In this place He heals our brokenness, becomes our defense and our vindication. We are enabled to submit to the Champion of our salvation, which we are working out with fear and trembling (Phil. 2:12).

Adults who grew up in judgmental, critical homes where they were never allowed to express themselves sometimes carry much hurt and anger into their relationships. Often they were not permitted to have their own feelings without being condemned; they were not permitted to explore any ideas different than their parents' or caregivers'. There was an eye watching their every move. Any punishment they received was justified. Their parents were incapable of making a mistake.

Adult children of religiously rigid environments were led to believe that any slip, error in judgment, or mistake was a sin that would send them straight to hell; the parents' religious doctrine was the only way to heaven, and to deviate from it would lead to destruction. Forgiveness could be attained only after much sorrow, penance, and retribution. Death before the completion of repentance led to an eternity in hell.

People raised in such oppressive home environments were never allowed to find themselves or to travel their own individual spiritual journeys leading to truth. The head of the home, usually the father, was considered God in the flesh. Conflict resolution was never taught or practiced. Whatever the head of the household said was law — and disobedience to his law was not discussed, but beaten out of the child. The wife was subservient and was not allowed to question the dictates of the husband.

When these adults marry, they often feel that they have finally found a platform from which to express themselves. They have escaped a place of abiding fear, constant condemnation, and continual criticism. Having no communication skills, they often have difficulty expressing themselves properly. When anyone disagrees with them, they tend to react as they were taught. Only now, the marriage partner or friend does not submit to dogmatic, manipulative words. Frustration develops. The adult child seeks to make himself or herself understood, resulting in more frustration. Anger is fed, and the individual continues to be in bondage to the idea that he or she should never have been born. The person either retreats to a silent corner, refusing to talk, or uses words to build walls of defense — shutting others out. He or she resides inside emotional isolation, attempting to remove himself or herself from more hurt and criticism.

There is a way of escape. God sent His Word to heal us and to deliver us from all our destructions (Ps. 107:20). We must determine to listen, to learn, and to change with the help of the Holy Spirit — our Teacher, our Guide, and our Intercessor. The anointing is upon Jesus to bind up and heal our emotional wounds (Luke 4:18). His anointing destroys every yoke of bondage (Isa. 10:27), setting the captives free.

PRAYER

Father, I am Your child. Jesus said that if I pray to You in secret, You will reward me openly.

Father, I desire with all my heart to walk in love, but I am ever sabotaging my own efforts and failing in my relationships. I know that without faith it is impossible to please and be satisfactory to You. I am coming near to You, believing that You exist and that You are the Rewarder of those who earnestly and diligently seek You.

Show "me" to me. Uncover me — bring everything to the light. When anything is exposed and reproved by the light, it is made visible and clear; and where everything is visible and clear, there is light.

Heal the past wounds and hurts that have controlled my behavior and my speech. Teach me to guard my heart with all diligence, for out of it flow the very issues of life. Teach me to speak the truth in love in my home, in my church, with my friends, and in all my relationships. Also, help me to realize that others have a right to express themselves. Help me to make room for their ideas and their opinions, even when they are different than mine.

Words are powerful. The power of life and death is in the tongue, and You said that I would eat the fruit of it.

Father, I realize that words can be creative or destructive. A word out of my mouth may seem of no account, but it can accomplish nearly anything — or destroy it! A careless or wrongly placed word out of my mouth can set off a forest fire. By my speech I can ruin the world, turn harmony to chaos, throw mud on a reputation, send the whole world up in smoke, and go up in smoke with it — smoke right from the pit of hell. This is scary!

Father, forgive me for speaking curses. I reacted out of past hurts and unresolved anger. At times I am dogmatic, even boasting that I am wise; sometimes unknowingly I have twisted the truth to make myself sound wise; at times I have tried to look better than others or get the better of another; my words have contributed to things falling apart. My human anger is misdirected and works unrighteousness.

Father, forgive me. I cannot change myself, but I am willing to change and walk in the wisdom that is from above.

Father, I submit to that wisdom from above that begins with a holy life and is characterized by getting along with others. It is gentle and reasonable, overflowing with mercy and blessings, not hot one day and cold the next, not two-faced. Use me as Your instrument to develop a healthy, robust community that lives right with You. I will enjoy its results only if I do the hard work of getting along with others, treating them with dignity and honor.

With the help of the Holy Spirit and by Your grace, I will not let any unwholesome talk come out of my mouth, but only what is helpful for building others up according to their needs, that it may benefit those who listen.

My heart overflows with a goodly theme; I address my psalm to You, the King. My tongue is like the pen of a ready writer. Mercy and kindness shut out all hatred and selfishness, and truth shuts out all deliberate hypocrisy or falsehood; and I bind them about my neck, write them upon the tablet of my heart.

I speak excellent and princely things; and the opening of my lips shall be for right things. My mouth shall utter truth, and wrongdoing is detestable and loathsome to my lips. All the words of my mouth are righteous (upright and in right standing with You, Lord); there is nothing contrary to truth or crooked in them. My tongue is as choice silver, and my lips feed and guide many. I open my mouth in skillful and godly wisdom, and on my tongue is the law of kindness [giving counsel and instruction].

Father, thank You for loving me unconditionally. I thank You for sending Your Son, Jesus, to be my Friend and elder Brother and for giving me Your Holy Spirit to teach me and to bring all things to my remembrance. I am an overcomer by the blood of the Lamb and by the word of my testimony.

In the name of Jesus I pray, amen.

Scripture References

1 John 3:1	Ephesians 4:29 NIV
Matthew 6:6	Psalm 45:1 AMP
Hebrews 11:6 AMP	Proverbs 3:3 AMP

Ephesians 5:13 AMP

Proverbs 4:23

Ephesians 4:15

Proverbs 18:21

James 3:5,6 MESSAGE

James 3:9-16 MESSAGE

James 3:17

James 3:17,18 MESSAGE

Proverbs 8:6-8 AMP

Proverbs 10:20,21 AMP

Proverbs 31:26 AMP

Romans 8:31-39 NIV

Hebrews 2:11 NIV

John 15:15 NIV

John 14:26

Revelation 12:11

$\mathcal{P}$rosperity

$\mathcal{F}$ather, I come to You in the name of Jesus concerning my financial situation. You are a very present help in trouble, and You are more than enough. Your Word declares that You shall supply all my need according to Your riches in glory by Christ Jesus.

(*If you have not been giving tithes and offerings, include this statement of repentance in your prayer.*) Forgive me for robbing You in tithes and offerings. I repent and purpose to bring all my tithes into the storehouse that there may be food in Your house. Thank You for wise financial counselors and teachers who are teaching me the principles of good stewardship.

Lord of hosts, You said, "Try Me now in this, and I will open the windows of heaven and pour out for you such a blessing that there will not be room enough to receive it." You will rebuke the devourer for my sake, and my heart is filled with thanksgiving.

Lord, my God, I shall remember that it is You Who give me the power to get wealth, that You may establish Your covenant. In the name of Jesus, I worship You only, and I will have no other gods before me.

You are able to make all grace — every favor and earthly blessing — come to me in abundance, so that I am always, and in all circumstances, furnished in abundance for every good work and charitable donation. Amen.

Scripture References

Psalm 56:1

Philippians 4:19

Malachi 3:8-12

Deuteronomy 8:18,19

2 Corinthians 9:8 AMP

25TH ANNIVERSARY COMMEMORATIVE EDITION

*D*edication for Your Tithes

I profess this day unto the Lord God that I have come into the inheritance which the Lord swore to give me. I am in the land which You have provided for me in Jesus Christ, the Kingdom of Almighty God. I was a sinner serving Satan; he was my god. But I called upon the name of Jesus, and You heard my cry and delivered me into the Kingdom of Your dear Son.

Jesus, as my Lord and High Priest, I bring the firstfruits of my income to You and worship the Lord my God with it.

I rejoice in all the good which You have given to me and my household. I have hearkened to the voice of the Lord my God and have done according to all that He has commanded me. Now look down from Your holy habitation from heaven and bless me as You said in Your Word. I thank You, Father, in Jesus' name. Amen.

Scripture References

Deuteronomy 26:1,3,   Colossians 1:13
  10,11,14,15 AMP   Hebrews 3:1,7,8
Ephesians 2:1-5

Selling Real Estate

Father, I thank You for the skillful and godly wisdom needed in offering my house (or other real estate) to be sold. I am preparing my house (property) in excellence that it may be beautiful and desirable, as though I am preparing it for Your habitation. I am asking a fair and competitive market price and will not take advantage of a potential buyer.

Father, I ask that You prepare and send a ready, willing, and able buyer to purchase my house (property) — a person who has the funds available to pay the fair market value, pre-qualified and approved by a lending institution; one who has perfect timing of possession that fits into my need and his/hers.

Thank You for going before me and preparing the way. In the name of Jesus, I seek and pursue peace, thanking You that the spirit of truth shall prevail in our deliberations. I declare and decree that everyone involved speaks truly, deals truly, and lives truly.

Should there be anything that is hidden, I ask that it be revealed and brought to the light. Truth and mercy are written upon the tablets of my heart, and I have favor, good understanding, and high esteem in Your sight and in the sight of the potential buyer.

In the name of Jesus, amen.

Scripture References

Proverbs 2:6,9,12,15 AMP

1 Corinthians 4:5 AMP

1 Corinthians 2:9

Proverbs 3:3,4 AMP

Ephesians 4:15 AMP

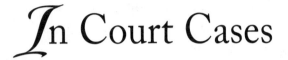n Court Cases

ather, in the name of Jesus, it is written in Your Word to call on You and You will answer me and show me great and mighty things. I put You in remembrance of Your Word and thank You that You watch over it to perform it.

I say that no weapon formed against me shall prosper, and any tongue that rises against me in judgment I shall show to be in the wrong. This peace, security, and triumph over opposition is my inheritance as Your child. This is the righteousness I obtain from You, Father, which You impart to me as my justification. I am far from even the thought of destruction; for I shall not fear, and terror shall not come near me.

Father, You say You will establish me to the end — keep me steadfast, give me strength, and guarantee my vindication; that is, be my warrant against all accusation or indictment. Father, You contend with those who contend with me, and You perfect that which concerns me. I dwell in the secret place of the Most High, and this secret place hides me from the strife of tongues, for a false witness who breathes out lies is an abomination to You.

I am a true witness, and all my words are upright and in right standing with You, Father. By my long forbearing and calmness of spirit the judge is persuaded, and my soft speech breaks down the most bone-like resistance. Therefore, I am not anxious beforehand how I shall reply in defense or what I am to say, for the Holy Spirit teaches me *in that very hour* and moment what I ought to say to those in the outside world. My speech is seasoned with salt.

As a child of the light, I enforce the triumphant victory of my Lord Jesus Christ in this situation, knowing that all of heaven is backing me. I am strong in You, Lord, and in the power of Your might. Thank You for the shield of faith that quenches every fiery dart of the enemy. I am increasing in wisdom and in stature and in years, and in favor with You, Father, and with man. Praise the Lord! Amen.

Scripture References

Jeremiah 33:3

Jeremiah 1:12 AMP

Isaiah 43:26 AMP

Isaiah 54:17 AMP

Isaiah 54:14 AMP

1 Corinthians 1:8 AMP

Isaiah 49:25

Psalm 138:8

Psalm 91:1

Psalm 31:20

Proverbs 6:19

Proverbs 14:25

Proverbs 8:8 AMP

Proverbs 25:15 AMP

Luke 12:11,12 AMP

Colossians 4:6

Matthew 18:18

Ephesians 6:10,16

Luke 2:52 AMP

Protection for Travel

Father, today, in Jesus' name, I confess Your Word over my travel plans and know that Your Word does not go out and return to You void, but it accomplishes what You say it will do. I give You thanks for moving quickly to perform Your Word and fulfill its promises.

As I prepare to travel, I rejoice in the promises that Your Word holds for protection and safety of the righteous. Only You, Father, make me live in safety. I trust in You and dwell in Your protection. If I face any problems or trouble, I will run to You, Father, my Strong Tower and Shelter in time of need. Believing in the written Word of God, I speak peace, safety, and success over my travel plans, in Jesus' name.

As a child of God, my path of travel is preserved, and angels keep charge over me and surround my car/airplane/train/ship. I will proceed with my travel plans without fear of accidents, problems, or any type of frustrations. I have the peace of God and will allow fear no place as I travel; the Lord delivers me from every type of evil and preserves me for His Kingdom. I stand confident that my travel plans will not be disrupted or confused.

Thank You, Father, that in every situation You are there to protect me. No matter in what means of transportation I choose to travel, You have redeemed me and will protect me. The earth and all things on it are under Your command. You are my Heavenly

Father. Through my faith in You, I have the power to tread on serpents and have all power over the enemy. No food or water will harm me when I arrive at my destination. My travel is safe.

Father, I give You the glory in this situation. Thank You that as I keep Your ways before me, I will be safe. Your mercy is upon me and my family, and our travels will be safe. Not a hair on our heads shall perish. Thank You, Father, for Your guidance and safety — You are worthy of all praise! Amen.

Scripture References

Isaiah 55:11	Isaiah 43:1-3
Jeremiah 1:12	2 Timothy 4:18
Psalm 4:8	Hosea 2:18
Psalm 91:1	Luke 10:19
Proverbs 18:10	Psalm 91:13
Proverbs 29:25	Luke 21:18
Mark 11:23,24	Mark 16:18
Proverbs 2:8	Matthew 18:18
Psalm 91:11,12	John 14:13
2 Timothy 4:18	Daniel 9:18
Philippians 4:7	Luke 1:50
2 Timothy 1:7	

$\mathcal{A}$biding in Jesus

INTRODUCTION

Let no one say when he is tempted, I am tempted from God; for God is incapable of being tempted by [what is] evil and He Himself tempts no one.

But every person is tempted when he is drawn away, enticed and baited by his own evil desire (lust, passions).

Then the evil desire, when it has conceived, gives birth to sin, and sin, when it is fully matured, brings forth death.

James 1:13-15 AMP

$\mathcal{S}$ingle people sometimes express the difficulty of keeping themselves pure. (See the following prayers on purity.) Some have asked, "Doesn't God understand that we are only human? Why did He create us with desires? Surely He understands and excuses us when we fall into temptation. If He wants me to avoid sexual temptation, then why doesn't He send me the spouse I have asked Him to give me?"

The Scriptures condemn premarital sex, fornication, adultery, and all forms of sexual perversion (Matt. 15:19; Mark 7:21 AMP; Gal. 5:19-21; Col. 3:5,6). Although sexual desires are not a sin, if not properly controlled, those desires can lead to sin.

According to James 1:13-15, sin begins with a thought conceived from lust. Lust is not limited to sex. It is possible to lust after many things that can cause sin. That's why it is so important to take control over the mind and heart to keep them pure and holy — in spite of temptation.

One of the myths that has ensnared many single people is the mistaken idea that marriage will automatically release them from the temptation to sin. Without repentance and the renewing of the mind, those who have a problem with lustful thoughts before they are married will have the same problem after they are married, just as those who have a problem with sexual perversion before marriage will continue to have the same problem after marriage.

One married man shared his testimony of deliverance from pornography. He was having to continually guard himself from mental images that kept reappearing.

Marriage is not a cure-all for sexual sins or any other sin.

Yes, God does understand. With every temptation He has provided a way of escape (1 Cor. 10:13).

Yes, there is forgiveness for sin (1 John 1:9) — through God's abounding grace (Rom. 5:20). The question is, "...Are we to remain in sin in order that God's grace (favor and mercy) may multiply and overflow? Certainly not! How can we who died to sin live in it any longer?" (Rom. 6:1,2 AMP).

We who are in Christ desire to bring glory to the Father. We cannot do so in our own strength. It is abiding in union with Jesus and loving as Jesus loves that ensures answered prayers. (John 15:7-9). If our prayers are not being answered, it is time to check our love walk. We must ask ourselves, "Are we keeping ourselves in the love of God — remaining vitally united with Jesus?"

We know [absolutely] that anyone born of God does not [deliberately and knowingly] practice committing sin, but the One Who was begotten of God carefully watches over and protects him [Christ's divine presence within him preserves him against the evil], and the wicked one does not lay hold (get a grip) on him or touch [him].

1 John 5:18 AMP

This verse says that the wicked one cannot touch us. What is the condition? Having Christ's presence within, staying united with Him — abiding in Him and allowing His Word to abide in us.

If you want to abide in Christ and have His Word abide in you, pray the following prayer with a sincere and believing heart.

PRAYER

Lord, I am abiding in Your Word [holding fast to Your teachings and living in accordance with them]. It is my desire to be Your true disciple. I am abiding in (vitally united to) the vine. I cannot bear fruit unless I abide in You.

Lord, because You are the Vine and I am a branch living in You, I bear much (abundant) fruit. Apart from You [cut off from vital union with You] I can do nothing. Your Son, Jesus, said, "If you live in Me [abide vitally united to Me] and My words remain in you and continue to live in your hearts, ask whatever you will, and it shall be done for you" (John 15:7 AMP).

When I bear (produce) much fruit, You, Father, are honored and glorified. By Your grace that I have received, I will show and prove myself to be a true follower of Your Son, Jesus. He has loved me, [just] as You, Father, have loved Him. I am abiding in that love.

Lord, You have assured me that if I keep Your commandments [if I continue to obey Your instructions], I will abide in Your love and live in it, just as Your Son, Jesus, obeyed Your commandments and lived in Your love. He told me these things, that Your joy and delight may be in me and that my joy and gladness may be of full measure and complete and overflowing. This is Your commandment: that we love one another [just] as You have loved us.

Father, thank You for Your Word — it is the truth that makes me free. I am born (begotten) of You, Lord, and I do not [deliberately, knowingly, and habitually] practice sin. Your nature abides in me [Your principle of life remains permanently within me]; and I cannot practice sinning because I am born (begotten) of You. I have hidden Your Word in my heart that I might not sin against You.

May Christ through my faith [actually] dwell (settle down, abide, make His permanent home) in my heart! It is my desire to be rooted deep in love and founded securely on love, that I may have the power and be strong to apprehend and grasp with all the saints [Your devoted people, the experience of that love] what is the breadth and length and height and depth [of it].

I pray, in the name of Jesus, that I may know this love that surpasses knowledge — that I may be filled to the measure of all Your fullness. Now to You Who is able to do immeasurably more than all I ask or imagine, according to Your power that is at work within me, to You be glory in the Church and in Christ Jesus throughout all generations, forever and ever! Amen.

Scripture References

John 8:31 AMP	1 John 3:9 AMP
John 15:4,5 AMP	Psalm 119:11
John 15:7-12 AMP	Ephesians 3:17,18 AMP
John 8:32	Ephesians 3:19-21 NIV
John 17:17	

$\mathcal{K}$nowing God's Plan for Marriage

$\mathcal{U}$nto You, O Lord, do I bring my life. O my God, I trust in, lean on, rely on, and am confident in You. Let me not be put to shame or [my hope in You] be disappointed; let not my enemies (rejection, hurt, inferiority, unworthiness) triumph over me.

Father, it is written, "For I know the thoughts and plans that I have for you, says the Lord, thoughts and plans for welfare and peace and not for evil, to give you hope in your final outcome. Then you will call upon Me, and you will come and pray to Me, and I will hear and heed you. Then you will seek Me, inquire for, and require Me [as a vital necessity] and find Me when you search for Me with all your heart. I will be found by you, says the Lord"(Jer. 29:11-14 AMP).

In the name of Jesus, I always pray and do not turn coward (faint, lose heart, and give up).

Father, I am looking for Your plan, Your answer for my life. It is my desire to be married. But I must be sure in my decision that I am living as You intend and accepting whatever situation You have put me into. According to Your Word, marriage will bring extra problems that I may not need to face at this time in my life.

All the ways of a man or woman are pure in his or her own eyes, but You, Lord, weigh the spirits (the thoughts and intents of the heart). Therefore, I roll my works upon You, [commit and trust them wholly to You; You will cause my thoughts to become agreeable to Your will, and] so shall my plans be established and succeed.

Because You, Lord, are my Shepherd, I have everything I need!

You let me rest in the meadow grass and lead me beside the quiet streams. You give me new strength. You help me do what honors You the most.

Even when walking through the dark valley of death, I will not be afraid, for You are close beside me, guarding and guiding me all the way.

You provide delicious food for me in the presence of my enemies. You have welcomed me as Your guest; my blessings overflow!

Your goodness and unfailing kindness shall be with me all of my life, and afterward I will live with You forever in Your home.

In Jesus' name I pray, amen.

Scripture References

Psalm 25:1,2 AMP   Proverbs 16:2,3 AMP

Luke 18:1 AMP   Psalm 23:1-6 TLB

1 Corinthians 7:1,2 TLB

*F*inding a Mate

INTRODUCTION

*I*n our ministry we hear from many men and women who desire to be married. If that is your desire, we encourage you to ask the Lord to prepare you for marriage. Submit to God's future plans for your life, and purpose to please Him. Do not make your deliberations, without knowing His will, at the expense of your personal spiritual growth and transformation. Going from glory to glory (2 Cor. 3:18) is not dependent on having a spouse.

Most of the time, each partner brings a lot of emotional baggage into the marriage relationship. As you prepare for marriage, remember that the anointing that was upon Jesus (Luke 4:18,19) is within you. This anointing will destroy every yoke of bondage (Isa. 10:27) as God exposes emotional wounds and heals your brokenness.

Knowing the reality of your completeness in Christ Jesus will enable you to enter into a healthy relationship, one in which both you and your partner will grow together spiritually and in every other area of life. Seeking first the Kingdom of God and His righteousness (Matt. 6:33), doing those things that are pleasing in His sight (1 John 3:22), will prepare you to be the person designed by Him to fulfill the role of husband or wife.

This prayer is written for your own growth and benefit.

PRAYER

Father, I come before You in the name of Jesus, asking for Your will to be done in my life as I look to You for a marriage partner. I submit to the constant ministry of transformation by the Holy Spirit, making my petition known to You.

Prepare me for marriage by bringing everything to light that has been hidden — wounded emotions, walls of denial, emotional isolation, silence or excessive talking, anger, or rigidity [*name any wall that separates you from healthy relationships and God's love and grace*]. The weapons of my warfare are not carnal, but mighty through You, Lord, to the pulling down of strongholds.

I know the One in Whom I have placed my confidence, and I am perfectly certain that the work, whether I remain unmarried or marry, is safe in Your hands until that day.

Because I love You, Lord, and because I am called according to Your plan, everything that happens to me fits into a pattern for good. In Your foreknowledge, You chose me to bear the family likeness of Your Son. You chose me long ago; when the time came You called me, You made me righteous in Your sight, and then You lifted me to the splendor of life as Your child.

I lay aside every weight, and the sins which so easily ensnare me, and run with endurance the race that is set before me, looking unto Jesus, the Author and Finisher of my faith, Who for the joy that was set before Him endured the cross, despising the shame, and has sat down at the right hand of the throne of God. I consider Him Who endured such hostility from sinners against Himself, lest I become weary and discouraged in my soul. He makes intercession for me.

FINDING A MATE

I turn my back on the turbulent desires of youth and give my positive attention to goodness, integrity, love, and peace in company with all those who approach You, Lord, in sincerity. I have nothing to do with silly and ill-informed controversies, which lead inevitably to strife. As Your servant, I am not a person of strife. I seek to be kind to all, ready and able to teach. I seek to be tolerant and have the ability to gently correct those who oppose Your message.

Father, I desire and earnestly seek (aim at and strive after) first of all Your Kingdom and Your righteousness (Your way of doing and being right), and then all these things taken together will be given me besides. So I do not worry and will not be anxious about tomorrow.

I am persuaded that I can trust You because You first loved me. You chose me in Christ before the foundation of the world. In Him the whole fullness of Deity (the Godhead) continues to dwell in bodily form [giving complete expression of the divine nature]; and I am in Him, made full and have come to the fullness of life [in Christ].

I am filled with the Godhead — Father, Son, and Holy Spirit — and I reach toward full spiritual stature. And He (Christ) is the Head of all rule and authority [of every angelic principality and power]. So, because of Jesus, I am complete; Jesus is my Lord.

I come before You, Father, expressing my desire for a Christian mate. I petition that Your will be done in my life. Now I enter into that blessed rest by adhering to, trusting in, and relying on You.

In Jesus' name, amen.

Scripture References

Matthew 6:10

1 Corinthians 4:5

2 Corinthians 10:4

2 Timothy 1:12 PHILLIPS

Romans 8:28-30 PHILLIPS

Hebrews 12:1-3 NKJV

Romans 8:34

2 Timothy 2:22-25 PHILLIPS

Matthew 6:33,34 AMP

1 John 4:19

Ephesians 1:4

Colossians 2:9,10 AMP

Matthew 6:10

Hebrews 4:10

John 14:1 AMP

Developing Patience

Father, I come before You in the name of Jesus. I desire to meditate, consider, and inquire in Your presence. Waiting patiently for a marriage partner has become a challenge — a trial, sometimes leading to temptation. I am asking for Your help in developing patience, quietly entrusting my future to Your will. It is to You that I submit my desire to be married.

By Your grace I surrender my life — all my desires, all that I am, and all that I am not — to the control of the Holy Spirit Who produces this kind of fruit in me: love, joy, peace, *patience*, kindness, goodness, faithfulness, gentleness, and self-control; and here there is no conflict. I belong to Jesus Christ, and I seek to live by the Holy Spirit's power and to follow the Holy Spirit's leading in every part of my life. [In exercising] self-control I [develop] steadfastness (patience, endurance), and in [exercising] steadfastness I [develop] godliness (piety).

By faith, I consider it wholly joyful whenever I am enveloped in, or encounter, trials of any sort or fall into various temptations. It is then that I am reminded to rest assured and understand that the trial and proving of my faith brings out endurance and steadfastness and patience. I purpose to let endurance and steadfastness and patience have full play and do a thorough work, so that I may be perfectly and fully developed [with no defects], lacking in nothing.

Father, fill me with the knowledge of Your will through all spiritual wisdom and understanding, that I may live a life worthy of You and may please You in every way: bearing fruit in every good work, growing in the knowledge of You, being strengthened with all power according to Your glorious might, so that I may have great endurance and patience, and joyfully give thanks to You Who qualified me to share in the inheritance of the saints in the Kingdom of light.

Father, I strip off and throw aside every encumbrance (unnecessary weight) and that sin which so readily (deftly and cleverly) clings to and entangles me, and I run with patient endurance and steady and active persistence the appointed course of the race that is set before me. I look away [from all that will distract] to Jesus, Who is the Leader and the Source of my faith [giving the first incentive for my belief] and is also its Finisher [bringing it to maturity and perfection].

With patience I am able to persevere through the difficult times — times of anxiety and worry — and overcome the fear that I may never be married. I am an overcomer by the blood of the Lamb and by the word of my testimony.

In Jesus' name, amen.

Scripture References

Psalm 3:4 AMP	James 1:2-4 AMP
Psalm 37:4,5	Colossians 1:9-12 NIV
Galatians 5:22-25 TLB	Hebrews 12:1,2 AMP
2 Peter 1:6 AMP	Revelation 12:11

Preparing Self for Marriage

Father, sometimes being single can be so lonely, so painful. Seeing people in pairs, laughing and having fun, makes me feel even more alone and different.

Lord, please comfort me in these times. Help me to deal with my feelings and thoughts in an appropriate way. Help me to remember to work hard on myself, so that I will be whole and mature when You bring the right person into my life.

Help me to remember that this is a time of preparation for the day when I will be joined to another human being for life. Show me how to be responsible for myself and how to allow others to be responsible for themselves.

Teach me about boundaries — what they are and how to establish them instead of walls. Teach me about love, Your love, and how to speak the truth in love, as Jesus did.

Father, I don't want to be a hindrance to my future spouse, to You, or to myself. Help me to take a good look at myself, at my self-image. Lead me to people — teachers, preachers, counselors — and to things — books, tapes, seminars — anyone and anything You can use to teach me Your ways of being and doing right and being whole.

Teach me how to choose the mate You would have for me. Give me the wisdom I need to see clearly and not to be double-minded. Help me to recognize the qualities You would have me look for in a mate.

Father, thank You for revealing to me that the choice of a mate is not to be based only on emotions and feelings, but that You have very definite guidelines in the Bible for me to use. I know that when I put these principles into practice, I will save myself a lot of pain and trouble.

Thank You that You are not trying to make things hard for me, but that You know me better than I know myself. You know my situation — You know the beginning from the end. You know the qualities and attributes that are needed in another person that will make me happy in our shared life together and will make that person happy with me.

I pray that You will keep my foot from being caught in a hidden trap of danger. I cast the care of this decision on You, knowing that You will cause my thoughts to come in line with Your will so that my plans will be established and succeed.

In Jesus' name I pray, amen.

Scripture References

1 Corinthians 1:3,4 NIV	James 1:5-8
Ephesians 4:15	Proverbs 3:26 AMP
Matthew 6:33 AMP	Proverbs 16:3 AMP

Committing to a Life of Purity

Father, I come before Your throne of grace in the name of Jesus. At one time I walked [habitually] following the course and fashion of this world [under the sway of the tendency of this present age]. I lived and conducted myself in the passions of my flesh [my behavior governed by my corrupt and sensual nature], obeying the impulses of the flesh and the thoughts of my mind [my cravings dictated by my senses and my dark imaginings].

But, God — You are so rich in Your mercy! Even when I was dead (slain) by [my own] shortcomings and trespasses, You made me alive together in union with Christ, and it is by Your grace (Your favor and mercy that I did not deserve) that I am saved (delivered from judgment and made a partaker of Christ's salvation). You raised me up together with Him and made us sit down together [giving me joint seating with Him] in the heavenly sphere in Christ Jesus (the Messiah, the Anointed One).

You are my Father; I am Your child. Since I am in Christ, I am a new creature; old things have passed away, and behold, all things have become new.

In accordance with Your Word, I rid myself of all malice and all deceit, hypocrisy, envy, and slander of every kind. Like a newborn baby, I crave pure spiritual milk so that by it I may grow up in my salvation, now that I have tasted that You, Lord, are good.

Father, forgive me for the years of watching, reading, and listening to vile things. I submit to Jesus Christ, Who loves me and gave Himself up for me, so that He might sanctify me, having cleansed me by the washing of water with the Word, that He might present me to Himself in glorious splendor, without spot or wrinkle or any such things [that I might be holy and faultless].

Thank You for the blood of Christ, Who through the eternal Spirit offered Himself unblemished to You, which cleanses my conscience from acts that lead to death, so that I may serve You, the living God! Thank You for the Holy Spirit Who indwells me. He is holy (chaste, pure).

I ask for and receive an impartation of the wisdom that comes from heaven — it is first of all pure; then peace-loving, considerate, submissive, full of mercy and good fruit, impartial, and sincere.

May my words issue from a pure heart, and may they be pleasing to You.

Lord, Your Holy Spirit is my Counselor — [change my impure language] and give to me a clear and pure speech from pure lips, that I may call upon Your name, to serve You.

I am transformed (changed) by the [entire] renewal of my mind, and I bring my thoughts into obedience to Your Word. I fix my thoughts on what is true and good and right. I determine to think about things that are pure and lovely, and dwell on the fine, good things in others. I think about all I can praise You for, and I am glad. I keep and guard my heart with all vigilance and above all that I guard, for out of it flow the springs of life.

What [an incredible] quality of love You have given (shown, bestowed upon) me, that I should [be permitted to] be named and called and counted a child of God! I am [even here and] now Your child; it is not yet disclosed (made clear) what I shall be [hereafter], but I know that when Jesus comes and is manifested, I shall [as Your child] resemble and be like Him, for I shall see Him just as He [really] is. I have this hope [resting] on Him, and I cleanse (purify) myself just as He is pure (chaste, undefiled, guiltless).

Through the power of the Holy Spirit given to me, I am an overcomer by the blood of the Lamb and by the word of my testimony!

In Jesus' name I pray, amen.

Scripture References

Ephesians 2:2-6 AMP	Proverbs 15:16 AMP
2 Corinthians 5:17	Zephaniah 3:9 AMP
1 Peter 2:1,2 NIV	Romans 12:2 AMP
Psalm 101:3 NIV	2 Corinthians 10:5
Ephesians 5:25-27 AMP	Philippians 4:8 TLB
Hebrews 9:14 NIV	Proverbs 4:23 AMP
1 Thessalonians 4:8 AMP	1 John 3:1-3 AMP
James 3:17 NIV	Revelation 12:11

I.
A MAN OF PURITY

Father, I attend to Your Word. I hide it in my heart that I might not sin against You. It is not wrong to have sexual desires.

You made me, You know me, and You bought me — I belong to You. I commit myself and all my natural affections to You, Father, and acknowledge the power of the Holy Spirit in my life. I give Him control and submit to Your will.

Forgive me for sinning against You, against myself, and against others. Thank You for Your grace that enables me to leave my gift at the altar when I remember that someone has a grievance against me. I will go and make peace with that person whenever possible and then come back and present my gift to You.

In the name of Jesus, I thank You for the power to shun immorality and all sexual looseness. I [flee from impurity in thought, word, or deed]. My body is the temple (the very sanctuary) of the Holy Spirit Who lives within me, Whom I have received [as a gift] from You. I am not my own. I was bought with a price [purchased with a preciousness and paid for, made Your own]. So then, I will honor You, Father, and bring glory to You in my body.

When I read Your Word, I receive the truth that makes me free. I have won my battle with Satan. I have learned to know You as my Father. I am strong with Your Word in my heart. I no longer love this evil world and all that it offers me, for when I love these things, I show that I do not really love You, Lord; for all these worldly things, these evil desires — the craze for sex, the ambition to buy everything that appeals to me, and the pride that comes from wealth and importance — are not from You, Father. They are from this evil world itself. This world is fading away, and these evil, forbidden things will go with it; but whoever keeps doing Your will, Lord, will live forever.

Thank You, Father, that I have been anointed by [I hold a sacred appointment from, and I have been given an unction from] the Holy One, and I know [the truth]. I have received the Holy Spirit, and He lives within me, in my heart, so that I don't need anyone to teach me what is right. For He teaches me all things, and He is the Truth and no liar; and so, just as He has said, I must live in Christ, never to depart from Him.

O Father, I stay in happy fellowship with You, so that when Your Son, Jesus, comes, I will be sure that all is well and will not have to be ashamed and shrink back from meeting Him. I know that You are always good and do only right, and I seek to be an imitator of You and do what is good and right.

In Jesus' name, amen.

Scripture References

Proverbs 4:20

Psalm 119:11

Matthew 5:23,24 AMP

1 Corinthians 6:18-20 AMP

John 8:32 AMP

1 John 2:12-17 TLB

1 John 2:20,27-29 TLB

Matthew 6:33 AMP

Ephesians 5:1 AMP

II.
A WOMAN OF PURITY

Father, on the authority of Your Word, I declare and decree that I am a new creation in Christ. I repent of my former sins, receive Your forgiveness, and renew my mind — replacing old thought patterns and habits with Your thoughts and plans for me.

I was a sinner, separated, (living apart) from Christ. But now in Christ Jesus, my Lord, I have been brought near through the blood of Christ. I confess that Jesus is my Lord and believe in my heart that You raised Him from the dead. Therefore, I am engrafted in Christ (the Messiah). Now, today, I am a new creation (a new creature altogether); the old [previous moral and spiritual condition] has passed away. Behold, the fresh and new has come!

Since I have confidence to enter the Most Holy Place by the blood of Jesus, by a new and living way opened for me through the curtain, that is, His body, and since I have a great Priest over the house of God, I draw near to You, Lord, with a sincere heart in full assurance of faith, having my heart sprinkled to cleanse me from a guilty conscience and having my body washed with pure water. I hold unswervingly to the hope I profess, for He Who promised is faithful. And I consider how I may spur others on toward love and good deeds. I will not give up meeting together, as some are in the habit of doing; but I will encourage others, and all the more as I see the Day approaching.

Father, I am Your daughter (Your handmaiden), and You have poured out Your Spirit upon me, and I shall prophesy [telling forth the divine counsels and predicting future events pertaining especially to Your Kingdom]. I seek (aim at and strive after) first of all Your Kingdom and Your righteousness (Your way of doing and being right), and then all these things taken together will be given me besides. I will not worry or be anxious about tomorrow, for tomorrow will have worries and anxieties of its own. Sufficient for each day is its own trouble.

As Your daughter, I thank You for enduing me with Your grace (free, spontaneous, absolute favor and loving-kindness).

COMMITTING TO A LIFE OF PURITY

With You, Father, nothing is ever impossible, and no word from You shall be without power or impossible of fulfillment.

Father, I submit to Your will for my life. Your ways are higher than my ways; Your thoughts higher than my thoughts. I commit my way to You, and You will cause my thoughts to become agreeable to Your will, and so shall my plans be established and succeed. I am Your handmaid; let it be done to me according to Your Word.

Since I have such a huge crowd of men and women of faith watching me from the grandstands, I strip off anything that slows me down or holds me back, and especially those sins that wrap themselves so tightly around my feet and trip me up; and I run with patience the particular race that You have set before me. I keep my eyes on Jesus, my Leader and Instructor.

Father, to the pure You show Yourself pure, and to the willful You show Yourself willful. The afflicted people You will deliver, but Your eyes are upon the haughty, whom You will bring down. For You, O Lord, are my Lamp; You, Lord lighten my darkness. For by You I run through a troop; by You I leap over a wall. As for You, Lord, Your way is perfect; Your Word is tried. You are my Shield, for I trust and take refuge in You.

O Father, that I might ascend the hill of the Lord and stand in Your Holy Place. I come with clean hands and a pure heart, refusing to lift up my soul to an idol or swear by what is false, that I may receive blessing and vindication from You, my God and my Savior. Surely, Lord God, You are good to those who are pure in heart.

In Jesus' name I pray, amen.

Scripture References

2 Corinthians 5:17	Luke 1:28,30,37 AMP
Romans 12:1,2 AMP	Isaiah 55:9 AMP
Jeremiah 29:11 AMP	Proverbs 16:3 AMP
Ephesians 2:12,13 AMP	Luke 1:38 AMP
Romans 10:9	Hebrews 12:1,2 TLB
2 Corinthians 5:17 AMP	2 Samuel 22:27-31 AMP
Hebrews 10:19-25 NIV	Psalm 24:3-5 NIV
Acts 2:17 AMP	Psalm 73:1 NIV
Matthew 6:33,34 AMP	

Letting Go of Bitterness

INTRODUCTION

In interviews with divorced men and women, I have been encouraged to write a prayer on overcoming bitterness.

Often the injustice of the situation in which these people find themselves creates deep hurts, wounds in the spirit, and anger that is so near the surface that the individuals involved risk sinking into the trap of bitterness and revenge. Their thoughts may turn inward as they consider the unfairness of the situation and dwell on how badly they have been treated.

In a family divorce situation, bitterness sometimes distorts ideas of what is best for the child/children involved. One parent (and sometimes both parents) will use the child/children against the other.

Unresolved anger often moves one marriage partner to hurt the one he or she holds responsible for the hurt and sense of betrayal which they feel.

There is healing available. There is a way of escape for all who will turn to the Healer, obeying Him and trusting Him.

181

PRAYER

Father, life seems so unjust, so unfair. The pain of rejection is almost more than I can bear. My past relationships have ended in strife, anger, rejection, and separation.

Lord, help me to let go of all bitterness and indignation and wrath (passion, rage, bad temper) and resentment (anger, animosity).

You are the One Who binds up and heals the broken-hearted. I receive Your anointing that destroys every yoke of bondage. I receive emotional healing by faith, and I thank You for giving me the grace to stand firm until the process is complete.

Thank You for wise counselors. I acknowledge the Holy Spirit as my wonderful Counselor. Thank You for helping me work out my salvation with fear and trembling, for it is You, Father, Who works in me to will and to act according to Your good purpose.

In the name of Jesus, I choose to forgive those who have wronged me. I purpose to live a life of forgiveness because You have forgiven me. With the help of the Holy Spirit, I get rid of all bitterness, rage, anger, brawling, and slander, along with every form of malice. I desire to be kind and compassionate to others, forgiving them, just as in Christ You forgave me.

With the help of the Holy Spirit, I make every effort to live in peace with all men and to be holy, for I know that without holiness no one will see You, Lord. I purpose to see to it that I do not miss Your grace and that no bitter root grows up within me to cause trouble.

I will watch and pray that I enter not into temptation or cause others to stumble.

Thank You, Father, that You watch over Your Word to perform it and that whom the Son has set free is free indeed. I declare that I have overcome resentment and bitterness by the blood of the Lamb and by the word of my testimony.

In Jesus' name, amen.

Scripture References

Ephesians 4:31 AMP	Ephesians 4:31,32 NIV
Luke 4:18	Hebrews 12:14,15 NIV
Isaiah 10:27	Matthew 26:41
Proverbs 11:14	Romans 14:21
John 15:26 AMP	Jeremiah 1:12 AMP
Philippians 2:12,13 NIV	John 8:36
Matthew 5:44	Revelation 12:11

Single Believer

_____ is united to the Lord and has become one spirit with Him. _____ shuns immorality and all sexual looseness. _____ flees from impurity in thought, word, or deed.

_____ will not sin against his/her body by committing sexual immorality. His/her body is the temple of the Holy Spirit, Whom he/she has received as a gift from God. _____ is not his/her own. _____ was bought for a price and made God's own. _____ will honor God and bring glory to Him in his/her spirit, soul, and body, which are God's.

_____ shuns youthful lusts and flees from them and aims at and pursues righteousness — all that is virtuous and good, right living, conformity to the will of God in thought, word, and deed. He/she aims at and pursues faith, love, and peace — which is harmony and concord with others — in fellowship with all Christians who call upon the name of the Lord out of a pure heart.

_____ shrinks from whatever might offend You, Father, or discredit the name of Christ. _____ shows himself/herself to be a blameless, guileless, innocent, and uncontaminated child of God, without blemish (faultless) in the midst of a crooked and wicked generation, among whom _____ is seen as a bright light shining out clearly in the dark world, holding out to it and offering to all the Word of Life. Thank You, Father, that Jesus is Lord.

In Jesus' name, amen.

Scripture References (AMP)

1 Corinthians 6:17-20   Philippians 2:12,15,16
2 Timothy 2:22

*C*omplete in Him as a Single

*F*ather, we thank You that _____ desires and earnestly seeks first after the things of Your Kingdom. We thank You that he/she knows that You love him/her and that he/she can trust Your Word.

For in Jesus the whole fullness of Diety (the Godhead) continues to dwell in bodily form — giving complete expression of the Divine Nature, and _____ is in Him and has come to the fullness of life in Christ. He/she is filled with the Godhead — Father, Son, and Holy Spirit — and he/she reaches full spiritual stature. And Christ is the Head of all rule and authority — of every angelic principality and power.

So because of Jesus, _____ is complete; Jesus is his/her Lord. He/she comes before You, Father, desiring a born-again, Christian mate. We petition that Your will be done in his/her life. Now we enter into that blessed rest by adhering, trusting in, and relying on You, in the name of Jesus. Amen.

Scripture References (AMP)

Matthew 6:33　　　　　Hebrews 4:10

Colossians 2:9,10

*S*ingle Female Trusting God for a Mate

*F*ather, in the name of Jesus, I believe that You are providing Your very best for _____ and that the man who will be united with _____ in marriage has awakened to righteousness. Father, as You have rejoiced over Jerusalem, so shall the bridegroom rejoice over _____. Thank You, Father, that he will love _____ as Christ loves the Church. He will nourish, carefully protect, and cherish _____.

Father, I believe, because he is Your best, that doubts, wavering, and insincerity are not a part of him; but he speaks forth the oracles of God, acknowledging Your full counsel with all wisdom and knowledge. He does not speak or act contrary to the Word. He walks totally in love, esteeming and preferring others higher than himself.

Father, I believe that everything not of You shall be removed from _____'s life. And I thank You for the perfecting of Your Word in her life that she may be thoroughly furnished unto all good works. Father, I praise You for the performance of Your Word in her behalf. Amen.

Scripture References

Isaiah 62:5 AMP

Ephesians 5:25

James 3:17 AMP

Proverbs 8:8

Jeremiah 1:12 AMP

Single Male Trusting God for a Mate

*F*ather, in the name of Jesus, I believe that You are providing a suitable helpmate for _____ — Father, according to Your Word, one who will adapt herself to _____, respect, honor, prefer, and esteem him, stand firmly by his side, united in spirit and purpose, having the same love and being in full accord and of one harmonious mind and intention.

Father, You say in Your Word that a wise, understanding, and prudent wife is from You, and he who finds a true wife finds a good thing and obtains favor of You.

Father, I know that _____ has found favor in Your sight, and I praise You and thank You for Your Word, knowing that You watch over it to perform it. Amen.

Scripture References

Ephesians 5:22,33 AMP   Philippians 2:2 AMP

Proverbs 18:22   Jeremiah 1:12 AMP

Proverbs 19:14

$\mathcal{H}$usbands

$\mathcal{F}$ather, in the beginning You provided a partner for man. Now I have found a wife to be my partner, and I have obtained favor from the Lord. I will not let mercy and truth forsake me. I bind them around my neck and write them on the tablet of my heart, and so I find favor and high esteem in the sight of God and man.

In the name of Jesus, I purpose to provide leadership to my wife the way Christ does to His Church, not by domineering, but by cherishing. I will go all out in my love for her, exactly as Christ did for the Church — a love marked by giving, not getting. We are the Body of Christ, and when I love my wife, I love myself.

It is my desire to give my wife what is due her, and I purpose to share my personal rights with her. Father, I am neither anxious nor intimidated, but I am a good husband to my wife. I honor her and delight in her. In the new life of God's grace, we are equals. I purpose to treat my wife as an equal so that our prayers will be answered.

Lord, I delight greatly in Your commandments, and my descendants will be mighty on earth, and the generation of the upright will be blessed. Wealth and riches will be in our house, and my righteousness will endure forever. In the name of Jesus, amen.

HUSBANDS

Scripture References

Matthew 18:18

Genesis 2:18 NEB

Proverbs 18:22 NKJV

Proverbs 3:3,4 NKJV

Proverbs 31:28-31 NLB

Ephesians 5:22,23 MESSAGE

1 Corinthians 7:3-5 PHILLIPS

1 Peter 3:7-9 MESSAGE

Psalm 112:1-4 NKJV

$\mathcal{W}$ives

$\mathcal{I}$n the name of Jesus, I cultivate inner beauty, the gentle, gracious kind that God delights in. I choose to be a good, loyal wife to my husband and address him with respect. I will not be overanxious and intimidated. I purpose to be, by God's grace, agreeable, sympathetic, loving, compassionate, and humble. I will be a blessing and also receive blessings.

By the grace of God, I yield to the constant ministry of transformation by the Holy Spirit. I am being transformed into a gracious woman who retains honor, and a virtuous woman who is a crown to my husband. I purpose to walk wisely that I may build my house. Houses and riches are the inheritance of fathers: and a prudent wife is from the Lord. In Christ I have redemption through His blood, the forgiveness of sins, according to the riches of His grace which He made to abound toward me in all wisdom and prudence.

Holy Spirit, I ask You to help me understand and support my husband in ways that show my support for Christ. *Teach me to function so that I preserve my own personality while responding to his desires. We are one flesh, and I realize that this unity of persons that preserves individuality is a mystery, but that is how it is when we are united to Christ. So I will keep on loving my husband and let the miracle keep happening!

Just as my husband gives me what is due me, I seek to be fair to my husband. I share my rights with my husband.

Strength and dignity are my clothing, and my position in my household is strong. My family is in readiness for the future. The bread of idleness (gossip, discontent, and self-pity) I will not eat. I choose to conduct the affairs of my household wisely, realizing that wisdom from above is pure, peaceable, gentle, willing to yield, full of mercy and good fruits, without partiality and without hypocrisy. Amen.

Scripture References

Matthew 16:19 NKJV	Proverbs 19:14
1 Peter 3:1-5, 8,9 MESSAGE	Ephesians 1:7,8 NKJV
Psalm 51:10 NKJV	Ephesians 5:22,33 MESSAGE
2 Corinthians 3:18	1 Corinthians 7:2-5 PHILLIPS
Proverbs 11:6	Proverbs 31:25-27 AMP
Proverbs 12:4	James 3:17,18 NKJV
Proverbs 14:1	

---

* *The Heart of Paul,* Ben Campbell Johnson. Copyright © 1976 by A Great Love, Inc., Toccoa, GA.

Compatibility in Marriage

Father, in the name of Jesus, the love of God is shed abroad in our hearts by the Holy Spirit Who indwells us. Therefore, my spouse and I are learning to endure long and are patient and kind; we are never envious and never boil over with jealousy. We are not boastful or vainglorious, and we do not display ourselves haughtily. We are not conceited or arrogant and inflated with pride. We are not rude and unmannerly, and we do not act unbecomingly. We do not insist on our own rights or our own way, for we are not self-seeking or touchy or fretful or resentful. We take no account of the evil done to us and pay no attention to a suffered wrong. We do not rejoice at injustice and unrighteousness, but we rejoice when right and truth prevail.

We bear up under anything and everything that comes. We are ever ready to believe the best of each other. Our hopes are fadeless under all circumstances. We endure everything without weakening. *Our love never fails* — it never fades out or becomes obsolete or comes to an end.

We are no longer children tossed to and fro, carried about with every wind of doctrine, but we speak the truth in love, dealing truly and living truly. We are enfolded in love, growing up in every way and in all things. We esteem and delight in one another, forgiving one another readily and freely as God in Christ

194

has forgiven us. We are imitators of God and copy His example as well-beloved children imitate their father.

Thank You, Father, that our marriage grows stronger each day because it is founded on Your Word and on Your kind of love. We give You the praise for it all, Father, in the name of Jesus. Amen.

Scripture References

1 Corinthians 13:4-8 AMP   Ephesians 4:14,15,32

1 Corinthians 14:1   Ephesians 5:1,2 AMP

*T*he New Creation Marriage

*T*he following prayer was given to me by the Holy Spirit for my husband and me.

Husband, you may pray the part for the wife in the third person.

Wife, you may pray the part for the husband in the third person.

Find time to pray together if both parties are willing and receptive.

PRAYER

The couple prays together:

Father, in the name of Jesus, we rejoice and delight ourselves in one another. We are in Christ, the Messiah, and have become (new creatures altogether) new creations; the old (previous moral and spiritual condition) has passed away. Behold, the fresh and new has come! May our family be seen as bright lights — stars or beacons shining out clearly — in the [dark] world. We are willing to receive suggestions from each other. Our relationships in our individual families can benefit from the analogy of the family of God in Ephesians 5. In this relationship we are learning to function so that each preserves his or her own personality while responding to the desires of each other. This unity of persons that preserves individuality is a mystery, but that is how it is when we are united to Christ. So we love each other and let the miracle keep happening!

We will walk in agreement on the authority of Your Word and seek to understand one another. That is more important than being understood. We will be quick to listen, slow to speak, and slow to anger, in the name of Jesus.

The husband prays:

*Father, I take responsibility for my family just as Christ does for the Church. I am a provider for my family. Marriage calls for reciprocal giving, so I love my wife with the self-giving love that Christ showed for His family, the Church.

You are helping me provide leadership to my wife the way Christ does to His Church, not by domineering, but by cherishing. I will go all out in my love for her, exactly as Christ did for the Church — a love marked by giving, not getting.

Christ's love makes the Church whole. His words evoke her beauty. Everything He does and says is designed to bring the best out of her, dressing her in dazzling white silk, radiant with holiness. And that is how I want to love my wife. I realize that I am doing myself a favor — since we are already "one" in marriage. Christ feeds and pampers the Church since we are part of His Body. And this is why I left my father and mother and cherish my wife. We are no longer two, but we have become "one flesh." This is a huge mystery, and I don't pretend to understand it all. What is clearest to me is the way Christ treats the Church. And this provides a good picture of how I am to treat my wife, loving myself in loving her.

The wife prays:

*Father, in the name of Jesus, I purpose to understand and support my husband in ways that show my support for Christ. As the Church is totally responsive to Christ, I respond to my husband in every aspect of our relationship.

I am being transformed by the entire renewing of my mind, and I am a good wife to my husband, appropriately responsive to his needs. I thank You for my inner disposition that reflects the glory of God. I cultivate inner beauty, the gentle, gracious kind that God delights in. The holy women of old were beautiful before God that way, and were good, loyal wives to their husbands. I resist the temptation to become anxious and intimidated. When I speak, I have something worthwhile to say, and I say it with kindness.

In Jesus' name, amen.

Scripture References

2 Corinthians 5:17 AMP	2 Corinthians 5:18
Philippians 2:15 AMP	Ephesians 1:4,6,8 AMP
Ephesians 5:25-30 AMP	Ephesians 5:22,33 AMP
1 Peter 2:6 AMP	1 Corinthians 11:7 AMP
1 Peter 2:23 AMP	Proverbs 31:11,12 AMP
2 Corinthians 3:6	Matthew 19:5,6 AMP

---

* Excerpts from *The Heart of Paul* by Ben Campbell Johnson, published by A Great Love, Inc., Toccoa, GA.

Harmonious Marriage

Father, in the name of Jesus, it is written in Your Word that love is shed abroad in our hearts by the Holy Ghost Who is given to us. Because You are in us, we acknowledge that love reigns supreme. We believe that love is displayed in full expression, enfolding and knitting us together in truth, making us perfect for every good work to do Your will, working in us that which is pleasing in Your sight.

We live and conduct ourselves and our marriage honorably and becomingly. We esteem it as precious, worthy, and of great price. *We commit ourselves to live in mutual harmony and accord with one another,* delighting in each other, being of the same mind and united in spirit.

Father, we believe and say that we are gentle, compassionate, courteous, tenderhearted, and humble-minded. We seek peace, and it keeps our hearts in quietness and assurance. Because we follow after love and dwell in peace, our prayers are not hindered in any way, in the name of Jesus. We are heirs together of the grace of God.

Our marriage grows stronger day by day in the bond of unity because it is founded on Your Word and rooted and grounded in Your love. Father, we thank You for the performance of it, in Jesus' name. Amen.

Scripture References

Romans 5:5	Ephesians 4:32
Philippians 1:9	Isaiah 32:17
Colossians 3:14	Philippians 4:7
Colossians 1:10	1 Peter 3:7
Philippians 2:13	Ephesians 3:17,18
Philippians 2:2	Jeremiah 1:12

*W*hen Desiring To Have a Baby

*O*ur Father, my spouse and I bow our knees unto You. Father of our Lord Jesus Christ, of Whom the whole family in heaven and on earth is named, we pray that You would grant to us according to the riches of Your glory, to be strengthened with might by Your Spirit in the inner man. Christ dwells in our hearts by faith, that we — being rooted and grounded in love — may be able to comprehend with all the saints what is the breadth and length and depth and height of the love of Christ, which passes knowledge, that we might be filled with all the fullness of God.

Hallelujah, we praise You, O Lord, for You give children to the childless wife, so that she becomes a happy mother. And we thank You that You are the One Who is building our family. As Your children and inheritors through Jesus Christ, we receive Your gift — the fruit of the womb, Your child as our reward.

We praise You, our Father, in Jesus' name, for we know that whatsoever we ask, we receive of You, because we keep Your commandments and do those things that are pleasing in Your sight.

Thank You, Father, that we are a fruitful vine within our house; our children will be like olive shoots around our table. Thus shall we be blessed because we fear the Lord.

In Jesus' name we pray, amen.

Scripture References

Ephesians 3:14-19	1 John 3:22,23 AMP
Psalm 113:9 AMP	Psalm 128:3,4 AMP
Psalm 127:3	

The Unborn Child

Father, in Jesus' name, I thank You for my unborn child. I treasure this child as a gift from You. My child was created in Your image, perfectly healthy and complete. You have known my child since conception and know the path he/she will take with his/her life. I ask Your blessing upon him/her and stand and believe in his/her salvation through Jesus Christ.

When You created man and woman, You called them blessed and crowned them with glory and honor. It is in You, Father, that my child will live and move and have his/her being. He/she is Your offspring and will come to worship and praise You.

Heavenly Father, I thank and praise You for the great things You have done and are continuing to do. I am in awe at the miracle of life You have placed inside of me. Thank You! Amen.

Scripture References

Psalm 127:3	Matthew 18:18
Genesis 1:26	John 14:13
Jeremiah 1:5	Galatians 3:13
2 Peter 3:9	1 John 3:8
Psalm 8:5	Psalm 91:1
Acts 17:28,29	

*G*odly Order in Pregnancy and Childbirth

*F*ather, in Jesus' name, I confess Your Word this day over my pregnancy and the birth of my child. I ask You to quickly perform Your Word, trusting that it will not go out from You and return to You void, but rather that it will accomplish that which pleases You. Your Word is quick and powerful and discerns my heart intentions and the thoughts of my mind.

Right now I put on the whole armor of God so that I may be able to stand against the tricks and traps of the devil. I recognize that my fight is not with flesh and blood, but against principalities, powers, and the rulers of darkness and spiritual wickedness in high places. God, I stand above all, taking the shield of faith and being able to quench the attacks of the devil with Your mighty power. I stand in faith during this pregnancy and birth, not giving any room to fear, but possessing power, love, and a sound mind, as Your Word promises in 2 Timothy 1:7.

Heavenly Father, I confess that You are my Refuge; I trust You during this pregnancy and childbirth. I am thankful that You have put angels at watch over me and my unborn child. I cast all the care and burden of this pregnancy over on You, Lord. Your grace is sufficient for me through this pregnancy; You strengthen my weaknesses.

Father, Your Word declares that my unborn child was created in Your image, fearfully and wonderfully made to praise You. You have made me a joyful mother, and I am blessed with a heritage from You as my reward. I commit this child to You, Father, and pray that he/she will grow and call me blessed.

I am not afraid of pregnancy or childbirth because I am fixed and trusting upon You, Father. I believe that my pregnancy and childbirth will be void of all problems. Thank You, Father, that all decisions regarding my pregnancy and delivery will be godly, that the Holy Spirit will intervene. Lord, You are my Dwelling Place, and I rest in the knowledge that evil will not come near me and no sickness or infirmity will strike me or my unborn child. I know that Jesus died on the cross to take away my sickness and pain. Having accepted Your Son, Jesus, as my Savior, I confess that my child will be born healthy and completely whole. Thank You, Father, for the law of the Spirit of life in Christ Jesus that has made me and my child free from the law of sin and death!

Father, thank You for protecting me and my baby and for our good health. Thank You for hearing and answering my prayers. Amen.

Scripture References

Jeremiah 1:12	Proverbs 31:28
Isaiah 55:11	Psalm 112:7
Hebrews 4:12	Psalm 91:1,10
Ephesians 6:11,12,16	Matthew 8:17
Psalm 91:2,11	Romans 8:2

1 Peter 5:7   James 4:7

2 Corinthians 12:9   Ephesians 6:12

Genesis 1:26   John 4:13

Psalm 139:14   Matthew 18:18

Psalm 113:9   Jeremiah 33:3

Psalm 127:3

Adopting a Child

Father, in Jesus' name, we come boldly before Your throne of grace, that we may receive mercy and find grace to help in our time of need. We are trusting in You and seek to do good, so that we may dwell in the land and feed surely on Your faithfulness.

We delight ourselves also in You, and You give us the desires and secret petitions of our hearts. We believe our desire to adopt a child is from You, and we are willing to assume the responsibility of rearing this child in the ways of the Master.

Father, we commit our way to You [roll and repose each care of our load on You]. Our confidence is in You, and You will bring this adoption to pass according to Your purpose and plan.

Lord, Your Son, Jesus, demonstrated Your love for children when He said, "Let the children alone, don't prevent them from coming to me. God's kingdom is made up of people like these" (Matt. 19:14 MESSAGE). Then He laid hands on them and blessed them.

Use us as Your instruments of peace and righteousness to bless this child. We purpose in our hearts to train this child in the way that he/she should go.

Lord, we are embracing this child (Your best gift) as our very own with Your love, as Jesus said, "Whoever embraces one of these children as I do embraces me, and far more than me — God who sent me" (Mark 9:37 MESSAGE).

Father, take this child up and be a Father and Mother to him/her as we extend our hands and our hearts to embrace him/her. Thank You for the blood of Jesus that gives protection to this one whom we love.

We thank You for the man and woman who conceived this child and pray that You will bless them, cause Your face to shine upon them, and be merciful to them. If they do not know Jesus, we ask You, the Lord of the harvest, to send forth laborers to share truth with them that they may come out of the snare of the devil.

Mercy and truth are written upon the tablets of our hearts, and You cause us to find favor and good understanding with You and with man — the adoption agency staff, the judges, and all those who are involved in this decision-making process. May all be careful that they do not despise one of these little ones over whom they have jurisdiction — for they have angels who see Your face continually in heaven.

We believe that all our words are righteous (upright and in right standing with You, Father). By our long forbearing and calmness of spirit those in authority are persuaded, and our soft speech breaks down the most bone-like resistance.

Lord, we are looking to You as our Great Counselor and Mighty Advocate. We ask for Your wisdom for us and our attorneys.

Father, contend with those who contend with us, and give safety to our child and ease him/her day by day. We are calling on You in the name of Jesus, and You will answer us and show us great and mighty things. No weapon formed against us and this adoption shall prosper, and any tongue that rises against us in judgment we shall show to be in the wrong. This [peace, righteousness, security, and triumph over opposition] is our inheritance as Your children.

Father, we believe; therefore, we have spoken. May it be done unto us according to Your Word.

In Jesus' name, amen.

Scripture References

Hebrews 4:16	Matthew 18:10 PHILLIPS
Psalm 37:3	Proverbs 8:8 AMP
Psalm 37:4 AMP	Proverbs 25:15 AMP
Ephesians 6:4 MESSAGE	James 1:5
Psalm 37:5 AMP	Isaiah 49:25
Proverbs 22:6	Jeremiah 33:3
Psalm 67:1	Isaiah 54:17 AMP
Matthew 9:38	Psalm 116:10
2 Timothy 2:26	Luke 1:38
Proverbs 3:3,4	

The Home

Father, I thank You that You have blessed me with all spiritual blessings in Christ Jesus.

Through skillful and godly wisdom is my house (my life, my home, my family) built, and by understanding it is established on a sound and good foundation. And by knowledge shall the chambers (of its every area) be filled with all precious and pleasant riches — great priceless treasure. The house of the uncompromisingly righteous shall stand. Prosperity and welfare are in my house in the name of Jesus.

My house is securely built. It is founded on a rock — revelation knowledge of Your Word, Father. Jesus is my Cornerstone. Jesus is Lord of my household. Jesus is our Lord — spirit, soul, and body.

Whatever may be our task, we work at it heartily as something done for You, Lord, and not for men. We love each other with the God kind of love, and we dwell in peace. My home is deposited into Your charge, entrusted to Your protection and care.

Father, as for me and my house, we shall serve the Lord, in Jesus' name. Hallelujah! Amen.

Scripture References

Ephesians 1:3

Proverbs 24:3,4 AMP

Proverbs 15:6

Proverbs 12:7 AMP

Psalm 112:3

Luke 6:48

Acts 4:11

Acts 16:31

Philippians 2:10,11

Colossians 3:23

Colossians 3:14,15

Acts 20:32

Joshua 24:15

$\mathcal{B}$lessing the Household

INTRODUCTION

$\mathcal{A}$s the head of the family, it is your privilege and duty to pray for the household in your charge and those under your care and authority.

The following prayer was written to be prayed by a man or a woman. So often in today's society, the woman finds herself having to assume the responsibility and position of the head of the household.

I.
PRAYER OF BLESSING
FOR THE HOUSEHOLD

Father, as the priest and head of this household, I declare and decree, "As for me and my house, we shall serve the Lord."

Praise be to You, the God and Father of our Lord Jesus Christ, for You have blessed us in the heavenly realms with every spiritual blessing in Christ. We reverence You and worship You in spirit and in truth.

Lord, we acknowledge and welcome the presence of Your Holy Spirit here in our home. We thank You, Father, that Your

Son, Jesus, is here with us because we are gathered together in His name.

Lord God, Your divine power has given us everything we need for life and godliness through our knowledge of You Who called us by Your own glory and goodness.

As spiritual leader of this home, I declare on the authority of Your Word that my family will be mighty in the land; this generation of the upright will be blessed.

Father, You delight in the prosperity of Your people; and we thank You that wealth and riches are in our house and that our righteousness endures forever.

In the name of Jesus, amen.

Scripture References

Revelation 1:6	Matthew 18:20
Joshua 24:15	2 Peter 1:3 NIV
Ephesians 1:3 NIV	Psalm 112:2 NIV
John 4:23	Psalm 112:3

II.
PRAYER OF BLESSING AT THE TABLE

INTRODUCTION

This prayer was written for the head of the household to pray not only to thank and praise God for His blessings, but also to cleanse and consecrate the food received and to sanctify the family members who partake of it.

PRAYER

Father, thank You for giving to us our daily bread. We receive this food with thanksgiving and praise. You bless our bread and our water and take sickness out of the midst of us.

In the name of Jesus, we call this food clean, wholesome, and pure nourishment to our bodies. Should there be any deadly thing herein, it shall not harm us, for the Spirit of life in Christ Jesus makes us free from the law of sin and death.

In the name of Jesus, amen.

Scripture References

Matthew 6:11	Mark 16:18
1 Timothy 4:4 NIV	Romans 8:2
Exodus 23:25	

III.
HUSBAND'S PRAYER OF BLESSING FOR HIS WIFE

INTRODUCTION

It is positive reinforcement, validation, and affirmation for children to hear their father pray, blessing his wife and their mother. This is a method of honoring her and reaffirming her position in the home. Words are powerful, and the blessings for the wife in front of the children will promote appropriate self-esteem necessary for success in life.

Sometimes a wife will feel that she has failed because she is not fulfilling all the roles expressed in Proverbs 31. I believe that God had this passage written to encourage a woman to be all that

He created her to be. Out of her "being" — knowing herself, both her strengths and her weaknesses, developing her talents, seeing herself as God sees her, and looking to Christ for her completeness (wholeness) — comes the "doing."

"The woman described in this chapter has outstanding abilities. Her family's social position is high. In fact, she may not be one woman at all — she may be a composite portrait of ideal womanhood. Do not see her as a model to imitate in every detail; your days are not long enough to do everything she does! See her instead as an inspiration to be all you can be. We can't be just like her, but we can learn from her industry, integrity, and resourcefulness."[1]

PRAYER

Father, I thank You for my wife who is a capable, intelligent, and virtuous woman. Her worth is far more precious than jewels, and her value is far above rubies or pearls.

I thank You that she is a woman of strong character, great wisdom, many skills, and great compassion. Strength and dignity are her clothing, and her position is strong and secure. She opens her mouth with skillful and godly wisdom, and on her tongue is the law of kindness [giving counsel and instruction].

Our children rise up and call her blessed (happy, fortunate, and to be envied); and I boast of and praise her, [saying], "Many daughters have done virtuously, nobly, and well [with the strength of character that is steadfast in goodness], but you excel them all."

---

[1] *Life Application Bible*, New International Version edition (Wheaton, IL: Tyndale House Publishers, 1988, 1989, 1990, 1991), commentary at bottom of p. 1131.

Father, my wife reverently and worshipfully fears You; she shall be praised! Give her of the fruit of her hands, and let her own works praise her in the gates [of the city].

I respect, value, and honor my wife before our children.

In the name of Jesus, amen.

Scripture References (AMP)

Proverbs 31:10	Proverbs 31:28,29
Proverbs 31:25,26	Proverbs 31:30,31

IV.
PARENT'S PRAYER OF BLESSING
FOR CHILDREN

INTRODUCTION

"The [Hebrew] father's place in the [traditional Jewish] home is fittingly shown by the beautiful custom of blessing the children, a custom which dates back to Isaac and Jacob. To this day, in many homes, the father blesses his children on Friday nights, on Rosh Hashanah eve and on Yom Kippur before leaving for the synagogue....

In very ancient times, the father or patriarch was the ruler of home and family. He made laws and enforced them. Later, however, laws were instituted by teachers, parents, judges, and kings. The father, as the master of the house, was looked up to for support and depended on for guidance."[2]

---

[2] Ben M. Edidin, *Jewish Customs and Ceremonies* (New York: Hebrew Publishing Company, 1941), p. 23.

BLESSING THE HOUSEHOLD

The following prayer, based on a translation of the traditional Hebrew father's blessing upon his children, may be used by the head of the household, whether male or female.

PRAYER

Father, I receive, welcome, and acknowledge each of my children as a delightful blessing from You. I speak Your blessings upon them and over them.

Children, I bless you in the name of Jesus, proclaiming the blessings of God, my Redeemer, upon you. May He give you wisdom, a reverential fear of God, and a heart of love.

May He create in you the desire to attend to His words, a willing and obedient heart that you may consent and submit to His sayings and walk in His ways. May your eyes look straight ahead with purpose for the future. May your tongue be as the pen of a ready writer, writing mercy and kindness upon the tablets of your heart. May you speak the truth in love. May your hands do the works of the Father; may your feet walk the paths which He has foreordained for you.

I have no greater joy than this: to hear that my children are living their lives in the truth.

May the Lord prepare you and your future mate to love and honor one another, and may He grant to your union upright sons and daughters who will live in accordance with His Word. May your source of livelihood be honorable and secure, so that you will earn a living with your own hands. May you always worship God in spirit and in truth.

I pray above all things that you may always prosper and be in health, even as your soul prospers. "I know the thoughts and plans that I have for you, says the Lord, thoughts and plans for welfare and peace and not for evil, to give you hope in your final outcome" (Jer. 29:11 AMP).

In the name of Jesus, amen.

Scripture References

Psalm 127:3 AMP	Ephesians 2:10 AMP
Philippians 2:13 AMP	3 John 4 AMP
Proverbs 4:20	1 Thessalonians 4:11,12 NIV
Psalm 45:1	John 4:23
Proverbs 3:3 AMP	3 John 2
Ephesians 4:15	

$\mathcal{P}$eace in a Troubled Marriage

$\mathcal{F}$ather, in the name of Jesus, we bring _____ before You. We pray and confess Your Word over them, and as we do, we use our faith, believing that Your Word will come to pass.

Therefore we pray that _____ will let all bitterness, indignation, wrath, passion, rage, bad temper, resentment, brawling, clamor, contention, slander, abuse, evil speaking, or blasphemous language be banished from them, and also all malice, spite, ill will, or baseness of any kind. We pray that _____ have become useful and helpful and kind to each other, tenderhearted, compassionate, understanding, loving-hearted, forgiving one another readily and freely as You Father, in Christ, forgave them.

Therefore, _____ will be imitators of You, God. They will copy You and follow Your example as well-beloved children imitate their father. _____ will walk in love, esteeming and delighting in one another as Christ loved them and gave Himself up for them, a slain offering and sacrifice to You, God, so that it became a sweet fragrance.

Father, we thank You that _____ will be constantly renewed in the spirit of their minds, having a fresh mental and spiritual attitude. They have put on the new nature and are created

219

in God's image in true righteousness and holiness. They have come to their senses and escaped out of the snare of the devil who has held them captive and henceforth will do Your will, which is that they love one another with the God-kind of love, united in total peace and harmony and happiness.

Thank You for the answer, Lord. We know it is done now in the name of Jesus. Amen.

Scripture References

Ephesians 4:31,32 AMP	Ephesians 4:23,24
Ephesians 5:1,2	2 Timothy 2:26 AMP
Matthew 18:18	

$\mathcal{W}$hen Marriage Vows Are Broken

INTRODUCTION

$\mathcal{T}$his prayer was originally written for a wife whose husband had been unfaithful. If you are a husband who has been betrayed, simply change this prayer to fit your situation.

PRAYER

Lord, You made us one when we became husband and wife. You made us one in body and spirit, and You intended for us to have godly children. My husband has dishonored me; we are no longer equal partners of life, and our prayers have been disturbed. The rejection and betrayal is very painful.

Father, forgive us for speaking our marriage vows so casually and without understanding. I have covered Your altar with tears because our prayers have been hindered. You witnessed the vows we made to each other on our wedding day when we were young. Our marriage vows are broken, and I am abandoned. Father, I cannot encourage my husband's wayward behavior and become a partaker of his evil work.

Jesus was wounded for our transgressions, and bruised for our iniquities; the chastisement of our peace was upon Him, and by His stripes we are healed (Isa. 53:5). I ask You to forgive my shortcomings and failures concerning my marriage. Help me learn and grow spiritually and receive emotional wholeness, as I grow more intimately acquainted with You. Father, give me the grace to forgive my husband's infidelity.

You hate divorce, but You allow it when a spouse is unfaithful. You know my husband's heart and the decisions he will make concerning his future, and I am responsible to You and my children. _____ has behaved as an unbeliever in this situation, and if he desires to go, give me the grace to let him go.

Lord, I trust in You with all of my heart and lean not unto my own understanding. In all of my ways I acknowledge You, and You shall direct my path. Father, You promised to never leave me, abandon me, or leave me without support. I know that the preparations of the heart belong to man, but I desire the wise answer of the tongue that comes from You. In Jesus' name I pray, amen.

Scripture References (AMP)

Titus 2:4-6	Ephesians 5:21
Proverbs 5:15-19	Jeremiah 1:12
Hebrews 9:14	Hebrews 13:5
1 Corinthians 11:3	

*O*vercoming Rejection in Marriage

*F*ather, in the name of Jesus, _____ and _____ are delivered from this present evil age by the Son of the Living God, and whom the Son has set free is free indeed. Therefore, they are delivered from a spirit of rejection and accepted in the Beloved to be holy and blameless in His sight. They forgive all those who have wronged them, and their hurts from the past are healed, for Jesus came to heal the brokenhearted.

They are God's chosen people, holy and dearly loved. They clothe themselves with compassion, kindness, humility, gentleness, and patience. They bear with each other and forgive whatever grievances they may have against one another. They forgive as the Lord forgave them. Over all these virtues, they put on love, which binds them together in perfect unity.

When they were children, they talked like children, thought like children, and reasoned like children; but now they have become husband and wife, and they are done with childish ways and have put them aside. The blood of Christ, Who through the eternal Spirit offered Himself without spot to God, purges their consciences from dead works of selfishness, agitating passions, and moral conflicts, so they can serve the Living God. They touch not any unclean thing, for they are a son and daughter of the Most High God. Satan's power over them is broken, and his strongholds are torn down. Sin no longer has dominion over them and their household.

The love of God reigns supreme in their home, and the peace of God acts as an umpire in all situations. Jesus is their Lord — spirit, soul, and body. Amen.

Scripture References (AMP)

Galatians 1:4

John 8:36

Ephesians 1:16

Luke 4:18

Romans 6:18

Colossians 3:12-15 NIV

1 Corinthians 13:11 AMP

1 Thessalonians 5:23

Colossians 3:15 AMP

$\mathcal{P}$eace in the Family

$\mathcal{F}$ather, in the name of Jesus, I thank You that You have poured Your Spirit upon our family from on high. Our wilderness has become a fruitful field, and we value our fruitful field as a forest. Justice dwells in our wilderness, and righteousness [religious and moral rectitude in every area and relation] abides in our fruitful field. The effect of righteousness will be peace [internal and external], and the result of righteousness, quietness, and confident trust forever.

Our family dwells in a peaceable habitation, in safe dwellings, and in quiet resting places. And there is stability in our times, abundance of salvation, wisdom, and knowledge. There, reverent fear and worship of the Lord is our treasure and Yours.

O Lord, be gracious to us; we have waited [expectantly] for You. Be the Arm of Your servants — our Strength and Defense — every morning, our Salvation in the time of trouble.

Father, we thank You for our peace, our safety, and our welfare this day. Hallelujah! Amen.

Scripture References (AMP)

Isaiah 32:15-18   Isaiah 33:2,6

225

*H*andling Household Finances

INTRODUCTION

*T*he following prayers may be prayed individually or as a couple. In preparation for marriage it is great wisdom for the couple to discuss finances. Each party comes with an individual view of how to handle money — spending and/or saving. It is wise to set up a budget that is agreeable to both.

There is a danger in the tendency to assume that the other party has the same opinions and ideas about money or, in case of disagreement, that one's own way is right and the other person's is wrong. Financial differences are one of Satan's greatest weapons for introducing strife and bringing pressure to bear on a marriage. Spending money can quickly evolve into an emotional experience, causing many other problems.

God is *El-Shaddai,* God Almighty (Ex. 6:3 AMP) — the God Who is more than enough — and His intention is that His children enjoy good health and that all may go well with them, even as their souls are getting along well (3 John 2 NIV). Two people coming into agreement with God's financial plan will offset the enemy's schemes to divide and conquer.

If you and your beloved are planning to marry or to establish a financial plan in your existing marriage, listen to one another. Understand what each other is saying. Realize that there are differences in viewpoints about money and allow for those differences. Determine who is more astute in financial matters: balancing the checkbook, paying the bills on time and making wise investments. Set aside time in your schedules to keep each other informed, review goals, and make plans. Wisdom from above is willing to yield to reason; cooperate one with the other (James 3:17 AMP).

PRAYER

Father, we come before You in the name of Jesus. Thank You for the Holy Spirit Who is present with us as we discuss our financial future together. We thank You for bringing us to this place in our lives. You have started a good work in us and will perform it until the day of Christ. We welcome You as we prepare to set up a budget that is pleasing to You and to each of us.

Jesus is our Lord and our High Priest, and we purpose to bring Him the firstfruits of our income and worship You, the Lord our God, with them.

Father, You are Lord over our marriage — over this union that we believe has been ordained by You. We confess Your Word over our life together and our finances. As we do so, we say that Your Word will not return to You void, but will accomplish what it says it will do.

Therefore, we believe in the name of Jesus that all of our needs are met, according to Your riches in glory. We acknowledge

You as Lord over our finances by giving tithes and offerings to further Your cause.

Father, on the authority of Your Word, we declare that gifts will be given to us; good measure, pressed down, shaken together, and running over shall they be poured into our bosom. For with the same measure we deal out, it shall be measured back to us.

We remember that it is written in Your Word that he who sows sparingly and grudgingly will also reap sparingly and grudgingly, and he who sows generously [that blessings may come to someone] will also reap generously and with blessings.

Lord, remind us always, and we purpose to remember, that it is You Who gives us power to become rich, and You do it to fulfill Your promise to our ancestors. We will never feel that it was our own power and might that made us wealthy.

Father, not only do we give tithes and offerings to You, but we also give to those around us who are in need. Your Word also says that he who gives to the poor lends to You, and You pay wonderful interest on the loan! We acknowledge You as we give for the benefit of the poor.

Thank You, Father, that as You bless us and we bless others, they will praise You and give You thanks and bless others and the circle of Your love and blessing will go on and on into eternity.

In the name of Jesus we pray, amen.

Scripture References

John 14:17	Luke 6:38
Philippians 1:6	2 Corinthians 9:6 AMP

Hebrews 3:1   Deuteronomy 8:17,18 TLB

Deuteronomy 26:10,11   Proverbs 19:17 TLB

Isaiah 55:11   2 Corinthians 9:12-15 AMP,

Philippians 4:19   NIV, PHILLIPS

I.
SETTING ASIDE THE TITHE

Father, Your Word states, "Be sure to set aside a tenth of all that your fields produce each year....so that you may learn to revere the Lord Your God always" (Deut. 14:22,23 NIV). We purpose to set aside the tithe because it belongs to You, O God our Father.

It is our delight to bring all the tithes (the whole tenth of our income) into the storehouse, that there may be food in Your house. Lord of hosts, in accordance with Your Word, we prove You now by paying You the tithe. You are opening the windows of heaven for us and pouring us out such a blessing that there shall not be room enough to receive it.

Thank You, Father, for rebuking the devourer for our sakes; he shall not destroy the fruits of our ground, neither shall our vine drop its fruit before the time in the field.

We praise You, Lord, for recording our names in Your book of remembrance of those who reverence and worshipfully fear You and who think on Your name so that we may be Yours in the day when You publicly recognize and openly declare us to be Your jewels (Your special possession, Your peculiar treasure).

Thank You for bringing us out of the authority of darkness and translating us into the Kingdom of Your dear Son, Jesus Christ, our Lord.

In His name we pray, amen.

Scripture References

Malachi 3:10,11 AMP   Colossians 1:13

Malachi 3:16,17 AMP

II.
GIVING THE OFFERING

Father, we give offerings at the direction of the Holy Spirit. We are ever ready with a generous and willing gift. At Your instructions we remember this: He who sows sparingly and grudgingly will also reap sparingly and grudgingly, and he who sows generously [that blessings may come to someone] will also reap generously and with blessings.

We [give] as we make up our own minds and purpose in our hearts, not reluctantly or sorrowfully or under compulsion; for You, Lord, love (take pleasure in, prize above other things, and are unwilling to abandon or to do without) a cheerful (joyous "prompt to do it") giver [whose heart is in his giving].

Father, we thank You that You are able to make all grace (every favor and earthly blessing) come to us in abundance, so that we may always, under all circumstances and whatever the need, be self-sufficient [possessing enough to require no aid or support and furnished in abundance for every good work and charitable donation].

Father, [You] provide seed for our sowing and bread for our eating. Thank You for providing and multiplying [our resources], for sowing and increasing the fruits of our righteousness. Thus we will be enriched in all things and in every way, so that we can be generous, and [our generosity as it is] administered by us will bring forth thanksgiving to You.

We confess with the Psalmist David, we have not seen the righteous forsaken, nor his seed begging bread.

We thank You for food, clothing, and shelter. In the name of Jesus, we determine to stop being perpetually uneasy (anxious and worried) about our life together, what we shall eat and what we shall drink, or about our bodies, what we shall put on. Our life — individually and together — is greater [in quality] than food, and our bodies [far above and more excellent] than clothing.

The bread of idleness [gossip, discontent, and self-pity] we will not eat. We declare on the authority of Your Word that our family will be mighty in the land: this generation of the upright will be blessed.

Father, You delight in the prosperity of Your people; we thank You that wealth and riches are in our house and our righteousness endures forever.

Good comes to us for we are generous and lend freely and conduct our affairs with justice. When we lack wisdom, we will ask of You, and You will give generously without finding fault with us.

In the name of Jesus, amen.

Scripture References

2 Corinthians 9:5-11 AMP	Psalm 112:2,3
Psalm 37:25	Psalm 37:26 NIV
Matthew 6:25 AMP	2 Corinthians 9:9 AMP
Proverbs 31:27 AMP	James 1:5 NIV
Psalm 35:27	

*M*oving to a New Location

*F*ather, Your Word says that You will perfect that which concerns us. Your mercy and loving-kindness, O Lord, endure forever — forsake not the works of Your own hands. We bring to You our apprehensions concerning our relocation. We ask You to go before us to make the crooked places straight in finding a new home.

Give us wisdom to make wise decisions in choosing the movers and packers best suited to handle our possessions. We have favor, good understanding, and high esteem in the sight of You and man — with the utility companies, with the school systems, and with the banks — with everyone involved in this move.

Father, we thank You for supplying and preparing the new friends that You would want us to have. We are trusting You to direct us to a church where we can fellowship with like believers, in one accord, where we are free to worship and praise You and sing to You a new song.

Father, in the name of Jesus, we commit this move to You, knowing that You provide for Your children. We trust You and delight ourselves in You, and You will give us the desires of our hearts.

We make all these requests known unto You with thanksgiving, and the peace that passes all understanding shall guard our hearts and minds. You will keep us in perfect peace because our minds are stayed on You.

We trust in You, Father, with all of our hearts. We lean not unto our own understanding; but in all of our ways we acknowledge You, and You shall direct our paths.

Thank You, Father, for Your blessing on this move.

In the name of Jesus, amen.

Scripture References

Psalm 138:8	Psalm 40:3
Isaiah 45:2	Psalm 96:1
James 1:5	Psalm 98:1
Proverbs 3:4	Psalm 149:1
Hebrews 10:25	Psalm 37:4,5
Acts 2:1,46	Philippians 4:6,7
Acts 4:34	Isaiah 26:3
Philippians 2:2	Proverbs 3:5,6
Isaiah 42:10	

Seeking Safety in a Place of Violence

Father, I am Your child. I have been redeemed by the blood of the Lamb. My sins are forgiven.

As the head of my household, I pray according to Your Word, asking for Your protection for each of us. Give safety to my children and ease them day by day. Our life is exceedingly filled with the scorning and scoffing of those who are at ease and with the contempt of the proud (irresponsible tyrants who disregard Your law).

Lord, You see the violence that is in the streets and in our schools. The drug dealers and the gang members living in our neighborhoods are waiting to snare our children.

On the authority of Your Word, I ask that You destroy [their schemes]; O Lord, confuse their tongues, for I have seen violence and strife in the inner city. Day and night they go about on its walls; iniquity and mischief are in its midst. Violence and ruin are within it; fraud and guile do not depart from its streets and marketplaces. I am calling upon You, Lord, and You will save me and my household as well.

Father, in the name of Jesus, You, and You alone, are our safety and our protection. My household and I are looking to You, for our strength comes from You — the God Who made heaven and earth. You will not let us stumble. You are our Guardian God Who will not fall asleep. You are right at our side to protect us. You guard us from every evil, You guard our very lives. You guard us when we leave and when we return. You guard us now; You guard us always.

My household was chosen and foreknown by You, Father, and consecrated (sanctified, made holy) by the Spirit to be obedient to Jesus Christ (the Messiah) and to be sprinkled with [His] blood. We receive grace (spiritual blessing) and peace in ever-increasing abundance [that spiritual peace to be realized in and through Christ, freedom from fears, agitating passions, and moral conflicts].

Lord, Your Son, Jesus, became our Passover by shedding His own precious blood. He is the Mediator (the Go-between, Agent) of a new covenant, and His sprinkled blood speaks of mercy. On the authority of Your Word, I proclaim that the blood of Jesus is our protection, as it is written, "...when I see the blood, I will pass over you..." (Ex. 12:13). I declare and decree that I am drawing a bloodline around my children, and the evil one cannot cross it.

I know that none of the God-begotten make a practice of sin — fatal sin. The God-begotten are also the God-protected. The evil one can't lay a hand on my household. I know that we are held firm by You, Lord.

Father, thank You for Your divine protection. In the name of Jesus I pray, amen.[1]

Scripture References

1 John 3:1	Psalm 121:1-8 MESSAGE
1 Peter 1:18,19	1 Peter 1:2 AMP
1 John 2:12	Hebrews 12:24 AMP
Psalm 123:4 AMP	1 John 5:18,19 MESSAGE
Psalm 55:9-11,16 AMP	

---

[1] In addition to praying this prayer, read Psalm 91 aloud over your family each day.

Dealing With an Abusive Family Situation

INTRODUCTION

*I*n our ministry, we receive letters from women who are living in abusive situations. Since many of them do not feel or believe that they can leave, they request that we write prayers to cover this area of need. They are fearful of practicing tough love. A need for security plays a big role in their decision to remain where they are. Or, in certain cases, they fear increased or even more severe abuse should they try to leave. Others have asked the abuser to leave or have moved out themselves; yet, their request is for prayer for deliverance for the abuser and other family members.

When I am traveling, I often meet women who feel that it is safe to talk with me. At the close of a meeting a few years ago, I was approached by an attractive woman whom I recognized by her manner of dress as belonging to a certain denomination. As she shared her agony and emotional pain, I moaned inwardly. I took her in my arms, encouraging her to go to her pastor for counseling. Her answer grieved me. She had been told by both her husband and her pastor that the beatings were because of her "rebellious nature."

"I don't know what else I can do to stop the abuse," she confided. "I've tried to please my husband. Scripturally, I cannot leave him. What can I do but stay with him? I don't want to disobey God, but I want the abuse to stop."

When we turn to the Scriptures, we find that God is much more merciful than we human beings. Jesus is our Example, and in one incident He turned around and walked away from the crowd who would have thrown Him off a cliff (Luke 4:28-30). There are times to take action; change brings change. Often we want God to do something when all the time He is waiting for us to do something: "Trust God from the bottom of your heart; don't try to figure out everything on your own. Listen for God's voice in everything you do, everywhere you go; he's the one who will keep you on track" (Prov. 3:5,6 MESSAGE).

A testimony of deliverance from abusive behavior was shared by a young husband who had been born again for only a short time. His mother had given him a copy of *The Living Bible*. One day he picked it up and read Malachi 2:15,16: "You were united to your wife by the Lord. In God's wise plan, when you married, the two of you became one person in his sight. And what does he want? Godly children from your union. Therefore guard your passions! Keep faith with the wife of your youth. For the Lord, the God of Israel, says he hates divorce and cruel men. Therefore control your passions — let there be no divorcing of your wives."

The young man said, "When I read these verses, I realized that I was treating my wife cruelly and admitted to myself that the addictions in my life were controlling me. It wasn't so much that I wanted to stop doing drugs, but I did want to change the way that I was treating my wife. I cried out to God, and He heard me and delivered me."

DEALING WITH AN ABUSIVE
FAMILY SITUATION

The following prayer was written for Christian women who want to know how to pray prayers that avail much while in an abusive family situation.

PRAYER

Father, Your Word says that You loved me and my family so much that You sent Your very own Son, Jesus, to die for our sin so we could live with You forever. You said that You would give us a new life that is wonderful and rich. I pray that I may become like You, for I am Your child and You love me.

By Your grace, Father, I will live my life in love. Your love in me is not a feeling, but a decision requiring more than mere words. As a Christian I am "light," and I will live as a child of the Light. The Light produces in me all that is good and right and true.

Lord, lead me in paths of righteousness for Your name's sake. I purpose to live with a due sense of responsibility, not as others who do not know the meaning of life, but as one who does. Direct me by Your Holy Spirit that I may make the best use of my time, despite all the evils of these days.

Father, there was a time when You looked for an intercessor. I am willing to stand in the gap and make up the hedge so that my family will not suffer judgment. Send Your Holy Spirit to convict, convince, and demonstrate to us about sin, righteousness, and judgment. Give us a heart of flesh and send a laborer of the harvest to share with us the Gospel of the glory of Christ (the Messiah).

I thank You, Father, that each family member who is lost receives and confesses that Jesus is his/her Lord, and I ask that Your will be done in his/her life. It is You Who rescues him/her from the dominion of darkness, and You translate him/her into the Kingdom of the Son of Your love. In the name of Jesus, I ask that You help him/her to grow in grace, that he/she may experience Your love and trust You to be his/her Father.

Lord, reveal the steps that I should take to break what appears to be a generational curse. The sins of the fathers are being repeated in our household, and I do not want this curse passed down to my children.

Father, Your Word says that we are overcomers by the blood of the Lamb and by the word of our testimony. In the name of Jesus, I am committing my life to You — to obey You. Show me the path of life for me and my family.

Uncontrollable, irrational anger, rage, and abuse are a curse. Your Son, Jesus, was made a curse for us; therefore, I put on Your whole armor that I may be able to successfully stand against all the strategies and the deceits of the devil.

In the name of Jesus, I am the redeemed, and I plead the blood of Jesus over my family. I thank You that the evil power of abuse is broken, overthrown, and cast down out of my family. The abuse is exposed and reproved by the light — it is made visible and clear; and where everything is visible and clear, there is light.

You sent Jesus to bind up our heartaches and to heal our pain. The Bible says that You have sent Your Word to heal us and to deliver us from our own destructions. Give us the grace and faith to receive healing and to forgive those who have abused us; thank You for the courage to make amends to those whom we have harmed.

DEALING WITH AN ABUSIVE FAMILY SITUATION

Teach us how to guard our hearts with all diligence. I declare and decree that we are growing in grace and the knowledge of You, developing the trust we need to receive Your transforming power to change. I make my petitions known to You with thanksgiving, in the name of Jesus. Amen.

Scripture References

John 3:16

John 10:10

Ephesians 5:1 PHILLIPS

1 John 3:18 AMP

Ephesians 5:8,9 PHILLIPS

Psalm 23:3

Ephesians 5:15,16 PHILLIPS

Ezekiel 22:30

John 16:8 AMP

Ezekiel 11:19

Matthew 9:38

Matthew 6:10

Colossians 1:13

1 Peter 3:18

Revelation 12:11

Psalm 16:11

Galatians 3:13

Ephesians 6:11 AMP

Ephesians 5:13 AMP

Luke 4:18

Psalm 107:20

Matthew 5:44

Proverbs 4:23

Romans 12:2

Philippians 4:6 NIV

$\mathcal{O}$vercoming Weariness

$\mathcal{T}$his prayer is for everyone who is experiencing weariness. It is not limited to the unmarried who are awaiting a life-partner. Many spouses become weary with heartaches that they did not expect to encounter in marriage. Their expected marital bliss has turned into disappointment, additional wounds, and frustration. They are weary with waiting for the healing of the marriage relationship or the deliverance of a spouse, children, or other loved ones from various addictions or negative, destructive behaviors. They long for someone who will heal their wounds without judging them — someone who will love them unconditionally.

Each individual brings baggage into marriage, hoping for a miracle — each partner looking to the other for acceptance and approval.

According to the letters and comments we have received in our ministry, unmarried people experience weariness in matters that married couples may not encounter. Hopefully, we who are married share responsibilities — household chores. Married homeowners may divide the work up into inside and outside labor. Sometimes one spouse neglects his/her responsibility, and the other finds himself/herself doing the work of two. The single person is responsible at all times for "the work of two."

We who are married have another individual involved in the decision-making process, which can lead to conflict. Conflict is not always bad. Out of this conflict can come intimacy. We are not alone in financial decisions, in planning for the future. We may feel alone, but there is another with whom we can talk, with whom we can explore possibilities. We have another human being from whom we can draw strength. Ideally, we grow together.

Sometimes a married person may experience feelings of "aloneness," but there is another person in the house, someone who is going to return, someone whose presence — although in certain marriages noncommunicative — is experienced.

The unmarried often feel such weariness and dread going home to emptiness — to nothingness. They look for that individual who will be their soul mate, a life partner, someone who will be present and available in good times and bad, someone who will love them unconditionally.

(We must all ask ourselves, "Am I ready and willing to love another person unconditionally?")

If you have grown weary and are disappointed in your expectations, I encourage you to seek God for His plan for your life. Ask the Holy Spirit to help you trust God and not be afraid.

PRAYER

Father, You see my weariness, my uneasiness, proceeding from continual waiting and disappointed expectation. It seems that my patience is exhausted, and I am discouraged. I am weary of asking and waiting for _____.

My soul is weary with sorrow; strengthen me according to Your Word.

Lord, I come to You, and You give me rest. I take Your yoke upon me and learn of You, for You are gentle and humble in heart, and I will find rest for my soul. Your yoke is easy, and Your burden is light.

I look to You, Lord, and Your strength; I seek Your face always. You are my Refuge and Strength, an ever-present help in trouble. O my Strength, I watch for You; You, O God, are my Fortress, my loving God. O my Strength, I sing praises to You.

Father, You give strength to the weary and increase the power of the weak. Even youths grow tired and weary, and young men stumble and fall; but those who hope in You, Lord, will renew their strength. They will soar on wings like eagles; they will run and not grow weary. They will walk and not be faint. I purpose to wait for You, Lord; to be strong and take heart and wait for You.

Lord, You are my Strength and my Song; You have become my Salvation. You are my God, and I will praise You, my father's God, and I will exalt You. In Your unfailing love You will lead the people You have redeemed. In Your strength You will guide them to Your holy dwelling.

You, Sovereign Lord, have given me an instructed tongue to know the word that sustains the weary. You waken me morning by morning, waken my ear to listen like one being taught.

You are my Light and my Salvation — whom shall I fear or dread? You are the Refuge and Stronghold of my life — of whom shall I be afraid? You are a shield for me, my Glory, and the Lifter of my head. With my voice I cry to You, Lord, and You hear and answer me out of Your holy hill. Lord, You sustain me.

I consider it wholly joyful whenever I am enveloped in or encounter trials of any sort or fall into various temptations. I am assured and understand that the trial and proving of my faith bring out endurance and steadfastness and patience. I purpose to let endurance and steadfastness and patience have full play and do a thorough work, so that I may be perfectly and fully developed [with no defects], lacking in nothing. I will praise You with my whole heart; Your joy is my strength.

I determine to consider Him Who endured such opposition from sinful men, so that I will not grow weary and lose heart.

Father, Your grace is sufficient, and I will not grow weary in doing good, for at the proper time I will reap a harvest if I do not give up. I am strong in You, Lord, and in Your mighty power.

In the name of Jesus I pray, amen.[1]

Scripture References

Psalm 119:28 NIV	Psalm 27:1 AMP
Matthew 11:28-30 NIV	Psalm 3:3,4 AMP
1 Chronicles 16:11 NIV	James 1:2-4 AMP
Psalm 46:1 NIV	Psalm 9:1
Psalm 59:9,17 NIV	Nehemiah 8:10
Isaiah 40:29-31 NIV	Hebrews 12:3 NIV
Psalm 27:14 NIV	2 Corinthians 12:9
Exodus 15:2,13 NIV	Galatians 6:9 NIV
Isaiah 50:4 NIV	Ephesians 6:10 NIV

---

[1] For additional strength and guidance, I suggest reading and meditating on the following passages: Psalm 6, Psalm 18, Psalm 27, Psalm 28, Psalm 38, Psalm 71.

The Children

Father, in the name of Jesus, I pray and confess Your Word over my children and surround them with my faith — faith in Your Word that You watch over it to perform it! I confess and believe that my children are disciples of Christ, taught of the Lord and obedient to Your will. Great is the peace and undisturbed composure of my children, because You, God, contend with that which contends with my children, and You give them safety and ease them.

Father, You will perfect that which concerns me. *I commit and cast the care of my children once and for all over on You, Father.* They are in Your hands, and I am positively persuaded that You are able to guard and keep that which I have committed to You. You are more than enough!

I confess that my children obey their parents in the Lord as His representatives, because this is just and right. My children _____ honor, esteem, and value as precious their parents; for this is the first commandment with a promise: that all may be well with my children and that they may live long on earth. I believe and confess that my children choose life and love You, Lord, obey Your voice and cling to You; for You are their Life and the Length of their days. Therefore, my children are the head and not the tail, and they shall be above only and not beneath. They are blessed when they come in and when they go out.

I believe and confess that You give Your angels charge over my children to accompany and defend and preserve them in all their ways. You, Lord, are their Refuge and Fortress. You are their Glory and the Lifter of their heads.

As parents, we will not provoke, irritate, or fret our children. We will not be hard on them or harass them or cause them to become discouraged, sullen, or morose or to feel inferior and frustrated. We will not break or wound their spirits, but we will rear them tenderly in the training, discipline, counsel, and admonition of the Lord. We will train them in the way they should go, and when they are old, they will not depart from it.

O Lord, my Lord, how excellent (majestic and glorious) is Your name in all the earth! You have set Your glory on or above the heavens. Out of the mouth of babes and unweaned infants You have established strength because of Your foes, that You might silence the enemy and the avenger. I sing praises to Your name, O Most High. *The enemy is turned back from my children in the name of Jesus!* They increase in wisdom and in favor with God and man. Amen.

Scripture References

Jeremiah 1:12	Psalm 91:11
Isaiah 54:13	Psalm 91:2
Isaiah 49:25	Psalm 3:3
1 Peter 5:7	Colossians 3:21
2 Timothy 1:12	Ephesians 6:4
Ephesians 6:1-3	Proverbs 22:6
Deuteronomy 30:19,20	Psalm 8:1,2
Deuteronomy 28:13	Psalm 9:2,3
Deuteronomy 28:3,6	Luke 2:52

$\mathcal{D}$ealing With a Child With ADD/ADHD

INTRODUCTION

*I*n these last days Satan is working harder than ever to destroy our children. One of the areas of his attack is what psychologists and educators call Attention Deficit Disorder/Attention Deficit Hyperactivity Disorder. These disorders are tools of the enemy to disrupt households — causing confusion, frustration, division, and every evil work. Their effects are far reaching.

Children and adults with ADD/ADHD are thought of as bullies, unruly, destructive, overbearing, impulsive, defiant — and the list goes on. It has been estimated that about two to five percent of school-aged children are now diagnosed with the disorder, and many adults who have it have never been diagnosed. Many who might be helped if properly diagnosed are in mental institutions, jails, and prisons.[1]

---

[1] For additional information on ADD/ADHD, including instructional practices for use in dealing with this disorder, see "101 ways to help children with add learn, Tips from Successful Teachers," published by Division of Innovation and Development, Office of Special Education Programs, Office of Special Education and Rehabilitative Services, U.S. Department of Education.

DEALING WITH A CHILD WITH ADD/ADHD

Although working with children diagnosed with ADD/ADHD can sometimes be frustrating and discouraging, as believers we know that God's Word, prayer, understanding caretakers, Christian counseling, medication, and their peers can all help them become overcomers.

In our ministry to these special children, we must remember that, according to 2 Corinthians 10:4, "...the weapons of our warfare are not carnal, but mighty through God to the pulling down of strong holds." Psalm 107:20 AMP says of the Lord's intervention on behalf of those in need, "He sends forth His word and heals them and rescues them from the pit and destruction." Prayer, according to the Word of God, will avail much (James 5:16).

Declare and decree victory for the child as you teach and direct him/her through the following prayers.

The first two were written by a grandmother, one of our associates at Word Ministries, whose grandson has been diagnosed with ADD/ADHD. They pray together each morning before he leaves for school.

The third prayer and the following series of daily prayers were based on conversations and prayer times that I have had with this young man. He and I have cried and laughed together in my office, where we talk privately and confidentially.

At times, he asks to sit in a class where I am teaching, and later we discuss the subject matter. For instance, we may talk about abandonment issues and how Jesus felt when He was on the cross. He is not shy about asking for prayer when he is having a problem.

If you use any of these prayers, I encourage you when necessary to explain in simple language the meaning of the terms found in them. Remember, the child's imagination is creating pictures with the words he or she speaks and hears.

As the child prays, listen carefully, allowing him/her to express his/her feelings, fears, thoughts, and ideas. Ask the Holy Spirit for discernment — it can be difficult to separate seriousness from horseplay. If you give the child time, he/she will let you know the difference.

PRAYERS TO BE PRAYED BY THE CHILD

I.

COMING AGAINST ADD/ADHD

Father, in the name of Jesus, I come against ADD/ADHD and say that I have the mind of Christ (the Messiah) and hold the thoughts (feelings and purposes) of His heart; I am able to concentrate and stay focused on each task.

I am a disciple (taught by You, Lord, and obedient to Your will), and great is my peace and undisturbed composure. I do not have a spirit of fear, but [You have given me a spirit] of power and of love and of a calm, well-balanced mind and discipline and self-control.

In the name of Jesus, I come against my defiant behavior and tantrums and hyperactivity and speak peace and love to the situations in which I find myself. I cast down imaginations and every high thing that would exalt itself against the knowledge of You, Lord, and bring into captivity every thought to the obedience of Christ.

Father, I ask for Your wisdom to reside in me each day as I learn new techniques for handling stressful incidents.

Father, Your Word says not to worry about anything but to pray and ask You for everything I need and to give thanks when I pray, and Your peace will keep my heart and mind in Christ Jesus. The peace You give me is so great that I cannot understand it.

Thank You for keeping my mind quiet and at peace. I declare that I am an overcomer; I am in control.

In the name of Jesus, amen.

Scripture References

1 Corinthians 2:16 AMP   Philippians 4:6,7 ICB

Isaiah 54:13 AMP   Isaiah 26:3

2 Timothy 1:7 AMP   Revelation 12:11

2 Corinthians 10:5

II.
MAKING NEW FRIENDS

Father, I am asking You to supply me with good friends I can relate to, spend time with, and enjoy as You intended. I desire to develop relationships that will be lasting and helpful to both me and my friends.

Father, I will be sound-minded, self-restrained, and alert — above all things, I purpose to have intense and unfailing love for others, for I know love covers a multitude of sins [forgives and disregards the offenses of others].

I ask You to help me manage my behavior and attitude so others will want to be around me. I purpose to bridle my tongue and speak words of kindness. I will not insist on having my own way, and I will not act unbecomingly. When someone is unkind and falsely accuses me, help me to maintain a cool spirit and be slow to anger. I commit to plant seeds of love, and I thank You for preparing hearts ahead of time to receive me as a friend and as a blessing to their lives.

Father, thank You for causing me to find favor, compassion, and loving-kindness with others.

Thank You, Lord, for my new friends.

In Jesus' name, amen.

Scripture References

1 Peter 4:7,8 AMP	James 1:19 AMP
Proverbs 21:23	1 Corinthians 3:6
1 Corinthians 13:4,5	Daniel 1:9 AMP
Proverbs 18:24 AMP	

III.
HAVING A BAD DAY

Father, this was not a good day. My scores were low. It was a hard day for me at school and at home. I feel that I messed up a lot. Because I know that You love me unconditionally and You are not holding anything against me, I come to talk with You.

Father, You expect me to be accountable to You, my teachers, and my parents for my behavior.[2] I ask Your forgiveness

---

[2] NOTE TO PARENT: Effective reprimands should be brief and directed at the child's behavior, not at the character of the child. Direct him/her in assuming responsibility for his/her actions, acknowledging and asking forgiveness when appropriate.

for acting mean and disrespectful to _____. I acknowledge my misbehavior, and I ask You to forgive me for _____.

Thank You, Lord, for helping me as I learn good social skills and how to do unto others as I want them to do unto me.

Father, I release my disappointment to You, and I believe that tomorrow will be a great day! I look forward to the new day with its new beginnings.

In the name of Jesus, amen.

Scripture References

Romans 8:33-39 NIV	Matthew 15:4 NIV
2 Corinthians 5:18 TLB	1 John 1:9 TLB
Matthew 12:36 NIV	Luke 6:31 NIV
Romans 13:1-5 NIV	Proverbs 4:18

IV.
LIVING EACH DAY

MONDAY:

Father, in the name of Jesus, I thank You for giving me life. You picked me out for Your very own even before the foundation of the world — before I was ever born. You saw me while I was being formed in my mother's womb, and You know all about ADD/ADHD.

Lord, You see the weird things I do, and You know all my weird thoughts even before I think them. Thank You for loving me and helping me replace bad thoughts with good thoughts.

Help my parents, teachers — and, especially, the bus driver — to help me do right things. Help me to be kind to others.

In the name of Jesus, amen.

Scripture References

Ephesians 1:4 AMP   Psalm 139:2 TLB

Psalm 139:13-16 TLB   Ephesians 4:32 TLB

TUESDAY:

Father, Psalm 91 says that You have assigned angels to me — giving them [special] charge over me to accompany and defend and preserve me in all my ways.

Lord, I need Your help. Sometimes my weird thoughts scare me, and I don't like the way I behave. I become so frightened and confused that I have to do something: run, make noises — even scream or try to hurt someone. These actions separate me from playmates; and when they don't want to be my friends, I am hurt and disappointed and angry.

I am asking You, Father, to help me form new behavior patterns and successfully overcome the disobedience and defiance that cause my parents and teachers anguish. I don't like to see them all upset, even though I laugh about it sometimes.

Thank You for helping me overcome obsessive, compulsive actions that create confusion for me and others around me. Even when others don't want me around, You will never abandon me. You will always be with me to help me and give me support.

In the name of Jesus, amen.

Scripture References

Psalm 91:11 AMP   Psalm 27:10 TLB

Romans 7:21-25 TLB   Hebrews 13:5 AMP

WEDNESDAY:

Father, thank You for my parents, grandparents, wise counselors, and teachers who understand me and are helping me learn good behavior patterns. Help me to listen and develop good relationships with others — especially other children.

Thank You for giving me the ability to learn how to express my anger appropriately; I rejoice every time I have a victory. Your Son, Jesus, said that He has given me power to overcome all the obstacles that ADD/ADHD causes in my life.

In His name I pray, amen.

Scripture References

Ephesians 4:26 TLB   Luke 10:19 NIV

THURSDAY:

Father, I believe in my heart that Your Son, Jesus, is my Lord and Master and that He has come to live in my heart. Thank You for giving me the mind of Christ (the Messiah), His thoughts (feelings and purposes).

Lord, You are with me when my thoughts get jumbled up, and You have sent the Holy Spirit to help me concentrate and stay focused on each task at home and at school. I am a disciple [taught by You, Lord, and obedient to Your will], and great is my peace and undisturbed composure. Thank You for giving me Your helmet of salvation to protect my thought life.

In the name of Jesus, amen.

Scripture References

Romans 10:9,10 NIV   Isaiah 54:13 AMP

1 Corinthians 2:16 AMP   1 Thessalonians 5:8 NIV

John 16:13 NIV

FRIDAY:

Father, You have not given me a spirit of fear, but You have given me a spirit of power and of love and a calm, well-balanced mind and discipline and self-control. Thank You that as I grow in the grace and knowledge of Jesus Christ, You are creating in me a willing heart to be obedient.

Forgive me for throwing tantrums, and help me recognize and control the destructive ideas that cause them. The Holy Spirit is my Helper. Thank You for giving me the ability to channel hyperactivity in constructive, productive ways.

I choose to speak peace and love into the situations that confront me and make me feel uncomfortable and out of control.

In the name of Jesus, amen.

Scripture References

2 Timothy 1:7 AMP   Philippians 2:13

2 Peter 3:18   John 14:16 AMP

Exodus 35:5

SATURDAY:

Father, sometimes awful thoughts come to me, and I command the voices that tell me bad things to be quiet and leave me in the name of Jesus.

Lord, in Your Word You said that I can make choices. I choose to cast down imaginations that cause me to feel afraid and angry; these thoughts are not Your thoughts. You love me, and I will think on good things.

Father, I ask for Your wisdom to reside in me each day as I learn new techniques for handling stressful incidents.

In the name of Jesus, amen.

Scripture References

Deuteronomy 30:19,20 TLB   Isaiah 55:8 TLB

2 Corinthians 10:5   Philippians 4:8 TLB

SUNDAY:

Father, there are so many everyday things that worry and torment me. I feel so different from other people.

Lord, Your Word says not to worry about anything but to pray and ask You for everything I need and to give thanks when I pray, and Your peace will keep my heart and mind in Christ Jesus. The peace You give me is so great that I cannot understand it.

Thank You for keeping my mind quiet and at peace. I declare that I am an overcomer, and by submitting to Your control, I am learning self-control.

Father, I thank You for teaching me how to be a good friend to those You are sending to be my friends.

In the name of Jesus, amen.

Scripture References

Philippians 4:6,7 ICB   Revelation 12:11

Isaiah 26:3 AMP   Galatians 5:23 AMP

PRAYER TO BE PRAYED
BY THE CAREGIVER

INTRODUCTION

Caregivers of ADD/ADHD children often find themselves in situations that far exceed their parenting skills. Much prayer and faith are required to see the ADD/ADHD child as God sees him/her. The emotional turmoil and disruption to the household often become overwhelming, and caregivers sometimes discover that the challenges are greater than themselves.

Responsible adults involved in the life of an ADD/ADHD child need godly wisdom, spiritual discernment, and mental and emotional alertness to overcome weariness, bewilderment, and anxiety. Often, they second-guess themselves, processing confusing emotions and scenes of great conflict. Words spoken to the child and over him/her can comfort, giving him/her hope — or they can reinforce his/her belief that he/she is bad and that something terrible is wrong with him/her. Words can heal or words can wound.

The prayers of the ADD/ADHD child must be reinforced by those who love him/her. Often our image of another individual —

even our children — can only be changed as we pray according to God's will and purpose for him/her. The following personal prayer for the caregiver is a composite of things the Holy Spirit has directed me to pray for my friend and associate and her husband who are raising their ADD/ADHD grandson. I have observed in them the heartache, the delight, the exasperation — the full gamut of emotions involved in this challenging experience. But through it all, God is faithful!

PRAYER

Father, in the name of Jesus, I thank You for this very special child. You see my confusion, anxiety, frustration, and bewilderment as I attempt to rear him/her [tenderly] in the training and discipline and the counsel and admonition of the Lord. Forgive me for times when I knowingly or unknowingly irritate and provoke him/her to anger [exasperate him/her to resentment].

You see my intense pain when I observe the rejection this child suffers by adults who speak harsh words against him/her and our family. Children refuse to play with him/her, and it hurts even though I understand. I know that those who have never walked in our shoes cannot fully understand us.

But, Lord, where others are unmerciful and unkind, You are merciful and kind. Surely, goodness and mercy shall follow us all the days of our lives, and we shall dwell in Your house forever. Hide us in the secret place of Your presence and keep us secretly in Your pavilion from the strife of tongues.

Lord, perfect the fruit of my lips that I may offer to You effective praise and thanksgiving for this child who is a blessing from You. His/her intellect astounds me, and his/her wit is a delight. I ask You for divine intervention and guidance as I train him/her up in the way that he/she should go. I thank You for the awesomeness of Your handiwork and the techniques that You have given him/her to survive — to overcome emotional turmoil — and the ability to function in this world around us. Truly, this child is fearfully and wonderfully made. I plead the blood of Jesus over him/her to protect him/her in every situation.

You have a divine purpose for this child. You have foreordained steps that he/she is to walk in, works that he/she is to do. Help me to look at his/her strengths and weaknesses realistically, that I may know how to help him/her develop and demonstrate self-control techniques. Forgive me for times when I lose patience and berate him/her for his/her behavior. Sometimes, I lose sight of who he/she really is. Anoint my eyes to see him/her as You see him/her.

Father, help me to speak works of grace; anoint my lips to speak excellent and princely things over him/her, about him/her, and to him/her. May the opening of my lips be for right things. Help me to give him/her healthy doses of unconditional love, administer to him/her appropriate discipline for misbehavior, and reward him/her for his/her good behavior. Anoint my lips with coals of fire from Your altar that I may speak words that comfort, encourage, strengthen, and honor him/her. Keep watch at the door of my lips, and forgive me when my patience has come to an end.

Father, You are my Comforter, Counselor, Helper, Intercessor, Advocate, Strengthener, and Standby. Whatever comes my way, help me to consider it wholly joyful, allowing endurance and steadfastness and patience to have full play and do a thorough work, so that I may be perfectly and fully developed [with no defects], lacking in nothing. When I am deficient in wisdom, I will ask of You, and You will give wisdom to me liberally and ungrudgingly, without reproaching or finding fault in me.

I pray that I may be invigorated and strengthened with all power according to the might of Your glory, [to exercise] every kind of endurance and patience (perseverance and forbearance) with joy.

Father, You have seen the tears in the night season, and I know that I shall experience the joy that comes in the morning times. You are my Exceeding Joy! You are my Wisdom, Righteousness, Sanctification, and Redemption. Thank You for being a constant companion.

Lord, I see my child, _____, growing and becoming strong in spirit, increasing in wisdom (in broad and full understanding) and in stature and years and in favor with You and with man.

In the name of Jesus I pray, amen.

Scripture References

Ephesians 6:4 AMP	Isaiah 6:6,7
Psalm 117:2	Psalm 141:3 AMP
Psalm 23:6	John 14:16 AMP
Psalm 31:20 AMP	James 1:2,4,5 AMP
Hebrews 13:15	Colossians 1:11 AMP
Psalm 127:3 AMP	Psalm 22:2
Proverbs 22:6	Psalm 30:5
Psalm 139:14	Psalm 43:4
Ephesians 2:10	1 Corinthians 1:30
Proverbs 8:6 AMP	Luke 1:80; 2:52 AMP

DAILY AFFIRMATIONS FOR USE
BY THE CAREGIVER

INTRODUCTION

Often it is very difficult for ADD/ADHD children to learn, to develop new learning techniques in their lives and to change their negative behavior patterns. When working with them, it is so important that we love them with the God-kind of love and praise them for their accomplishments.

Following are examples of the kinds of positive daily affirmations that can be said to the ADD/ADHD child to help him/her develop a good self-image and to become all that God intends for him/her in this life.

AFFIRMATIONS

• Great job • Well done • I'm very proud of you • Good for you • Neat • Outstanding • That was a smart decision • You are smart • God loves you • I love you • I knew you could do it • I believe in you • I know you are trying • Super-duper • You are a good boy/girl • Way to go • What an imagination • You are growing up • Good memory • Amazing • Nice work • What a wise choice • You are a blessing to me • You are special to me • You are valuable • You are a gem, a precious jewel • You are more precious than gold • You are incredible • You are important • Outstanding performance • You are a winner • Remarkable • Nothing can stop you • Now you've got it • Excellent • You are catching on • Great • Wonderful • Good • Terrific • Beautiful • Now you are cooking • You are fantastic • Beautiful work • Outstanding • You are spectacular • You are a real trooper • You are unique • Great discovery • You try so hard • Good try • Good effort • Magnificent • You've got it • Super work • Phenomenal • Marvelous • Dynamite • You mean so much to me • You make me laugh • You brighten my day • Hurray for you • You are beautiful • You are handsome • You are a good friend • You are a loving son/daughter [grandson/granddaughter] • You light up my life • You belong • You are an important part of our family • We are family • You mean the world to me • That's right • You are correct • You are a success • Hurray • You are growing in wisdom every day • You are a beautiful creation • You are loved • I love you • WOW! • You are a success • You are an overcomer • You are a child of my love • You are victorious • You are a ray of sunshine • You are patient • You have a good attitude • You are a doer • You know how to get the job done • You are a chosen one • You give good hugs • Thank you for being a part of my life•

You are deserving of praise!

Scripture Passages for Meditation

A GOOD REPORT: Proverbs 15:30; Philippians 4:8

A SOFT ANSWER: Proverbs 15:1

PERFECT LOVE: 1 John 4:18

Children at School

Father, in Jesus' name, I confess Your Word this day concerning my children as they pursue their education and training at school. You are effectually at work in them, creating within them the power and desire to please You. They are the head and not the tail, above and not beneath.

I pray that my children will find favor, good understanding, and high esteem in the sight of God and their teachers and classmates. I ask You to give my children wisdom and understanding as knowledge is presented to them in all fields of study and endeavor.

Father, thank You for giving my children an appreciation for education and helping them to understand that the Source and beginning of all knowledge is You. They have the appetite of the diligent, and they are abundantly supplied with educational resources; their thoughts are those of the steadily diligent, which tend only to achievement. Thank You that they are growing in wisdom and knowledge. I will not cease to pray for them, asking that they be filled with the knowledge of Your will, bearing fruit in every good work.

Father, I thank You that my children have divine protection since they dwell in the secret place of the Most High. My children trust and find their refuge in You and stand rooted and grounded in Your love. They shall not be led astray by philosophies of men and teaching that is contrary to truth. You are their Shield and Buckler, protecting them from attacks or threats. Thank You for the angels whom You have assigned to them to accompany, defend, and preserve them in all their ways of obedience and service. My children are established in Your love, which drives all fear out of doors.

I pray that the teachers of my children will be godly men and women of integrity. Give our teachers understanding hearts and wisdom in order that they may walk in the ways of piety and virtue, revering Your holy name. Amen.

Scripture References

Philippians 2:13	Psalm 91:1,2
Deuteronomy 28:1,2,13	Ephesians 4:14
Proverbs 3:4 AMP	Psalm 91:3-11
1 Kings 4:29	Ephesians 1:17
Daniel 1:4	Psalm 112:8
Proverbs 1:4,7	Ephesians 3:17
Proverbs 3:13	Matthew 18:18
Proverbs 4:5	James 1:5
Colossians 1:9,10	

Child's Future

Father, Your Word declares that children are an inheritance from You and promises peace when they are taught in Your ways. I dedicate _____ to You today, that he/she may be raised as You would desire and will follow the path You would choose. Father, I confess Your Word this day over _____. I thank You that Your Word goes out and will not return unto You void, but will accomplish what it says it will do.

Heavenly Father, I commit myself, as a parent, to train _____ in the way he/she should go, trusting in the promise that he/she will not depart from Your ways, but will grow and prosper in them. I turn the care and burden of raising him/her over to You. I will not provoke my child, but I will nurture and leave him/her in Your care. I will do as the Word of God commands and teach my child diligently. My child will be upon my heart and mind. Your grace is sufficient to overcome my inabilities as a parent.

My child _____ is obedient and honors both his/her parents, being able to accept the abundant promises of Your Word of long life and prosperity. _____ is a godly child not ashamed or afraid to honor and keep Your Word. He/she stands convinced that You are the Almighty God. I am thankful that as _____ grows, he/she will remember You and not pass by the opportunity of a relationship with Your Son, Jesus. Your great blessings will be upon _____ for keeping Your ways. I thank You for Your blessings over every area of _____'s life, that You will see to the salvation and obedience of his/her life to Your ways.

Heavenly Father, I thank You now that laborers will be sent into _____'s path, preparing the way for salvation, as it is written in Your Word, through Your Son, Jesus. I am thankful that _____ will recognize the traps of the devil and will be delivered to salvation through the purity of Your Son. You have given _____ the grace and the strength to walk the narrow pathway to Your Kingdom.

I pray that just as Jesus increased in wisdom and stature, You would bless this child with the same wisdom and pour out Your favor and wisdom openly to him/her.

I praise You in advance for _____'s future spouse. Father, Your Word declares that you desire for children to be pure and honorable, waiting upon marriage. I speak blessings to the future union and believe that _____ will be well suited to his/her partner and their household will be in godly order, holding fast to the love of Jesus Christ. Continue to prepare _____ to be the man/woman of God that You desire him/her to be.

_____ shall be diligent and hard-working, never being lazy or undisciplined. Your Word promises great blessing to his/her house, and he/she shall always be satisfied and will always increase. Godliness is profitable unto his/her house, and _____ shall receive the promise of life and all that is to come.

Father, thank You for protecting and guiding my child.

In Jesus' name I pray, amen.

Scripture References

Psalm 127:3	Matthew 7:14
Isaiah 54:13	Luke 2:52
Isaiah 55:11	Hebrews 13:4
Proverbs 22:6	1 Thessalonians 4:3
1 Peter 5:7	Ephesians 5:22-25
Ephesians 6:4	2 Timothy 1:13
Deuteronomy 6:7	Proverbs 13:11
2 Corinthians 12:9	Proverbs 20:13
Ephesians 6:1-3	Romans 12:11
2 Timothy 1:12	1 Timothy 4:8
Proverbs 8:17,32	1 John 3:8
Luke 19:10	John 10:10
Matthew 9:38	Matthew 18:18
2 Corinthians 2:11	John 14:13
2 Timothy 2:26	Psalm 91:1,11
Job 22:30	

*P*rayer for a Teenager

*F*ather, in the name of Jesus, I affirm Your Word over my son/daughter. I commit _____ to You and delight myself also in You. I thank You that You deliver _____ out of rebellion into right relationship with us, his/her parents.

Father, the first commandment with a promise is to the child who obeys his/her parents in the Lord. You said that all will be well with him/her and he/she will live long on the earth. I affirm this promise on behalf of my child, asking You to give _____ an obedient spirit that he/she may honor (esteem and value as precious) his/her father and mother.

Father, forgive me for mistakes made out of my own unresolved hurts or selfishness, which may have caused _____ hurt. I release the anointing that is upon Jesus to bind up and heal our (parents' and child's) broken hearts. Give us the ability to understand and forgive one another, as God for Christ's sake has forgiven us. Thank You for the Holy Spirit Who leads us into all truth and corrects erroneous perceptions about past or present situations.

Thank You for teaching us to listen to each other and giving _____ an ear that hears admonition, for then he/she will be called wise. I affirm that I will speak excellent and princely things, and the opening of my lips shall be for right things. Father, I commit to train and teach _____ in the way that he/she is to go, and when _____ is old, he/she will not depart from sound doctrine and teaching, but will follow it all the days of his/her life. In the name of Jesus, I command rebellion to be far from the heart of my child and confess that he/she is willing and obedient, free to enjoy the reward of Your promises. _____ shall be peaceful, bringing peace to others.

Father, according to Your Word, we have been given the ministry of reconciliation, and I release this ministry and the word of reconciliation into this family situation. I refuse to provoke or irritate or fret my child; I will not be hard on him/her lest he/she becomes discouraged, feeling inferior and frustrated. I will not break his/her spirit, in the name of Jesus and by the power of the Holy Spirit. Father, I forgive my child for the wrongs he/she has done and stand in the gap until he/she comes to his/her senses and escapes out of the snare of the enemy (rebellion). Thank You for watching over Your Word to perform it, turning and reconciling the heart of the rebellious child to the parents and the hearts of the parents to the child. Thank You for bringing my child back into a healthy relationship with You and with me, that our lives might glorify You! Amen.

Scripture References

Psalm 55:12-14	Proverbs 8:6,7
1 Peter 5:7	Proverbs 22:6
Psalm 37:4	Isaiah 1:19
John 14:6	Isaiah 54:13
Ephesians 6:1-3	2 Corinthians 5:18,19
1 John 1:9	Colossians 3:21

PRAYER FOR A TEENAGER

Isaiah 61:1

John 16:13

Proverbs 15:31

Proverbs 13:1

John 20:23

Ezekiel 22:30

Jeremiah 1:12

Malachi 4:6

Group
Prayers

PART TWO

*I*ndividual Growth

*F*ather, in the name of Jesus, we in our prayer group desire that our prayers avail much. We are individuals who are [mutually dependent on one another], having gifts (faculties, talents, qualities) that differ according to the grace given us. We, who with unveiled faces all reflect Your glory, are being transformed into Your likeness with ever-increasing glory, which comes from You, Who are the Spirit.

Father, we realize that You know what we have need of before we ask and that we are not all growing in the same manner or on the same time schedule, but we are growing in the grace and knowledge of our Lord and Savior Jesus Christ.

We give each other space to grow, for we are becoming a patient people, bearing with one another and making allowances because we love one another. We acknowledge that we do not have dominion [over] each other, and we refuse to lord it over one another's faith; but we are fellow laborers [to promote] one another's joy, because it is by faith that we stand firm.

In Jesus' name, amen.

Scripture References

James 5:16	2 Peter 3:18
Romans 12:5,6 AMP	2 Corinthians 1:24 AMP
2 Corinthians 3:18 NIV	Ephesians 4:20
Matthew 6:32	

A Group Member Experiencing Grief or Loss

*F*ather, in the name of Jesus, we approach Your throne of grace, bringing _____ before You. We recognize that grieving is a human emotional process, and we give him/her the space that he/she needs to enter into the rest that You have for him/her.

Lord, Jesus bore _____'s griefs (sicknesses, weaknesses, and distresses) and carried his/her sorrows and pains; we know that Your Spirit is upon Jesus to bind up and heal _____'s broken heart. May he/she be gentle with himself/herself, knowing that he/she is not alone in his/her grief. You are with him/her, and You will never leave him/her without support.

Give us, _____'s friends and prayer partners, discernment, sympathy, and understanding so that we may bear (endure, carry) his/her burden of loss. We trust You to guide him/her, and we respect his/her decisions awaiting the manifestation of Your healing.

Father, we desire to be doers of Your Word, and not hearers only. Therefore, we make a commitment to rejoice with those who rejoice [sharing others' joy] and to weep with those who weep [sharing others' grief]. We pray that our love will give _____ great joy and comfort and encouragement, because he/she has cheered and refreshed the hearts of Your people.

Thank You, Father, for sending the Holy Spirit to comfort, counsel, help, intercede, defend, strengthen, and stand by _____ in this time of grief and sorrow.

In Jesus' name, amen.

Scripture References

Isaiah 53:4 AMP	James 1:22
Isaiah 61:1 AMP	Romans 12:15 AMP
Hebrews 13:5 AMP	Philemon 7 AMP
Galatians 6:2 AMP	John 14:26 AMP

*L*oving and Caring for Self

*F*ather, I realize that before I can love others as You have instructed, I must love myself. Help me to speak truly, deal truly, and live truly in harmony with You, myself, and others in my prayer group.

I am Your workmanship, created in Christ Jesus. I am fearfully and wonderfully made. Help me to remember that others do not always know what is best for me. I trust in You with all of my heart and lean not on my own understanding; in all of my ways I acknowledge You, and You will make my paths straight.

I look to You to cause my thoughts to be agreeable to Your will that I may make healthy choices. Give me the courage to say no when it is in my best interest according to Your purpose and plan for my life.

I take responsibility for myself and allow others in our prayer group to take responsibility for themselves, in the name of Jesus. This frees me so that I am not [merely] concerned with my own interests, but also with the interests of others.

I desire to do unto others as I would have them do unto me. I am walking uprightly before You; therefore, I consider, direct, and establish my way [with the confidence of integrity].

You are my confidence, and You will keep my foot from being snared. Your love is shed abroad in my heart, and I will love my neighbor as myself.

In Jesus' name, amen.

Scripture References

Romans 13:9	Philippians 2:4 AMP
Ephesians 4:15 AMP	Matthew 7:12
Ephesians 2:10	Proverbs 21:29 AMP
Psalm 139:14	Proverbs 3:26
Proverbs 3:5,6 NIV	Romans 5:5
Proverbs 16:3 AMP	Matthew 22:39

*P*erseverance in Prayer

*F*ather, the course that You have set before me is clear. You have called me into this prayer group to respond to the many prayer requests we receive from those who need agreement or who don't know how to pray for themselves.

Lord, You are the Vinedresser, Jesus is the Vine, and I am the branch. I remain in Him and He remains in me, and my prayers bear much fruit; apart from Him, I can do nothing.

Father, at times I am tempted to grow weary and overburdened with the pain and heartache of others. Help me to remember that Jesus said, "Come to me, all you who are weary and burdened, and I will give you rest" (Matt. 11:28 NIV). I take His yoke upon me and learn from Him, for He is gentle and humble in heart, and I will find rest for my soul. His yoke is easy, and His burden is light.

Lord, Jesus said that I ought always to pray and not to turn coward (faint, lose heart, or give up). I am earnest and unwearied and steadfast in my prayer [life], being [both] alert and intent [in my praying with thanksgiving].

Therefore, since I am surrounded by such a great cloud of witnesses, I throw off everything that hinders and the sin that so easily entangles, and I run with perseverance the race marked out for me. I fix my eyes on Jesus, the Author and Perfecter of my faith, Who for the joy set before Him endured the cross, scorning its shame, and sat down at the right hand of Your throne. I consider Him Who endured such opposition from sinful men, so that I will not grow weary and lose heart during times of intercession.

In His name I pray, amen.

Scripture References

John 15:1-7 AMP   Colossians 4:2 AMP

Matthew 11:29,30 NIV   Hebrews 12:1-3 NIV

Luke 18:1 AMP

$30.00

$\mathcal{P}$leasing God Rather Than Men

$\mathcal{F}$ather, I desire to please You rather than men. Forgive me for loving the approval and the praise and the glory that come from men [instead of and] more than the glory that comes from You. [I value my credit with You more than credit with men.]

In Jesus' name I declare that I am free from the fear of man, which brings a snare. I lean on, trust in, and put my confidence in You. I am safe and set on high.

I take comfort and am encouraged and confidently and boldly say, "The Lord is my Helper; I will not be seized with alarm [I will not fear or dread or be terrified]. What can man do to me?"

Father, just as You sent Jesus into the world, You have sent me. You are ever with me, for I always seek to do what pleases You.

In Jesus' name, amen.

Scripture References

John 12:43 AMP   John 17:18 AMP

Proverbs 29:25 AMP   John 8:29 AMP

Hebrew 13:6 AMP

Communication With Group Members

Father, to as many as received Jesus, You gave the power to become Your sons and daughters. I am learning to be straightforward in my communication with my brothers and sisters in Christ, my co-laborers in the Lord. I have the power to be direct, honestly expressing my feelings and desires, because Jesus has been made unto me wisdom. Wisdom from above is straightforward, impartial (unbiased, objective), and unfeigned (free from doubts, wavering, and insincerity).

I am Your creation, Father, and You created me to be active in sharing my faith, so that I will have a full understanding of every good thing we have in Christ. It is my prayer in Jesus' name that my conversation will always be full of grace, seasoned with salt, so that I may know how to answer everyone. I am content with my own reality (satisfied to the point where I am not disturbed or disquieted) in whatever state I am, so those around me can feel safe in my presence. I will speak truly, deal truly, and live truly, expressing the truth in love.

As Your children and co-laborers, we walk in the ever-developing maturity that enables us to be in perfect harmony and full agreement in what we say, perfectly united in our common understanding and in our opinions and judgments. And if on some point we think differently, You will make it clear to us. We live up to what we have already attained in our individual lives and in our group. We will let our yes be simply yes, and our no be simply no.

In Jesus' name, amen.

Scripture References

John 1:12	Philippians 4:11 AMP
1 Corinthians 1:30	Ephesians 4:15 AMP
James 3:17 AMP	1 Corinthians 1:10 AMP
Philemon 6 NIV	Philippians 3:15-17 NIV
Colossians 4:6 NIV	Matthew 5:37 AMP

$\mathcal{T}$he Body of Christ

$\mathcal{F}$ather, You put all things under the feet of Jesus and gave Him to be head over all things to the Church, which is His Body, the fullness of Him who fills all in all. We were dead in trespasses and sins, but You made us alive! Christ is our Peace, and we are no longer strangers and foreigners, but fellow citizens with the saints and members of the household of God. Jesus is our Cornerstone.

Father, You want us to grow up, to know the whole truth and tell it in love — like Christ in everything. We take our lead from Christ, Who is the Source of everything we do. He keeps us in step with each other. His very breath and blood flow through us, nourishing us so that we will grow up healthy in God, robust in love.

May we be filled with the knowledge of Your will in all wisdom and spiritual understanding. As the elect of God, holy and beloved, we put on tender mercies, kindness, humility, meekness, longsuffering; bearing with one another and forgiving one another. If we have a complaint against another, even as Christ forgave us, so we also must do. Above all things, we put on love, which is the bond of perfection, and let the peace of God rule in our hearts, to which also we were called in one Body, and we are thankful.

Full of belief, confident that we're presentable inside and out, we keep a firm grip on the promises that keep us going. Father, You always keep Your Word. Now we will see how inventive we can be in encouraging love and helping out, not avoiding worshiping together as some do, but spurring each other on, especially as we see the big Day approaching.

Since we are all called to travel on the same road and in the same direction, we will stay together, both outwardly and inwardly. We have one Master, one faith, one baptism, one God and Father of all, Who rules over all, works through all, and is present in all. Everything we are and think and do is permeated with oneness.

Father, we commit to pray for one another, keeping our eyes open and keeping each other's spirits up, so that no one falls behind or drops out. Also, we pray for our spiritual leaders that they will know what to say and have the courage to say it at the right time. We are one in the bond of love, in the name of Jesus.

Scripture References

Ephesians 1:22,23 NKJV

Hebrews 10:23-25 MESSAGE

Ephesians 4:15,16 MESSAGE

Ephesians 4:4-6 MESSAGE

Colossians 3:12-15 NKJV

Ephesians 6:18,19 MESSAGE

*U*nity and Harmony

ather, in the name of Jesus, this is the confidence that we have in You: that, if we ask anything according to Your will, You hear us; and since we know that You hear us, whatsoever we ask, we know that we have the petitions that we desire of You.

Holy Spirit, teach us how to agree (harmonize together, together make a symphony) about anything and everything — so that whatever we ask will come to pass and be done for us by our Father in heaven.

We pray that as members of the Body of Christ we will live as becomes us with complete lowliness of mind (humility) and meekness (unselfishness, gentleness, mildness), with patience, bearing with one another and making allowances because we love one another. In the name of Jesus, we are eager and strive earnestly to guard and keep the harmony and oneness of [produced by] the Spirit in the binding power of peace.

We commit, in the name of Jesus, and according to the power of God at work in us, to be of one and the same mind (united in spirit), sympathizing [with one another], loving [each other] as brethren (of one household), compassionate and courteous — tenderhearted and humble-minded. We will never return evil for evil or insult for insult scolding, tongue-lashing, berating; but, on the contrary, we will bless praying for their welfare, happiness, and protection and truly pitying and loving one another. For we know that to this we have been called, that we may ourselves inherit a blessing [from God] — obtain a blessing as heirs, bringing welfare and happiness and protection.

Father, thank You that Jesus has given to us the glory and honor that You gave Him, that we may be one, [even] as You and Jesus are one: Jesus in us and You in Jesus, in order that we may become one and perfectly united, that the world may know and [definitely] recognize that You sent Jesus and that You have loved them [even] as You have loved Jesus.

Father, Thy will be done in earth, as it is in heaven. Amen, and so be it.

Scripture References

John 5:14,15   1 Peter 3:8,9 AMP

1 Corinthians 1:10 AMP   John 17:22,23 AMP

Matthew 18:19 AMP   Matthew 6:10

Ephesians 4:2,3 AMP

$\mathcal{V}$ision for a Church

$\mathcal{F}$ather, in the name of Jesus, we come into Your presence thanking You for _____(name of church). You have called us to be saints in _____(name of city) and around the world. As we lift our voices in one accord, we recognize that You are God and everything was made by and for You. We call into being those things that be not as though they were.

We thank You that we all speak the same thing: There is no division among us; we are perfectly joined together in the same mind. Grant unto us, Your representatives here, a boldness to speak Your Word, which You will confirm with signs following. We thank You that we have workmen in abundance and all manner of cunning people for every manner of work. Each department operates in the excellence of ministry and intercessions. We have in our church the ministry gifts for the edifying of this Body till we all come into the unity of faith and knowledge of the Son of God unto a mature person. None of our people will be children, tossed to and fro and carried about with every wind of doctrine. We speak the truth in love.

We are a growing and witnessing Body of believers becoming _____(number) strong. We have every need met. Therefore, we meet the needs of people who come in spirit, soul, and body. We ask for the wisdom of God in meeting these needs. Father, we thank You for the ministry facilities that will more than meet the needs of the ministry You have called us to. Our church is prospering financially, and we have more than enough to meet every situation. We have everything we need to carry out Your Great Commission and reach the ___*kw*___ (name of city or county) area for Jesus. We are a people of love as love is shed abroad in our hearts by the Holy Spirit. We thank You that the Word of God is living big in all of us and Jesus is Lord!

We are a supernatural church, composed of supernatural people doing supernatural things, for we are laborers together with God. We thank You for Your presence among us, and we lift our hands and praise Your holy name! Amen.

Scripture References

Acts 4:24	Ephesians 4:11-15
Romans 4:17	Philippians 4:19
1 Corinthians 1:10	Romans 5:5
Acts 4:29	1 Corinthians 3:9
Mark 16:20	Psalm 63:4
Exodus 35:33	

This prayer was written by and used with the permission of T. R. King, Valley Christian Center, Roanoke, Virginia.

*P*ersonal Prayer of a Pastor for the Congregation

*F*ather, as the pastor of _____, I approach the throne of grace on behalf of the membership. I thank my God in all my remembrance of them. In every prayer of mine, I always make my entreaty and petition for them all with joy (delight). [I thank my God] for their fellowship — their sympathetic co-operation and contributions and partnership — in advancing the good news (the Gospel). And I am convinced and sure of this very thing: that You have begun a good work in them and will continue until the day of Jesus Christ — right up to the time of His return — developing [that good work] and perfecting and bringing it to full completion in them.

In the name of Jesus, it is right and appropriate for me to have this confidence and feel this way about them all, because even as they do me, I hold them in my heart as partakers and sharers — one and all with me — of grace (God's unmerited favor and spiritual blessing).

Father, You are my witness and know how I long for and pursue them all with love, in the tender mercies of Christ Jesus [Himself]!

PERSONAL PRAYER OF A PASTOR
FOR THE CONGREGATION

So this is my prayer: that their love will flourish and that they will not only love much, but love well and learn to love appropriately. May they use their heads and test their feelings so that their love is sincere and intelligent, not sentimental gush. Father, I pray that each one will live a lover's life, circumspect and exemplary, a life Jesus will be proud of: bountiful in fruits from the soul, making Jesus Christ attractive to all, getting everyone involved in the glory and praise of God.

Father, may the membership abound in and be filled with the fruits of righteousness (of right standing with God and right doing), which come through Jesus Christ, the Anointed One, to the honor and praise of God — that Your glory may be both manifested and recognized.

I commit myself to You, Father, anew and to them, for I am convinced of this: I shall remain and stay by them all to promote their progress and joy in believing, so that in me they may have abundant cause for exultation and glorifying in Christ Jesus. In the name of Jesus, they will be sure as citizens so to conduct themselves that their manner of life will be worthy of the good news (the Gospel) of Christ.

Thank You, Father, that they are standing firm in united spirit and purpose, striving side by side and contending with a single mind for the faith of the glad tidings (the Gospel). They are not for a moment frightened or intimidated in anything by their opponents and adversaries, for such [constancy and fearlessness] will be a clear sign (proof and seal) to their enemies of [their impending] destruction; but [a sure token and evidence] to the congregation of their deliverance and salvation, and that from You, God.

The membership of _____ fills up and completes my joy by living in harmony and being of the same mind and one in purpose, having the same love, being in full accord and of one harmonious mind and intention.

In Jesus' name, amen.

Scripture References

Philippians 1:4-7 AMP

Philippians 1:8-11 MESSAGE

Philippians 1:25-28 AMP

Philippians 2:2 AMP

$\mathcal{M}$inisters

$\mathcal{F}$ather, in the name of Jesus, we pray and confess that the Spirit of the Lord — the spirit of wisdom and understanding, the spirit of counsel and might, the spirit of knowledge — shall rest upon _____. We pray that as Your Spirit rests upon _____, He will make him/her of quick understanding because You, Lord, have anointed and qualified him/her to preach the Gospel to the meek, the poor, the wealthy, the afflicted. You have sent _____ to bind up and heal the brokenhearted, to proclaim liberty to the physical and spiritual captives, and to open the prison and the eyes to those who are bound.

_____ shall be called the priest of the Lord. People will speak of him/her as a minister of God. He/she shall eat the wealth of the nations.

We pray and believe that no weapon that is formed against _____ shall prosper and that any tongue that rises against him/her in judgment shall be shown to be in the wrong. We pray that You prosper _____ abundantly, Lord — physically, spiritually, and financially.

We confess that _____ holds fast and follows the pattern of wholesome and sound teaching in all faith and love, which is for us in Christ Jesus. _____ guards and keeps with the greatest love the precious and excellently adapted truth entrusted to him/her by the Holy Spirit, Who makes His home in _____.

Lord, we pray and believe that each and every day freedom of utterance is given _____, that he/she will open his/her mouth boldly and courageously as he/she ought to do to get the Gospel to the people. Thank You, Lord, for the added strength, which comes superhumanly, that You have given him/her.

We hereby confess that we shall stand behind _____ and undergird him/her in prayer. We will say only that good thing that will edify _____. We will not allow ourselves to judge him/her, but we will continue to intercede for him/her and speak and pray blessings upon him/her in the name of Jesus. Thank You, Jesus, for the answers. Hallelujah! Amen.

Scripture References

Isaiah 11:2,3	2 Timothy 1:13,14 AMP
Isaiah 61:1,6 AMP	Ephesians 6:19,20 AMP
Isaiah 54:17 AMP	1 Peter 3:12

*M*issionaries

*F*ather, we lift before You those in the Body of Christ who are out in the field carrying the good news of the Gospel not only in this country, but also around the world. We lift those in the Body of Christ who are suffering persecution — those who are in prison for their beliefs. Father, we know that You watch over Your Word to perform it, that Your Word prospers in the thing for which You sent it. Therefore, we speak Your Word and establish Your covenant on this earth. We pray here, and others receive the answer there by the Holy Spirit.

Thank You, Father, for revealing unto Your people the integrity of Your Word and that they must be firm in faith against the devil's onset, withstanding him. Father, You are their Light, Salvation, Refuge, and Stronghold. You hide them in Your shelter and set them high upon a rock. It is Your will that each one prospers, is in good health, and lives in victory. You set the prisoners free, feed the hungry, execute justice, rescue, and deliver.

We commission the ministering spirits to go forth and provide the necessary help for and assistance to these heirs of salvation. We and they are strong in the Lord and in the power of Your might, quenching every dart of the devil in Jesus' name.

Father, we use our faith, covering these in the Body of Christ with Your Word. We say that no weapon formed against them shall prosper, and any tongue that rises against them in judgment they shall show to be in the wrong. This peace, security, and triumph over opposition is their inheritance as Your children. This is the righteousness they obtain from You, Father, which You impart to them as their justification. They are far from even the thought of destruction; for they shall not fear, and terror shall not come near them.

Father, You say You will establish them to the end — keep them steadfast, give them strength, and guarantee their vindication, that is, be their Warrant against all accusation or indictment. They are not anxious beforehand how they shall reply in defense or what they are to say, for the Holy Spirit teaches them in that very hour and moment what they ought to say to those in the outside world, their speech being seasoned with salt.

We commit these, our brothers and sisters in the Lord, to You, Father, deposited into Your charge, entrusting them to Your protection and care, for You are faithful. You strengthen them and set them on a firm foundation and guard them from the Evil One. We join our voices in praise unto You, Most High, that You might silence the enemy and avenger. Praise the Lord! Greater is He that is in us than he that is in the world!

In Jesus' name we pray, amen.

Scripture References

Jeremiah 1:12	Ephesians 6:10,16
Isaiah 55:11	Isaiah 54:14,17
1 Peter 5:9	1 Corinthians 1:8
Psalm 27:1,5	Luke 12:11,12
3 John 2	Colossians 4:6
1 John 5:4,5	Acts 20:32

MISSIONARIES

Psalm 146:7

Psalm 144:7

Matthew 18:18

Hebrews 1:14

2 Thessalonians 3:3

Psalm 8:2

1 John 4:4

*C*hurch Teachers

*F*ather, we come in the name of Jesus, asking You for called teachers for our classes and choirs. We thank You for teachers who are filled with the Spirit of God, in wisdom and ability, in understanding and intelligence, in knowledge and in all kinds of craftsmanship, to devise skillful methods for teaching us and our children the Word of God. They are teachers who give themselves to teaching.

Father, may these teachers recognize that they must assume the greater accountability. According to Your Word, teachers will be judged by a higher standard and with greater severity [than other people]. We thank You that our teachers will not offend in speech — never say the wrong things — that they may be fully developed characters and perfect men and women, each one able to control his/her own body and to curb his/her entire nature.

Thank You that our teachers are part of the fivefold ministry who are perfecting and fully equipping the saints (God's consecrated people), [that they should do] the work of ministering toward building up Christ's Body (the Church), [that it might develop] until we all attain oneness in the faith and in the comprehension of the full and accurate knowledge of the Son of God; that [we might arrive] at really mature manhood — the completeness of personality, which is nothing less than the standard height of Christ's own perfection — the measure of the stature of the fullness of the Christ and the completeness found in Him.

Thank You, Father, that Your people at our church are no longer children, tossed [like ships] to and fro. They are enfolded in love, growing up in every way and in all things into Him, Who is the Head, [even] Christ, the Messiah, the Anointed One.

Father, You are effectually at work in our teachers — energizing and creating in them the power and desire — both to will and to work for Your good pleasure and satisfaction and delight. Father, in the name of Jesus, their power and ability and sufficiency are from You. [It is You] Who have qualified them (making them to be fit, worthy, and sufficient) as ministers and dispensers of a new covenant. They are not ministers of the law which kills, but of the (Holy) Spirit, which makes alive.

Father, we rejoice in the Lord over our teachers and commit to undergird them with our faith and love. We will not judge or criticize them, but speak excellent and princely things concerning them. The opening of our lips shall be for right things.

Thank You, Father, that the teachers live in harmony with the other members of our church, being in full accord and of one harmonious mind and intention. Each is not [merely] concerned for his/her own interests, but each for the interest of others. Jesus is our example in humility, and our teachers shall tend — nurture, guard, guide, and fold — the flock of God, which is [their responsibility], and they will be examples of Christian living to the flock (the congregation).

Thank You, Father, for the performance of Your Word in our midst, in the name of Jesus. Amen.

Scripture References (AMP)

Exodus 31:3,4	2 Corinthians 3:5,6 AMP
Romans 12:7	Proverbs 8:6
James 3:1,2	Philippians 2:2,4,5 AMP
Ephesians 4:12-15 AMP	1 Peter 5:2,3
Philippians 2:13	Jeremiah 1:12

$\mathcal{A}$ Christian Counselor

$\mathcal{F}$ather, in the name of Jesus, I pray for _____ to exhort and counsel the emotionally wounded. I ask in faith that Your Spirit will rest upon him/her — the Spirit of wisdom and understanding, the Spirit of counsel and might. Give him/her insight and knowledge for understanding his/her counselees' responses to circumstances.

Thank You, Father, that _____ is a good listener to the confessions of his/her counselees. Help him/her to comprehend the unfolding of those past hurts that influence reactions to current situations.

Lord, _____ will not judge by what he/she sees with his/her eyes or decide by what he/she hears with his/her ears. He/she will judge the needy and give decisions with justice. Righteousness will be his/her belt, and faithfulness the sash around his/her waist. He/she will be clothed with fairness and with truth.

Thank You that _____ is a promoter of peace and is filled with joy. Grant Your counselor, out of the rich treasury of Your glory, to be strengthened and reinforced with mighty power in the inner man by the [Holy] Spirit [Himself indwelling his/her innermost being and personality].

301

You will not leave _____ without support as he/she gives his/her time and concern, helping to complete the forgiveness process. He/she will be confident about his/her convictions, knowing excellent things, and will have the knowledge to assist Your children in knowing the certainty of the words of truth.

In Jesus' name, amen.

Scripture References

Isaiah 11:2,3 AMP	Ephesians 3:16 AMP
Isaiah 11:4,5 NIV	Proverbs 22:20,21 AMP
Isaiah 11:5 TLB	

*P*rosperity for Ministering Servants

*F*ather, how we praise You and thank You for Your Word, knowing that You watch over Your Word to perform it, and no Word of Yours returns void, but accomplishes that which You please, and it prospers in the thing for which You sent it.

Father, in the name of Jesus, we pray and believe that those in Your Body who have sown the seed of spiritual good among the people reap from the people's material benefits, for You directed that those who publish the good news of the Gospel should live and get their maintenance by the Gospel.

The people's gifts are the fragrant odor of an offering and sacrifice which You, Father, welcome and in which You delight. You will liberally supply, fill to the full, the people's every need according to Your riches in glory in Christ Jesus.

Father, it is Your will that those who receive instruction in the Word of God share all good things with their teachers, contributing to their support. We confess that Your people will not lose heart and grow weary and faint in acting nobly and doing right, for in due time and at the appointed season they shall reap, if they do not loosen and relax their courage and faint.

So then, as occasion and opportunity are open to the people, they do good to all people not only being useful and profitable to them, but also doing what is for their spiritual good and advantage.

We pray that Your people will be a blessing, especially to those of the household of faith — those who belong to God's family. Help us to remember that whoever sows generously will also reap generously.

God, You are then able to make all grace, every favor and earthly blessing, come to Your people in abundance, so that they are always and under all circumstances possessing enough to require no aid or support and furnished in abundance for every good work and charitable donation.

As Your people give, their deeds of justice and goodness and kindness and benevolence go on and endure forever. And, God, You provide the seed for the sower and bread for the eating, so You also will provide and multiply the people's resources for sowing and increase the fruits of their righteousness. Thus, Your people are enriched in all things and in every way so that they can be generous, and their generosity, as it is administered by Your teachers, will bring thanksgiving to God.

As it is written, "Give, and it shall be given unto you; good measure, pressed down, and shaken together, and running over, shall men give into your bosom" (Luke 6:38). Praise the Lord!

In Jesus' name, amen.

Scripture References

Jeremiah 1:12

Isaiah 55:11

1 Corinthians 9:11-14

Philippians 4:17-19

Galatians 6:6-10

2 Corinthians 9:6-11

Luke 6:38

A Ministry in Need of Finances

INTRODUCTION

This prayer was written in response to an appeal for help from a ministry in a financial crunch. This ministry reaches out to people addicted to drugs, alcohol, and other substances. After we had prayed the following prayer, it was given to our editor and prayer request correspondent. It can be used to pray for the needs of any ministry.

PRAYER

Father, in the name of Jesus, we believe that all of the needs of _____ are met, according to Philippians 4:19. We believe that — because this ministry has given tithes and offerings to further Your cause to help youth, adults, and families come to the knowledge of the truth — [gifts] will be given to them; good measure, pressed down, shaken together, and running over will they be poured into their bosom. For with the measure they deal out, it will be measured back to them.

Father, in the name of Jesus, we ask on the authority of Your Word that those in Your Body who have sown [the seed of] spiritual good among the people will reap from the people's material benefits, for You have directed that those who publish the good news of the Gospel should live and get their maintenance by the Gospel.

We confess that Your ministers with _____ Ministry seek and are eager for the fruit that increases to the people's credit [the harvest of blessing that is accumulating to their account]. The people's gifts are the fragrant odor of an offering and sacrifice that You, Father, welcome and in which You delight. You will liberally supply (fill to the full) the people's every need according to Your riches in glory in Christ Jesus.

Father, we call forth partners who will respond to Your call to support this ministry prayerfully and financially.

Lord, we thank You for directing the leader _____, who seeks Your ways, teaching him/her the fortitude of Your Word and the steadfastness of its truth. Your anointing, which destroys the yoke of bondage, abides within him/her permanently. Teach him/her to pray for the people and the government of our land. We thank You for Your Word, which brings freedom to the hearers, and we thank You for preparing their hearts to receive the good news of the Gospel.

Lord, strengthen (complete, perfect) and make _____ what he/she ought to be, equipping him/her with everything good that he/she may carry out Your will; [while You Yourself] work in him/her and accomplish that which is pleasing in Your sight, through Jesus Christ (the Messiah), to Whom be the glory forever and ever (to the ages of the ages).

In His name we pray, amen.

Scripture References

Luke 6:38 AMP

1 Corinthians 9:11,13 AMP

Philippians 4:17-19 AMP

Matthew 9:38 AMP

Isaiah 10:27

1 Timothy 2:1-3 AMP

John 8:32

Hebrews 13:21 AMP

*P*rayers for Ministry Partners

I.

*F*ather, we thank You for our partners and for their service and dedication to serve You. Thank You that they bring forth the fruit of the Spirit: love, joy, peace, longsuffering, gentleness, goodness, faith, meekness, and temperance.

Father, thank You that our partners are good ground, that they hear Your Word and understand it, and that the Word bears fruit in their lives. They are like trees planted by rivers of water that bring forth fruit in their season. Their leaf shall not wither, and whatever they do shall prosper.

From the first day we heard of our partners, we haven't stopped praying for them, asking God to give them wise minds and spirits attuned to His will, and so acquire a thorough understanding of the ways in which God works. Our partners are merciful as our Father is merciful. They will judge only as they want to be judged. They do not condemn, and they are not condemned. Our partners forgive others, and people forgive them.

They give, and men will give to them — yes, good measure, pressed down, shaken together, and running over will they pour into their laps. For whatever measure they use with other people, they will use in their dealings with them. In Jesus' name we pray, amen.

Scripture References

Colossians 1:9 MESSAGE   Matthew 7:1 AMP

Galatians 5:22,23   Luke 6:37,38

Psalm 1:3

II.

Father, we ask You to bless our partners with all spiritual blessings in heavenly places that goodwill might come to them. They are generous and lend freely. They conduct their affairs with justice.

Lord, Your Word says that surely they will never be shaken. They are righteous men and women who will be remembered forever. They will not fear bad news; their hearts are steadfast, trusting in You, Lord.

We ask that Your plans be fulfilled in their lives, and we thank You for Your mercies on their behalf.

In the name of Jesus, amen.

Scripture References

Psalm 112:5-8 NIV   Jeremiah 29:11 NIV

Colossians 1:9 MESSAGE

Overcoming Prejudice

INTRODUCTION

The previous few days in Miami had been exceptionally cool. Jan, my traveling companion, and I did not consider it coat weather, but the Floridians shivered, all bundled up in their winter wear.

The prayer seminar had gone well, and it was now our last service before leaving for home. The preparation for the Sunday morning worship service had been difficult, and I found myself at the mercy of the Holy Spirit. (Not a bad place to be!)

During the preliminaries and the praise and worship service, I was crying out inwardly, just for a starting Scripture that I could read.

The sanctuary was packed as I stood before the congregation of beautiful skin tones — from almost white to light chocolate to black velvet. Their faces looked back at me. I smiled and began to read a psalm — making comments as I felt prompted by the Holy Spirit.

Where is the flow of the Spirit? I wondered. *God, what is it You want to do in this church today?*

The tension within me grew, and I felt helpless.

At last, I knew. (Sometimes it is good that we do not know what we will say beforehand. We might mess it all up, working to be politically correct, writing and rewriting to make sure that we cross every "t" and dot every "i" with the correct flourish.)

The love of God began to rise within me. I spoke from my heart of hearts:

"You cannot really know me unless I choose to share myself — my thoughts, my ideas, and my feelings. Obviously, I am a Southern white woman. I grew up in cotton mill towns in North Georgia. There I attended the all-white Pentecostal churches where my dad served as pastor. I attended all-white schools and lived in all-white neighborhoods. The only black people I knew were Smut and Clarabell, tenants on my uncle's farm.

"I don't know if I have any racial prejudice — it has never been tested. I know that at one time I was filled with intellectual prejudice, because God exposed it in a very dramatic way. If I have any racial prejudice, I want the Holy Spirit to uncover it and deliver me. All I know is that I love you, and we are one — one blood. In Christ Jesus there is neither Jew nor Greek, male nor female, black nor white. There is that one new man created in Him."

The barriers came tumbling down. My newly found friends, brothers and sisters in the Lord, no longer hugged from a distance. Many smothered me in bear hugs after the benediction. The unity of the Spirit had prevailed (Eph. 4:3).

Jesus is our peace, and I believe that the Scriptures written by the Apostle Paul in Galatians and Ephesians apply today.

Ethnic groups are assuming responsibility for the sins of the forefathers and asking forgiveness for past wrongs done to one another. We are accountable to God and each other as members of one household, and by the blood of the Lamb and through good communication we are overcoming the dividing schemes of the devil. God is bringing His people together. Red and yellow, black and white — we are coming together — and we are precious in His sight.

We are no longer outsiders or aliens, but fellow citizens with every other Christian — we belong now to the household of God (Eph. 2:19 PHILLIPS).

PRAYER

Father, in the name of Jesus, we come before You, asking Your forgiveness for being intolerant of one another because of the colors of our skin. Forgive us for tolerating prejudice in the household of faith. Set us free from the influence of public opinion that we may live out our glorious, Christ-originated faith.

Forgive us for segregating ourselves by color, by a measure of wealth or intellect. We are all Your children, the sheep of Your pasture. You made us, and not we ourselves.

We are one blood, redeemed by the blood of the Lamb, Who was slain before the foundation of the world. We are baptized "into" Christ and have put on the family likeness of Christ.

We call for an end to division and segregation in Christ's family — may there be no division into Jew and non-Jew, slave and free, male and female. Among us we are all equal. That is, we are all in a common relationship with Jesus Christ.

OVERCOMING PREJUDICE

Thank You, Father, for bringing us together in Christ through His death on the cross. The cross got us to embrace, and that was the end of the hostility.

Lord, Jesus came and preached peace to us outsiders and peace to us insiders. He treated us as equals and so made us equals. Through Him we share the same Spirit and have equal access to You, Father.

The Kingdom of faith is now our home country, and we are no longer strangers or outsiders. We *belong* here.

Lord, You are building a home. You are using us all — irrespective of how we got here — in what You are building. You are fitting us in with Christ Jesus as the Cornerstone Who holds all the parts together. We see it taking shape day after day — a holy temple built by You, Father, all of us built into it, a temple in which You are quite at home.

Father, You have called us all to travel on the same road and in the same direction, so we will stay together, both outwardly and inwardly. We have one Master, one faith, one baptism, one God and Father of all — Who rules over all, works through all, and is present in all. Everything we are and think and do is permeated with oneness.

Father, we imitate You. We walk in love, [esteeming and delighting in one another]. We walk as children of the light [leading the lives of those native-born to the light]. We look carefully how we walk! We live purposefully and worthily and accurately, making the very most of the time [buying up each opportunity], because the days are evil.

We speak out to one another in psalms and hymns and spiritual songs, offering praise with voice [and instruments] and making melody with all our hearts to You, Lord, at all times and for everything, giving thanks in the name of our Lord Jesus Christ to You, Father. By love we serve one another.

Thank You, Father, that prejudice is being rooted out of the Body of Christ, in the name of Jesus. Amen.

Scripture References

James 2:1 MESSAGE	Ephesians 2:13-22 MESSAGE
Psalm 100:3	Ephesians 4:3-6 MESSAGE
1 Peter 1:18,19 NIV	Ephesians 5:1,2,8 AMP
Galatians 3:27,28 PHILLIPS	Ephesians 5:15,16,19,20 AMP
Galatians 3:28 MESSAGE	Galatians 5:13 AMP

*O*ffice Staff

INTRODUCTION

*O*ur prayer coordinator wrote this prayer for our ministry. It may be used for the members of any ministry or outreach that depends upon the Holy Spirit to go before it and prepare the way for its labor with and for the Lord.

PRAYER

Father, we begin this day rejoicing in You. We thank You for Your goodness, mercy, and grace toward us as individuals and as a ministry. We confess and proclaim that this is the day that You have made, and we purpose to rejoice and be glad in it.

Father, we lift up the day with its activities, its relationships, its decisions and creativity. We offer it all up to You, acknowledging Jesus as Lord of all and asking You by Your Holy Spirit to use it for Your glory and honor. We pray for Your will to be done in us individually and as a ministry.

We plead the blood of Jesus over this property, all staff members, every telephone contact, every person who enters these doors, and the entire ministry network, including all those for whom we pray. We thank You for delivering us from the authority of darkness and translating us into the Kingdom of Your dear Son. We are living and growing up in the Kingdom of light.

Father, You have given us choices. We choose life and blessings. You are our Strength, our Confidence, and our Courage. We are courageous, boldly proclaiming that Your anointing — Your burden-removing, yoke-destroying power — is abiding in us individually and collectively. This anointing is working in, on, and through us this day to accomplish Your will. May You be glorified in all that we do.

Thank You for Your love. We are imitators of You — walking in love, in truth, in light, and in wisdom inside and outside these offices. We are well-balanced and enduring in all things.

We are asking for and expecting the former and latter rains to be poured out on this ministry to fulfill Your assignments. You have called us by Your grace for such a time as this. We rejoice in the outpouring of Your Spirit on this ministry.

In the name of Jesus, amen.

Scripture References

Psalm 33:1	1 John 2:27
Psalm 118:24	1 Corinthians 6:20
1 Corinthians 12:3	Ephesians 5:1,2 AMP
Matthew 6:10	James 5:7
Colossians 1:13	1 Peter 5:10
Deuteronomy 30:19	Esther 4:14
Isaiah 10:27	Acts 2:17

Ministry in Nursing Homes

Father, thank You for calling me to minister to Your children in nursing homes. I purpose to keep on going by Your power, for You first saved me and then called me to this holy work. I had nothing to do with it. It was Your idea, a gift prepared for me in Jesus long before I knew anything about it.

But I know it now. Since the appearance of our Savior, nothing could be plainer; death defeated, life vindicated in a steady blaze of light — all through the work of Jesus. I couldn't be more sure of my ground — the One I've trusted in can take care of what He's trusted me to do right to the end.

Thank You for Your Word — the entrance of Your Word brings light, and Your light is the life of men. The words that I speak are spirit and life, and I pray that the light of the Gospel will illumine the minds of those to whom I minister.

Father, Your anointing abides within me [permanently] — thank You for [an unction from] the Holy One. You have touched my hands with Your anointing, and when I lay hands on the sick, they shall experience the healing that flows from Your throne and recover.

Thank You, Lord, for those who welcome me, reaching out for prayer, encouragement, and hugs. I pray that the light in my eyes will bring joy to their hearts. Help me to exhort and teach them to continue in their desire to be useful, fulfilling Your call on their lives.

Father, You have a purpose for them — it is not Your will that they be set aside. You want them to continue bringing forth fruit in their old age. Help me to bring understanding to them.

O Father, I pray for those who are in fetal positions, not speaking or opening their eyes. Arise, O Sun of righteousness, with healing in Your wings and minister to these souls who will soon meet You face to face. I yield my body to You to be used as an instrument of righteousness, bringing salvation, wholeness, healing, deliverance, and comfort to the sick and the elderly.

Father, You execute justice for the fatherless and the widow, and You are a judge and protector (champion) of the widow. You protect, preserve, and uphold the fatherless and widow, and You set them upright. I am claiming these promises for all those I minister to, believing You to watch over Your Word to perform it.

Lord, Your arm is not shortened that You cannot save, and nothing is too hard for You. I ask You for the wisdom and common sense I need to be a vessel of honor, sanctified and fitting for Your use and prepared for every good work.

I do not go in my own strength, but in the divine energy that You provide. It is my purpose to always be obedient to James 1:27 AMP — "External religious worship...that is pure and unblemished in the sight of God the Father is this: to visit and help and care for the orphans and widows in their affliction and need..." — and to reach out to the homeless and loveless in their plight.

Thank You, Lord, that I eat the good of the land because I am willing and obedient. I serve You with a glad heart and a joyous spirit. Whatever You call me to do, You equip me with all that I need to accomplish it.

In the name of Jesus, amen.

Scripture References

2 Timothy 1:8-10 MESSAGE	Romans 6:13
Deuteronomy 10:18 AMP	Psalm 68:5 AMP
Psalm 119:130	Psalm 146:9 AMP
John 1:4	Jeremiah 1:12 AMP
John 6:63	Isaiah 39:1
2 Corinthians 4:4 AMP	Genesis 18:14
1 John 2:20,27 AMP	James 1:15
Mark 16:18	2 Timothy 2:21
Psalm 92:14	Isaiah 1:19
Mark 4:2	

$\mathcal{M}$inisters to the Incarcerated

INTRODUCTION

$\mathcal{T}$his prayer was written in response to a letter from an inmate. He had received Jesus, started a Bible study, and wanted to know how to pray for God-called teachers and preachers to come and teach the inmates. He was praying for prisoners who did not know Jesus, believing that revival was coming to the correctional facility where he was housed.

PRAYER

Father, You said that whoever calls upon the name of the Lord will be saved. How shall the inmates at this correctional facility/prison call on Him in Whom they have not believed? And how shall they believe in Him of Whom they have not heard? And how shall they hear without a preacher? And how shall they preach unless they are sent? We ask You, the Lord of the harvest, to send Your chosen laborers to preach deliverance to the captives of this prison.

Father, we thank You for Your ministers who are willing to go and preach deliverance to the incarcerated. May You grant to them out of the rich treasury of Your glory to be strengthened and reinforced with mighty power in the inner man by the [Holy]

Spirit [Himself indwelling their innermost being and personality]. Anoint their lips to preach the good news of the Gospel.

Father, send Your Holy Spirit to go before the ministers, anoint the ears of the hearers, and prepare their hearts to hear, receive, love, and obey Your Word. Thank You that the light of the Gospel shines in their hearts so as to beam forth the light for the illumination of the knowledge of Your majesty and glory so that everyone who calls on Your name shall be saved.

Father, thank You for creating a desire within Your ministers to diligently study Your Word that they might show themselves approved unto You, workmen who will not be put to shame, rightly dividing Your Word of truth. They are living witnesses to those who are not yet obedient to the Gospel.

Father, we thank You for an outpouring of Your Spirit upon the staff and inmates of this facility. We know that faith comes by hearing, and hearing by Your Word. We thank You for the salvation and deliverance of all those who call upon Your name.

In the name of Jesus, we thank You for sending the Holy Spirit Who reveals truth to sinners, convicting and convincing them of sin, righteousness, and judgment.

We release Your mercy, Your love, and Your grace to those within these walls that they might be saved through faith, and that not of themselves; it is Your gift.

Thank You, Lord, for hearing our prayer on behalf of the people at this correctional facility/prison.

In Jesus' name, amen.

Scripture References

Romans 10:13,14

Matthew 9:38

Ephesians 3:16 AMP

2 Corinthians 4:6 AMP

Romans 10:13

2 Timothy 2:15

Romans 15:18

Acts 2:18

Romans 10:17

John 16:8,13

Ephesians 2:8

Revival

Father, in the name of Jesus, You have revived us again that Your people may rejoice in You. Thank You for showing us Your mercy and loving-kindness, O Lord, and for granting us Your salvation. You have created in us a clean heart, O God, and renewed a right, persevering, and steadfast spirit within us. You have restored unto us the joy of Your salvation, and You are upholding us with a willing spirit. Now we will teach transgressors Your ways, and sinners shall be converted and return to You.

We therefore cleanse our ways by taking heed and keeping watch [on ourselves] according to Your Word [conforming our lives to it]. Since Your [great] promises are ours, we cleanse ourselves from everything that contaminates and defiles our bodies and spirits and bring [our] consecration to completeness in the (reverential) fear of God. With our whole hearts have we sought You, inquiring for You and of You and yearning for You; O let us not wander or step aside [either in ignorance or willfully] from Your commandments. Your Word have we laid up in our hearts, that we might not sin against You.

Jesus, thank You for cleansing us through the Word — the teachings — which You have given us. We delight ourselves in Your statutes; we will not forget Your Word. Deal bountifully with Your servants, that we may live; and we will observe Your Word [hearing, receiving, loving, and obeying it].

Father, in the name of Jesus, we are doers of the Word and not merely listeners to it. It is You, O Most High, Who has revived and stimulated us according to Your Word! Thank You for turning away our eyes from beholding vanity [idols and idolatry] and restoring us to vigorous life and health in Your ways. Behold, we long for Your precepts; in Your righteousness, give us renewed life. This is our comfort and consolation in our affliction: that Your Word has revived us and given us life.

We strip ourselves of our former natures — put off and discard our old unrenewed selves — which characterized our previous manner of life. We are constantly renewed in the spirit of our minds — having a fresh mental and spiritual attitude; and we put on the new nature (the regenerate self), created in God's image, (Godlike) in true righteousness and holiness. Though our outer man is (progressively) decaying and wasting away, our inner self is being (progressively) renewed day after day. Hallelujah! Amen.

Scripture References (AMP)

Psalm 85:6,7	James 1:22
Psalm 51:10,12,13	Psalm 119:25
Psalm 119:9-11	Psalm 119:37,40,50
2 Corinthians 7:1	Ephesians 4:22-24
John 15:3	2 Corinthians 4:16
Psalm 119:16,17	

Success of a Meeting

Father, in the name of Jesus, we approach the throne of grace boldly and confidently. May the Word of God come forth accurately and in love during the _____ meeting. We ask You to anoint each speaker to teach and preach the Word of God in simplicity, with boldness and with accuracy during the entire meeting. We ask that those who hear will not be able to resist the wisdom and the inspiration of the Holy Spirit that will be spoken through Your ministers of the Gospel.

As Your Word is taught, we ask You to cause people to open their spiritual eyes and ears that they might turn from darkness to light — from the power of Satan to You, Father — and that they will personally confess Jesus as their Lord.

We commit this meeting to You, Father; we deposit it into Your charge — entrusting this meeting, the people who will hear, and the people who will speak into Your protection and care. We commend this meeting to the Word — the commands and counsels and promises of Your unmerited favor. Father, we know that Your Word will build up the people and cause them to realize that they are joint-heirs with Jesus.

We believe, Father, that as Your Word comes forth, an anointing will be upon the speaker(s), and _____(name) will be submitted completely to the Holy Spirit, for the Word of God that is spoken is alive and full of power, making it active, operative, energizing and effective, being sharper than any two-edged sword. We ask You to meet the need of every person spiritually, physically, mentally, and financially.

We thank You, Father, and praise You that, because we have asked and agreed together, these petitions have come to pass. Let these words with which we have made supplication before the Lord be near to the Lord our God day and night, that He may maintain the cause and right of His people in the _____(meeting) as each day of it requires! We believe that all the earth's people will know that the Lord is God and there is no other! Hallelujah! Amen.

Scripture References (AMP)

James 5:16	Acts 26:18
Matthew 18:19	Acts 20:32
Ephesians 6:19	Hebrews 4:12
Acts 6:10	Philippians 4:19
Ephesians 1:18	1 Kings 8:59,60

Success of a Conference

Father, we pray that those who hear the messages at the _____ conference will believe — adhere to and trust in and rely on Jesus as the Christ, and that all those You have called to attend the conference will be there and receive what You have for them.

Let it be known and understood by all that it is in the name and through the power and authority of Jesus Christ of Nazareth and by means of Him that this conference is successful.

Father, Jesus said whatever we bind on earth is bound in heaven, and whatever we loose on earth is loosed in heaven. In His name we bind the will of each person — psalmists, speakers, ushers, and workers — to Your will, their minds to the mind of Christ, and their emotions to the control of the Holy Spirit. When the people see the boldness and unfettered eloquence of the speakers, they shall marvel and recognize that they have been with Jesus. Everybody shall be praising and glorifying God for what shall be occurring. By the hands of the ministers, numerous and startling signs and wonders will be performed among the people.

Father, in the name of Jesus, we thank You that You have observed the enemy's threats and have granted us, Your bondservants, full freedom to declare Your message fearlessly — while You stretch out Your hand to cure and perform signs and wonders through the authority and by the power of the name of Your Holy Child and Servant, Jesus.

We thank You, Father, that when we pray, the place in which we are assembled will be shaken; and we shall all be filled with the Holy Spirit, and Your people shall continue to speak the Word of God with freedom and boldness and courage.

By common consent, we shall all meet together at the conference. More and more individuals shall join themselves with us — a crowd of both men and women. The people shall gather from the north, south, east, and west, bringing the sick and those troubled with foul spirits, and they shall all be cured.

I pray for each one participating in this conference. May every attitude be an expression of the fruit of the Spirit: love, joy, peace, patience, kindness, goodness, faithfulness, gentleness, and self-control. Lord, I pray that each one will release rivers of living water, an outflowing of the anointing of Your Holy Spirit.

Thank You, Father, for the performance of Your Word, in the name of Jesus! Amen.

Scripture References (AMP)

Acts 4:10,13,21	Acts 5:12,13,16
Matthew 18:18	Acts 6:3,10
Acts 5:12	Galatians 5:22
Acts 4:29-31	

$\mathcal{P}$rotection and Deliverance of a City

$\mathcal{F}$ather, in the name of Jesus, we have received Your power — ability, efficiency, and might — because the Holy Spirit has come upon us; and we are Your witnesses in _____ and to the ends — the very bounds — of the earth.

We fearlessly and confidently and boldly draw near to the throne of grace that we may receive mercy and find grace to help in good time for every need — appropriate help and well-timed help, coming just when we in the city of _____ need it.

Father, thank You for sending forth Your commandments to the earth; Your Word runs very swiftly throughout _____. Your Word continues to grow and spread.

Father, we seek — inquire for, require, and request — the peace and welfare of _____, in which You have caused us to live. We pray to You for the welfare of this city and do our part by getting involved in it. We will not let [false] prophets and diviners who are in our midst deceive us; we pay no attention and attach no significance to our dreams that we dream or to theirs. Destroy [their schemes], O Lord; confuse their tongues, for we have seen violence and strife in the city.

Holy Spirit, we ask You to visit our city and open the eyes of the people, that they may turn from darkness to light and from the power of Satan to God, so that they may thus receive forgiveness and release from their sins and a place and portion among those who are consecrated and purified by faith in Jesus.

Father, we pray for deliverance and salvation for those who are following the course and fashion of this world — who are under the sway of the tendency of this present age — following the prince of the power of the air.

Father, forgive them, for they know not what they do.

Father, You see the regional and cultural strongholds that would hinder the Gospel. You have told us to declare Your works. So we say boldly that the prince of the power of the air, the god of this world who blinds the unbelievers' minds (that they should not discern the truth), is a defeated foe. We declare on the authority of Your Word that You have disarmed the powers and authorities; You made a public spectacle of them, triumphing over them by the Cross. Thank You, Father, for the spreading of the Gospel.

Thank You, Father, for the guardian angels assigned to this place who war for us in the heavenlies.

In the name of Jesus, we stand victorious over the principalities, powers, rulers of the darkness of this world, and spiritual wickedness in high places over _____.

We ask the Holy Spirit to sweep through the gates of our city and convince the people and bring demonstration to them about sin and about righteousness — uprightness of heart and right standing with God — and about judgment.

Father, You said, "For I know the thoughts and plans that I have for you...thoughts and plans for welfare and peace, and not for evil, to give you hope in your final outcome" (Jer. 29:11 AMP). By the blessing of the influence of the upright and God's favor [because of them], the city of _____ is exalted. Amen.

Scripture References

Acts 1:8 AMP

Hebrews 4:16 AMP

Psalm 147:15 AMP

Acts 12:24 AMP

Jeremiah 29:7,8 AMP

Psalm 55:9 AMP

Acts 26:18 AMP

Ephesians 2:2 AMP

Luke 23:34 AMP

2 Corinthians 4:4 AMP

Ephesians 6:12

Psalm 101:8 AMP

John 16:8 AMP

Jeremiah 29:11 AMP

Proverbs 11:11 AMP

$\mathcal{P}$rotection From Terrorism

$\mathcal{F}$ather, in the name of Jesus, we praise You and offer up thanksgiving because the Lord is near — He is coming soon. Therefore, we will not fret or have any anxiety about the terrorism that is threatening the lives of those who travel and those stationed on foreign soil or at home. But in this circumstance and in everything by prayer and petition [definite requests] with thanksgiving we continue to make our wants known to You.

Father, our petition is that terrorism in the heavenlies and on earth be stopped before it spreads to other countries and comes to our land, _____.

Jesus, You have given us the authority and power to trample upon serpents and scorpions and (physical and mental strength and ability) over all the power that the enemy [possesses], and nothing shall in any way harm us.

In the name of Jesus, we take authority over a spirit of timidity — of cowardice, of craven and cringing and fawning fear (of terrorism) — for [God has given us a spirit] of power and of love and of a calm and well-balanced mind and discipline and self-control.

332

We shall not be afraid of the terror of the night, nor of the arrow [the evil plots and slanders of the wicked] that flies by day, nor of the pestilence that stalks in darkness, nor of the destruction and sudden death that surprise and lay waste at noonday.

Therefore, we establish ourselves on righteousness, rightness — [right], in conformity with God's will and order; we shall be far from even the thought of oppression or destruction, for we shall not fear, and from terror, for it shall not come near us.

Holy Spirit, thank You for writing this Word upon the tablets of our hearts so that we can speak it out of our mouths, for we will order our conversation aright, and You will show us the salvation of God. Hallelujah! Amen.

Scripture References

Philippians 4:5,6 AMP	Romans 8:31
Luke 10:19 AMP	2 Timothy 1:7 AMP
Ephesians 6:10 AMP	Psalm 91:5,6 AMP
Ephesians 2:2 AMP	Isaiah 54:14 AMP
Ephesians 6:12 AMP	Proverbs 3:3 AMP
Matthew 16:19	Psalm 50:23
Psalm 56:9 AMP	

$\mathcal{S}$alvation of the Lost

$\mathcal{F}$ather, it is written in Your Word, "First of all, then, I admonish and urge that petitions, prayers, inter-cessions, and thanksgivings be offered on behalf of all men" (1 Tim.2:1 AMP).

Therefore, Father, we bring the lost of the world this day — every man, woman, and child from here to the farthest corner of the earth — before You. As we intercede, we use our faith, believing that thousands this day have the opportunity to make Jesus their Lord.

Father, we know that Satan would prevent these from hearing truth, if possible. We are human, but we don't wage war with human plans and methods. We use God's mighty weapons to knock down the devil's strongholds. With these weapons we break down every proud argument that keeps people from knowing God. With these weapons we conquer their rebellious ideas and teach them to obey Christ.

We ask the Lord of the harvest to thrust the perfect laborers across these lives this day to share the good news of the Gospel in a special way so that they will listen and understand it. We believe that they will not be able to resist the wooing of the Holy Spirit, for You, Father, bring them to repentance by Your goodness and love.

We confess that they shall see who have never been told of Jesus. They shall understand who have never heard of Jesus. And they shall come out of the snare of the devil who has held them captive. They shall open their eyes and turn from darkness to light — from the power of Satan to You, God!

In Jesus' name, amen.

Scripture References

1 Timothy 2:1,2 AMP   Romans 2:4

2 Corinthians 10:3-5 NLT   Romans 15:21 AMP

Matthew 9:38   2 Timothy 2:26 AMP

*N*ations and Continents

*F*ather, Jesus is our Salvation. He is the God-revealing light to the non-Jewish nations and the light of glory for Your people Israel. As members of the Body of Christ, we are asking You to give us the nations for an inheritance and the ends of the earth for our possession. All kings shall fall down before You; all nations shall serve You. In the name of Jesus, we bring before You the nation (or continent) of _____ and her leaders. We ask You to rebuke leaders for our sakes, so that we may live a quiet and peaceable life in all godliness and honesty.

We pray that skillful and godly wisdom will enter the heart of _____'s leaders and that knowledge shall be pleasant to them, that discretion will watch over them, and that understanding will keep them and deliver them from the way of evil and from the evil men.

We pray that the upright shall dwell in the government(s), that men and women of integrity, blameless and complete in Your sight, Father, shall remain; but the wicked shall be cut off and the treacherous shall be rooted out. We pray that those in authority winnow the wicked from among the good and bring the threshing wheel over them to separate the chaff from the grain, for loving-kindness and mercy, truth, and faithfulness preserve those in authority, and their offices are upheld by the people's loyalty.

Father, we ask that You direct the decisions made by these leaders, and that present leaders who are men and women of discernment, understanding, and knowledge will remain in office so the stability of _____ will long continue. We pray that the uncompromisingly righteous will be in authority in _____ so the people can rejoice.

Father, it is an abomination for leaders to commit wickedness. We pray that their offices be established and made secure by righteousness and that right and just lips are a delight to those in authority and that they love those who speak what is right.

We pray and believe that the good news of the Gospel is published in this land. We thank You for laborers of the harvest to publish Your Word that Jesus is Lord in _____. We thank You for raising up intercessors to pray for _____ in Jesus' name. Amen.

Scripture References

1 Timothy 2:1,2	Proverbs 28:2 AMP
Psalm 105:14	Proverbs 29:2 AMP
Proverbs 2:10-15 AMP	Acts 12:24
Proverbs 2:21,22 AMP	Psalm 68:11
Proverbs 20:26,28 AMP	Luke 2:30-32 MESSAGE
Proverbs 21:1	Psalm 2:8
Proverbs 16:10,12,13 AMP	Psalm 72:11

Here is a list of continents and nations to help you as you pray for the world:

CONTINENTS:

Africa	Europe
Antarctica	North America
Asia	South America
Australia	

NATIONS:

Abkha Republic	Belgium
Afghanistan	Belize
Albania	Benin
Algeria	Bermuda
Andorra	Bhutan
Angola	Bolivia
Anguilla	Bosnia-Herzegovina
Antigua and Barbuda	Botswana
Argentina	Brazil
Armenia	British Antarctic Territory
Aruba	British Indian Ocean Territory
Austria	Brunei
Azerbaijan	Bulgaria
Bahamas	Burkina Faso
Bahrain	Burma
Bangladesh	Burundi
Barbados	Cambodia
Belarus	Cameroon

Canada

Cape Verde

Cayman Islands

Central African Republic

Chad

Chile

China, People's Republic
  of Colombia

Comoros

Congo

Costa Rica

Cote d'Ivoire

Croatia

Cuba

Cyprus

Czech Republic

Denmark

Djibouti

Dominica

Dominican Republic

East Timor

Eastern Europe

Ecuador

Egypt

El Salvador

Equatorial Guinea

Eritrea

Estonia

Ethiopia

Faeroe Islands

Falkland Islands

Fiji

Finland

France

Gabon

The Gambia

Georgia

Germany

Ghana

Gibraltar

Great Britain

Greece

Greenland

Grenada

Guadeloupe

Guam

Guatemala

Guinea

Guinea-Bissau

Guyana	Kuwait
Haiti	Kyrgyzstan
Honduras	Laos
Hong Kong	Latvia
Hungary	Lebanon
Iceland	Lesotho
India	Liberia
Indonesia	Libya
Iran	Liechtenstein
Iraq	Lithuania
Ireland	Luxembourg
Isle of Man	Macau
Israel	Macedonia
Italy	Madagascar
Jamaica	Malawi
Japan	Malaysia
Jersey	Maldives
Jordan	Mali
Kazakhstan	Malta
Kenya	Marshall Islands
Kiribati	Mauritania
North Korea	Mauritius
South Korea	Mexico
Kosovo	Micronesia

Moldova	Palestinian Aut.
Monaco	Panama
Mongolia	Papua New Guinea
Montserrat	Paraguay
Morocco	Peru
Mozambique	Philippines
Myanmar	Pitcairn Island
Nagorno-Karabakh	Poland
Namibia	Portugal
Nauru	Puerto Rico
Nepal	Qatar
Netherlands	Romania
New Caledonia	Russia
New Zealand	Rwanda
Nicaragua	Saint Helena
Niger	Saint Kitts-Nevis
Nigeria	St. Lucia
Niue	Saint Vincent and the
Northern Ireland	Grenadines
Northern Mariana Islands	San Marino
Norway	São Tomé E Príncipe
Oman	Saudi Arabia
Pakistan	Senegal
Palau	Serbia
	Seychelles

Sierra Leone

Singapore

Slovakia

Slovenia

Soloman Islands

Somalia

South Africa

South Georgia & The
South Sandwich Islands

Spain

Sri Lanka

Sudan

Suriname

Swaziland

Sweden

Switzerland

Syria

Taiwan

Tajikistan

Tanzania

Thailand

Tibet

Togo

Tonga

Trinidad & Tobago

Tunisia

Turkey

Turkmenistan

Turks & Caicos Islands

Tuvalu

Uganda

Ukraine

United Arab Emirates

United Kingdom

United States of America

Uruguay

Uzbekistan

Vanuatu

Vatican City State

Venezuela

Vietnam

British Virgin Islands

Western Sahara

Western Samoa

Yemen

Yugoslavia

Zaire

Zambia

Zimbabwe

$\mathcal{T}$he People of Our Land

$\mathcal{F}$ather, in the name of Jesus, we come before You to claim Your promise in 2 Chronicles 7:14 AMP: "If My people, who are called by My name shall humble themselves, pray, seek, crave, and require of necessity My face and turn from their wicked ways, then will I hear from heaven, forgive their sin, and heal their land."

We are Your people, called by Your name. Thank You for hearing our prayers and moving by Your Spirit in our land. There are famines, earthquakes, floods, natural disasters, and violence occurring. Men's hearts are failing them because of fear.

Lord, Your Son, Jesus, spoke of discerning the signs of the times. With the Holy Spirit as our Helper, we are watching and praying.

We desire to humble ourselves before You, asking that a spirit of humility be released in us. Thank You for quiet and meek spirits, for we know that the meek shall inherit the earth.

Search us, O God, and know our hearts; try us, and know our thoughts today. See if there be any wicked way in us, and lead us in the way everlasting.

Forgive us our sins of judging inappropriately, complaining about, and criticizing our leaders. Cleanse us with hyssop, and we will be clean; wash us, and we will be whiter than snow. Touch our lips with coals from Your altar that we may pray prayers that avail much for all men and women everywhere.

Lord, we desire to release rivers of living water for the healing of the nations.

In the name of Jesus, amen.

Scripture References

Luke 21:11,25,26	Psalm 51:7 NIV
Matthew 16:3	Isaiah 6:6,7 NIV
Matthew 26:41	James 5:16
James 4:10	1 Timothy 2:1
1 Peter 3:4	John 7:38
Matthew 5:5	Revelation 22:1,2
Psalm 139:23	

*A*merican Government

*F*ather, in Jesus' name, we give thanks for the United States and its government. We hold up in prayer before You the men and women who are in positions of authority. We pray and intercede for the president, the representatives, the senators, the judges of our land, the policemen and the policewomen, as well as the governors and mayors, and for all those who are in authority over us in any way. We pray that the Spirit of the Lord rests upon them.

We believe that skillful and godly wisdom has entered into the heart of our president and knowledge is pleasant to him. Discretion watches over him; understanding keeps him and delivers him from the way of evil and from evil men.

Father, we ask that You compass the president about with men and women who make their hearts and ears attentive to godly counsel and do that which is right in Your sight. We believe You cause them to be men and women of integrity who are obedient concerning us that we may lead a quiet and peaceable life in all godliness and honesty. We pray that the upright shall dwell in our government — that men and women blameless and complete in Your sight, Father, shall remain in these positions of authority, but the wicked shall be cut off from our government and the treacherous shall be rooted out of it.

Your Word declares that "blessed is the nation whose God is the Lord" (Ps. 33:12). We receive Your blessing. Father; You are our Refuge and Stronghold in times of trouble (high cost, destitution, and desperation). So we declare with our mouths that Your people dwell safely in this land, and we *prosper* abundantly. We are more than conquerors through Christ Jesus!

It is written in Your Word that the heart of the king is in the hand of the Lord and that You turn it whichever way You desire. We believe the heart of our leader is in Your hand and that his decisions are divinely directed of the Lord.

We give thanks unto You that the good news of the Gospel is published in our land. The Word of the Lord prevails and grows mightily in the hearts and lives of the people. We give thanks for this land and the leaders You have given to us, in Jesus' name.

Jesus is Lord over the United States! Amen.

Scripture References

1 Timothy 2:1-3	Deuteronomy 28:10,11
Proverbs 2:10-12,21,22	Romans 8:37 AMP
Psalm 33:12	Proverbs 21:1
Psalm 9:9	Acts 12:24

School Systems and Children

*F*ather, we thank You that the entrance of Your Word brings light and that You watch over Your Word to perform it. Father, we bring before You the _____ school system(s) and the men and women who are in positions of authority within the school system(s).

We ask You to give them skillful and godly wisdom, that Your knowledge might be pleasant to them. Then discretion will watch over them; understanding will keep them and deliver them from the way of evil and from evil men. We pray that men and women of integrity, blameless and complete in Your sight, remain in these positions, but that the wicked be cut off and the treacherous be rooted out in the name of Jesus. Father, we thank You for born-again, Spirit-filled people in these positions.

Father, we bring our children, our young people, before You. We speak forth Your Word boldly and confidently, Father, that we and our households are saved in the name of Jesus. We are redeemed from the curse of the law, for Jesus was made a curse for us. *Our sons and daughters are not given to another people.* We enjoy our children, and they shall not go into captivity, in the name of Jesus.

As parents, we train our children in the way they should go, and when they are old they shall not depart from it.

Our children shrink from whatever might offend You, Father, and discredit the name of Christ. They show themselves to be blameless, guileless, innocent, and uncontaminated children of God, without blemish (faultless, unrebukable), in the midst of a crooked and wicked generation, holding out to it and offering to all the Word of Life. Thank You, Father, that You give them knowledge and skill in all learning and wisdom and bring them into favor with those around them.

Father, we pray and intercede that these young people, their parents, and the leaders in the school system(s) separate themselves from contact with contaminating and corrupting influences and cleanse themselves from everything that would contaminate and defile their spirits, souls, and bodies. We confess that they shun immorality and all sexual looseness — flee from impurity in thought, word, or deed — and they live and conduct themselves honorably and becomingly as in the open light of day. We confess and believe that they shun youthful lusts and flee from them in the name of Jesus.

Father, we ask You to commission the ministering spirits to go forth and police the area, dispelling the forces of darkness.

Father, we thank You that in Christ all the treasures of divine wisdom (of comprehensive insight into the ways and purposes of God) and all the riches of spiritual knowledge and enlightenment are stored up and lie hidden for us, and we walk in Him.

We praise You, Father, that we shall see _____ walking in the ways of piety and virtue, revering Your name, Father. Those who err in spirit will come to understanding, and those who murmur discontentedly will accept instruction in the way, Jesus, to Your will and carry out Your purposes in their lives; for You, Father, occupy first place in their hearts. We surround _____ with our faith.

Thank You, Father, that You are the delivering God. Thank You that the good news of the Gospel is published throughout our school system(s). Thank You for intercessors to stand on Your Word and for laborers of the harvest to preach Your Word in Jesus' name. Praise the Lord! Amen.

Scripture References

Psalm 119:130	2 Timothy 2:21 AMP
Jeremiah 1:12	2 Corinthians 7:1 AMP
Proverbs 2:10-12 AMP	1 Corinthians 6:18 AMP
Proverbs 2:21,22 AMP	Romans 13:13 AMP
Acts 16:31	Ephesians 5:4
Galatians 3:13	2 Timothy 2:22
Deuteronomy 28:32,41	Matthew 18:18
Proverbs 22:6 AMP	2 Timothy 2:26
Philippians 2:15,16 AMP	Hebrews 1:14
Daniel 1:17 AMP	Colossians 2:3 AMP
Daniel 1:9	Isaiah 29:23,24 AMP
1 John 2:16,17 AMP	

$\mathcal{M}$embers of the Armed Forces

$\mathcal{F}$ather, our troops have been sent into _____ as peacekeepers. We petition You, Lord, according to Psalm 91, for the safety of our military personnel.

This is no afternoon athletic contest that our armed forces will walk away from and forget about in a couple of hours. This is for keeps, a life-or-death fight to the finish against the devil and all his angels. We look beyond human instruments of conflict and address the forces and authorities and rulers of darkness and powers in the spiritual world. As children of the Most High God, we enforce the triumphant victory of our Lord Jesus Christ.

Our Lord stripped principalities and powers, making a show of them openly. Thank you, Jesus, for defeating the evil one and his forces of darkness for us, and giving us authority to proclaim your name that is above every name. All power and authority both in heaven and earth belong to you. Righteousness and truth shall prevail, and nations shall come to the light of the Gospel.

We petition heaven to turn our troops into a real peacekeeping force by pouring out the glory of God through our men and women in that part of the world. Use them as instruments of righteousness to defeat the plans of the devil.

Lord, we plead the power of the blood of Jesus, asking You to manifest Your power and glory. We entreat You on behalf of the citizens in these countries on both sides of this conflict. They have experienced pain and heartache; they are victims of the devil's strategies to steal, kill, and destroy. We pray that they will come to know Jesus, Who came to give us life and life more abundantly.

We stand in the gap for the people of the war-torn, devil-overrun land. We expect an overflowing of Your goodness and glory in the lives of those for whom we are praying. May they call upon Your name and be saved.

You, Lord, make known Your salvation; Your righteousness You openly show in the sight of the nations.

Father, provide for and protect the families of our armed forces. Preserve marriages; cause the hearts of the parents to turn toward their children and the hearts of the children to turn toward the fathers and mothers. We plead the blood of Jesus over our troops and their families. Provide a support system to undergird, uplift, and edify those who have been left to raise children by themselves. Jesus has been made unto these parents wisdom, righteousness, and sanctification. Through Your Holy Spirit, comfort the lonely and strengthen the weary.

Father, we are looking forward to that day when the whole earth shall be filled with the knowledge of the Lord as the waters cover the sea.

In Jesus' name, amen.

A portion of this prayer was taken from a letter dated January 22, 1996, written by Kenneth Copeland of Kenneth Copeland Ministries in Fort Worth, Texas, and sent to his partners. Used by permission.

Scripture References

Ephesians 6:12 MESSAGE   Psalm 98:2 AMP

Colossians 2:15   Malachi 4:6

John 10:10   1 Corinthians 1:30

Ezekiel 22:30   Isaiah 11:9

Acts 2:21

The Nation and People of Israel

Lord, You will not cast off nor spurn Your people, neither will You abandon Your heritage. You have regard for the covenant [You made with Abraham]. Father, remember Your covenant with Abraham, Isaac, and Jacob.

Father, we pray for the peace of Jerusalem. May they prosper who love you [the Holy City]. May peace be within your walls and prosperity within your palaces! For our brethren and companions' sake, we will now say, "Peace be within you!" For the sake of the house of the Lord our God, we will seek, inquire for, and require your good.

Father, we thank You for bringing the people of Israel into unity with each other and for bringing Your Church (both Jew and Gentile) into oneness — one new man. Thank You for the peace treaties with Israel's former enemies. May these treaties be used for good to make way for the good news of the Gospel as we prepare for the coming of our Messiah.

We intercede for those who have become callously indifferent (blinded, hardened, and made insensible to the Gospel). We pray that they will not fall to their utter spiritual ruin. It was through their false step and transgression that salvation has come to the Gentiles. Now, we ask that the eyes of their understanding be enlightened that they may know the Messiah Who will make Himself known to all of Israel.

We ask You to strengthen the house of Judah and save the house of Joseph. Thank You, Father, for restoring them because You have compassion on them. They will be as though You had not rejected them, for You are the Lord their God, and You will answer them. We thank You for Your great mercy and love to them and to us, in the name of Yeshua, our Messiah.

Father, thank You for saving Israel and gathering them from the nations, that they may give thanks to Your holy name and glory in Your praise. Praise be to You, Lord, the God of Israel, from everlasting to everlasting. Let all the people say, "Amen!" Praise the Lord.

In Jesus' name, amen.

Scripture References

Psalm 94:14 AMP	Romans 11:7 AMP
Psalm 74:20 AMP	Romans 11:11 AMP
Leviticus 46:22	Ephesians 1:18
Psalm 122:6-9 AMP	Zechariah 10:6,12 NIV
Ephesians 2:14 AMP	Psalm 106:47,48 NIV

*P*eace of Jerusalem

*F*ather, in the name of Jesus and according to Your Word, I long and pray for the peace of Jerusalem, that its inhabitants may be born again. I pray that You, Lord, will be a refuge and a stronghold to the children of Israel. Father, Your Word says "multitudes, multitudes are in the valley of decision" and whoever calls upon Your name shall be delivered and saved.

Have mercy upon Israel and be gracious to them, O Lord, and consider that they fight for their land to be restored. You, Lord, are their Strength and Stronghold in their day of trouble. We pray that they are righteous before You and that You will make even their enemies to be at peace with them. Your Word says You will deliver those for whom we intercede, who are not innocent, through the cleanness of our hands. May they realize that their defense and shield depend on You.

We thank You for Your Word, Lord, that You have a covenant with Israel and that You will take away their sin. They are Your beloved. Your Word also says that Your gifts are irrevocable, that You never withdraw them once they are given, and that You do not change Your mind about those to whom You give Your grace or to whom You send Your call. Though they have been disobedient and rebellious toward You, Lord, we pray that now they will repent and obtain Your mercy and forgiveness through Your Son, Jesus. We praise You, Lord, for Your compassion and Your forgiveness to Your people. We praise You that they are under Your protection and divine guidance, that they are Your special possession, Your peculiar treasure, and that You will spare them; for we have read in Your Word that all Israel shall be saved!

I commit to pray for the peace of Jerusalem! Thank You, Father, for delivering us all from every evil work and for the authority You have given us with the name of Jesus. We love You and praise You. Every day, with its new reasons, we praise You!

Pray for the peace of Jerusalem! May they prosper that love you, "the Holy City"! Peace be within your walls and prosperity within your palaces! Amen.

Scripture References

Joel 3:14	Romans 11:29 AMP
Job 22:30 AMP	Isaiah 45:17

*S*pirit-Controlled Life

*F*ather, I pray for all saints everywhere. Help us remain teachable that we may receive instruction from the apostles, prophets, evangelists, pastors, and teachers. We will be Your children equipped for the work of ministry, for the edifying of the Body of Christ. Bring us to the unity of faith and knowledge of the Son of God, to a perfect man, to the measure of the stature of the fullness of Christ.

Father, there is now no condemnation to those who walk according to the Spirit, because through Christ Jesus the law of the Spirit of life sets us free from the law of sin and death. Grant us the grace to live the life of the Spirit. Father, You condemned sin in the flesh [subdued, overcame, deprived it] of its power over us. Now the righteous and just requirement of the Law is fully met in us who live and move in the ways of the Spirit—our lives governed and controlled by the Holy Spirit.

We purpose to live according to the Spirit, and we are controlled by the desires of the Spirit. We set our minds on and seek those things which gratify the Holy Spirit. We no longer live the life of the flesh; we live the life of the Spirit. The Holy Spirit of God really dwells within us, directing and controlling us.

On the authority of Your Word, we declare that we are more than conquerors and are gaining a surpassing victory through Jesus Who loves us. We refuse to let ourselves be overcome with evil, but we will overcome and master evil with good. We have on the full armor of light, clothed with the Lord Jesus Christ, the Messiah, and make no provision for indulging the flesh.

May we always be doers of God's Word. We have God's wisdom, and we draw it forth with prayer. We are peace-loving, full of compassion and good fruits. We are free from doubts, wavering, and insincerity. We are subject to God, our Father.

We are strong in the Lord and the power of His might. Therefore, we take our stand against the devil and resist him; he flees from us. We draw close to God, and God draws close to us. We do not fear, for God never leaves us.

In Christ, we are filled with the Godhead: Father, Son, and Holy Spirit. Jesus is our Lord!

Scripture References

Romans 8:2,4,9,14,31,37 AMP	James 3:17 AMP
Romans 12:21	Hebrews 13:5
Romans 13:12,14	Ephesians 6:10
James 1:22	James 4:7,8
James 3:17 AMP	Colossians 2:10

Renew Fellowship

Father, You hasten Your Word to perform it. I believe that _____ is a disciple of Christ, taught of You, Lord, and obedient to Your will. Great is his/her peace and undisturbed composure. _____ has You in person for his/her Teacher. He/she has listened and learned from You and has come to Jesus.

_____ continues to hold to things he/she has learned and of which he/she is convinced. From childhood he/she has had knowledge of and been acquainted with the Word, which is able to instruct him/her and give him/her the understanding of the salvation that comes through faith in Christ Jesus. Father, You will heal _____, lead _____ and recompense _____, and restore comfort to _____.

Jesus gives _____ eternal life. He/she shall never lose it or perish throughout the ages, to all eternity. _____ shall never by any means be destroyed. You, Father, have given _____ to Jesus. You are greater and mightier than all else; no one is able to snatch _____ out of Your hand.

I pray and believe that _____ comes to his/her senses and escapes out of the snare of the devil who has held him/her captive and that _____ would judge himself/herself.

_____ has become a fellow-heir with Christ, the Messiah, and shares in all He has for him/her and holds the first newborn confidence and original assured expectation, firm and unshaken to the end. _____ casts not away his/her confidence, for it has great recompense of reward.

Thank You for giving _____ wisdom and revelation — quickening him/her to Your Word. Thank You that _____ enjoys fellowship with You and Jesus and with fellow believers.

In Jesus' name, amen.

Scripture References

Jeremiah 1:12	2 Timothy 2:26 AMP
John 6:45	1 Corinthians 11:31
Isaiah 54:13 AMP	Matthew 18:18
2 Timothy 3:14,15	Hebrews 3:14 AMP
Isaiah 57:18	Hebrews 10:35 AMP
John 10:28,29	Ephesians 1:17
1 John 5:16	1 John 1:3

$\mathcal{D}$eliverance From Satan and His Demonic Forces

If the person for whom you are interceding has not confessed Jesus as Savior and Lord, pray specifically for his/her salvation if you have not already done so. Stand and thank the Father that it is done in the name of Jesus. Then pray:

Father, in the name of Jesus, I come boldly to Your throne of grace and present _____ before You. I stand in the gap and intercede in behalf of _____, knowing that the Holy Spirit within me takes hold together with me against the evils that would attempt to hold _____ in bondage. I unwrap _____ from the bonds of wickedness with my prayers and take my shield of faith and quench every fiery dart of the adversary that would come against _____.

Father, You say that whatever I bind on earth is bound in heaven, and whatever I loose on earth is loosed in heaven. You say for me to cast out demons in the name of Jesus.

"In the name of Jesus, I bind _____'s body, soul, and spirit to the will and purposes of God for his/her life. I bind _____'s mind, will, and emotions to the will of God. I bind him/her to the truth and to the blood of Jesus. I bind his/her mind to the mind of Christ, that the very thoughts, feelings, and purposes of His heart would be within his/her thoughts.

I loose every old, wrong, ungodly pattern of thinking, attitude, idea, desire, belief, motivation, habit, and behavior from him/her. I tear down, crush, smash, and destroy every stronghold associated with these things. I loose any stronghold in his/her life that has been justifying and protecting hard feelings against anyone. I loose the stronghold of unforgiveness, fear, and distrust from him/her. I bind and loose these things in Jesus' name."[1]

Father, I ask You to commission Your ministering spirits to go forth and provide the necessary help and assistance for _____.

Father, I have laid hold of _____'s salvation and his/her confession of the Lordship of Jesus Christ. I speak of things that are not as though they were, for I choose to look at the unseen — the eternal things of God. I say that Satan shall not get an advantage over _____, for I am not ignorant of Satan's devices. I resist Satan, and he has run in terror from _____ in the name of Jesus. I give Satan no place in _____. I plead the blood of the Lamb over _____, for Satan and his cohorts are overcome by that blood and Your Word. I thank You, Father, that I tread on serpents and scorpions and over all the power of the enemy in _____'s behalf. _____ is delivered from this present evil world. He/she is delivered from the powers of darkness and translated into the Kingdom of Your dear Son!

Father, I ask You now to fill those vacant places within _____ with Your redemption, Your Word, Your Holy Spirit,

Your love, Your wisdom, Your righteousness, and Your revelation knowledge in the name of Jesus.

I thank You, Father, that _____ is redeemed out of the hand of Satan by the blood of Jesus. He/she is justified and made righteous by the blood of Jesus and belongs to You — spirit, soul, and body. I thank You that every enslaving yoke is broken, for he/she will not become the slave of anything or be brought under its power in the name of Jesus. _____ has escaped the snare of the devil who has held him/her captive and henceforth does Your will, Father, which is to glorify You in his/her spirit, soul, and body.

Thank You, Father, that Jesus was manifested that He might destroy the works of the devil. Satan's works are destroyed in _____'s life in the name of Jesus. Hallelujah! _____ walks in the Kingdom of God, which is righteousness, peace, and joy in the Holy Spirit! Praise the Lord! Amen.

Note: This prayer may be prayed as many times as necessary. It takes time to realize the faith that leads you into a position of praise and thanksgiving. Stand firm, fixed, unmovable, and steadfast, remembering that greater is He that is in you than he that is in the world.

Scripture References

Hebrews 4:16	2 Corinthians 2:11
Ezekiel 22:30	James 4:7
Romans 8:26	Ephesians 4:27
Isaiah 58:6	Revelation 12:11
Ephesians 6:16	Luke 10:19
Matthew 18:18	Galatians 1:4

Mark 16:17	Colossians 1:13
Ephesians 6:12	Matthew 12:43-45
Colossians 2:15	1 Corinthians 6:12
Matthew 12:29	2 Timothy 2:26
Hebrews 1:14	1 John 3:8
Romans 4:17	Romans 14:17
2 Corinthians 4:18	

---

[1] *Shattering Your Strongholds,* Copyright © 1992 by Liberty Savard, Bridge-Logos Publishers, North Brunswick, NJ (pp. 171-172).

$\mathcal{D}$eliverance From Cults

$\mathcal{F}$ather, in the name of Jesus, we come before You in prayer and in faith, believing that Your Word runs swiftly throughout the earth, for the Word of God is not chained or imprisoned. We bring before You _____ (those, and families of those, involved in cults).

Father, stretch forth Your hand from above; rescue and deliver _____ out of great waters, from the land of hostile aliens whose mouths speak deceit and whose right hands are right hands raised in taking fraudulent oaths. Their mouths must be stopped, for they are mentally distressing and subverting _____ and whole families by teaching what they ought not teach for the purpose of getting base advantage and disreputable gain. But, praise God, they will not get very far, for their rash folly will become obvious to everybody!

Execute justice, precious Father, for the oppressed. Set the prisoners free, open the eyes of the blind, lift up the bowed down, heal the brokenhearted, and bind up their wounds. Lift up the humble and downtrodden, and cast the wicked down to the ground in the mighty name of Jesus.

Turn back the hearts of the disobedient, incredulous, and unpersuadable to the wisdom of the upright and the knowledge of the will of God, in order to make ready for You, Lord, a people perfectly prepared in spirit, adjusted, disposed, and placed in the right moral state.

Father, You say in Your Word to refrain our voices from weeping and our eyes from tears, for our prayers shall be rewarded and _____ shall return from the enemy's land and come again to his/her own country. You will save our offspring from the land of their exile; from the east and the west — sons from afar and daughters from the ends of the earth. We shall see _____ walking in the ways of piety and virtue, revering Your name, Father. Those who err in spirit will come to understanding. Those who murmur discontentedly will accept instruction in the Way, Jesus. Father, You contend with those who contend with us, and You give safety to _____.

In the name of Jesus, I bind _____'s feet to the paths of righteousness, that his/her steps would be steady and sure. I bind _____ to the work of the Cross, with all of its mercy, grace, love, forgiveness, and dying to self.

I loose the power and effects of deceptions and lies from him/her. I loose the confusion and blindness of the god of this world from _____'s mind that have kept him/her from seeing the light of the gospel of Jesus Christ. I call forth every precious word of Scripture that has ever entered into his/her mind and heart, that it would rise up in power within him/her. I loose the power and effects of any harsh or hard words (word curses) spoken to, about, or by _____.

Jesus gave me the keys and the authority to bind and loose these things in His name. Thank You, Lord, for the truth.[1]

Father, we ask You to commission the ministering spirits to go forth and dispel these forces of darkness and bring _____ home in the name of Jesus.

Father, we believe and confess that _____ has had knowledge of and been acquainted with the Word, which was able to instruct him/her and give him/her the understanding for salvation that comes through faith in Christ Jesus. Lord, we pray and believe that You certainly will deliver _____ from every assault of evil and draw _____ to Yourself and preserve and bring _____ safe into Your heavenly Kingdom. Glory to You, Father, Who deliver those for whom we intercede in Jesus' name! Amen.

Note: Pray this prayer until faith arises in you. Then you will know that God shall perform His Word in the life of the one for whom you are interceding. The Holy Spirit is your Helper. When you perceive the intercession is completed, surround the individual with songs and shouts of deliverance in your prayer closet.

Scripture References

Psalm 147:15	Isaiah 43:5,6
2 Timothy 2:9	Isaiah 29:23,24
Psalm 144:7,8	Isaiah 49:25
Titus 1:11	Matthew 18:18
2 Timothy 3:9	2 Timothy 3:2-9
Psalm 146:7,8	Hebrews 1:14
Psalm 147:3-6	2 Timothy 3:15
Luke 1:17	2 Timothy 4:18
Jeremiah 31:16,17	Job 22:30
Jeremiah 46:27	

---

[1] *Shattering Your Strongholds*, Copyright © 1992 by Liberty Savard, Bridge-Logos Publishers, North Brunswick, NJ (pp. 171-172).

$\mathcal{D}$eliverance From Habits

$\mathcal{F}$ather, in the name of Jesus and according to Your Word, I believe in my heart and say with my mouth that Jesus is Lord of my life. Since all truth is in Jesus, I strip myself of my former nature [put off and discard my old, unrenewed self]. I desire to be free from the habit(s) of _____ in the name of Jesus. Father, the habit(s) is/are not helpful (good for me, expedient, and profitable when considered with other things). I no longer desire to be the slave of wrong habits and behaviors or be brought under their power.

Father, these self-destructive habits are symptoms of a flaw in my soul, my character, and I confess them as sin. I don't want to habitually make the same mistakes over and over. Father, Your Word exposes the wrong thought patterns that are driving me to continue acting out in ways that are contrary to Your Word. I desire to be continually filled with, and controlled by, the Holy Spirit.

Thank You, Father, for translating me into the Kingdom of Your dear Son. Now I am Your garden under cultivation. In the name of Jesus, I throw all spoiled virtue and cancerous evil into the garbage. In simple humility, I purpose to let You, my Gardener, landscape me with the Word, making a salvation-garden of my life.

I arm myself with the full armor of God, that armor of a heavily armed soldier which God has supplied for me — the helmet of salvation...loins girded with truth...feet shod with the preparation of the gospel of peace...the shield of faith...and the Sword of the Spirit, which is the Word of God. With God's armor on, I am able to stand up against all the strategies and deceits and fiery darts of Satan, in the name of Jesus.

Clothed in Your armor, I discipline my body and subdue it. With every temptation I choose the way of escape that You provide. Greater is He that is in me than he that is in the world.

Thank You, Lord. I praise You that I am growing spiritually and that Your engrafted Word is saving my soul. I strip away the old nature with its habits, and I put on the new man created in Christ Jesus. Hallelujah! Amen.

Scripture References

Romans 10:9,10	1 Corinthians 10:13
Ephesians 4:21,22 AMP	Ephesians 6:13-17
1 Corinthians 6:12 AMP	1 John 4:4
1 Corinthians 3:9 AMP	2 Corinthians 5:17
James 1:21 MESSAGE	

Deliverance From Corrupt Companions

Father, in the name of Jesus, I ask You to open the eyes of
_____'s understanding, that he might not be deceived by
the influence of corrupt and depraved people. Thank You for
causing him to come alive and awakening him that he might
return to sober sense and his right mind.

Father, I forgive his sins and come before You asking for
mercy — mercy that triumphs over judgment. Thank You for
drawing him to Yourself with cords and bands of love and for
leading him to repentance with Your goodness. Then he will
separate himself from contact with contaminating influences and
cleanse himself from everything that would defile his spirit, soul,
and body.

In the name of Jesus, I bind his mind to the mind of Christ,
that he might live and conduct himself honorably and becomingly
as in the open light of the day. I loose him from the wrong thought
patterns of his former lifestyle that were controlled by a set of
values inspired by the adversary, who misleads those who have not
come alive to Christ.

I ask You to give him a willing heart, that he might be loyally
subject (submissive) to the governing (civil) authority — not
resisting nor setting himself up against them. He shall be

obedient, prepared, and willing to do any upright and honorable work. He shall walk as a companion with wise men, and he shall be wise.

_____ is pardoned through the name of Jesus and because he confesses His name. He is victorious over the wicked one because he has come to know and recognize and be aware of the Father.

As _____'s mind is renewed by the Word, the Word dwells and remains in him, and he dwells in the Son and in the Father always. God's nature abides in _____ — His principle of life remains permanently within him, and he cannot practice sinning because he is born of God. The law of the Spirit of life in Christ Jesus has made _____ free from the law of sin and death. Thank You, Father, for watching over Your Word to perform it, in Jesus' name! Amen.

Scripture References

1 Corinthians 15:33,34	Proverbs 28:7
2 Timothy 2:21 AMP	1 Thessalonians 5:22
2 Corinthians 7:1	1 John 2:12-16 AMP
Romans 13:13 AMP	1 John 2:21,24
1 Peter 2:1	1 John 3:9 AMP
Romans 13:1,2 AMP	Romans 8:2
Titus 3:1 AMP	Jeremiah 1:12
Proverbs 13:20	

*D*eliverance From Mental Disorder

*F*ather, in the name of Jesus, I fearlessly and confidently and boldly draw near to the throne of grace, that I may receive mercy and find grace to help in good time for _____1_____.

Father, I commit to pray on _____2_____'s behalf, making up the hedge and standing in the gap before You for him/her, that Your mercy might triumph over judgment. Jesus, You defeated the devil for _____2_____, and we take back everything Satan has stolen from him/her.

It is You, Father, Who deliver _____5_____ from the pit and corruption of _____7_____(name of disorder: schizophrenia, paranoia, manic depression, etc.). Father, You have not given _____4_____ a spirit of timidity — of cowardice, of craven and cringing and fawning fear — but [You have given him/her a spirit of] power and of love and of a calm and well-balanced mind and discipline and self-control.

In the name of Jesus, I forgive his/her sins and stand in the gap for him/her until he/she comes to his/her senses [and] escapes out of the snare of the devil, who has held him/her captive.

Because Jesus defeated principalities and powers and made a show of them openly, I stand against the forces of darkness, which have been assigned to _____6_____. Thank you Father for delivering _____*the*_____ from the authority of darkness, and translating him/her into the Kingdom of your dear Son

I decree and declare that the law of the Spirit of life in Christ Jesus has made _____*you*_____ free from the law of sin and death. _____*eat*_____ shall no longer be of two minds — hesitating, dubious, irresolute — unstable and unreliable and uncertain about everything (he/she thinks, feels, and decides). _____*at*_____ shall get rid of all uncleaness and the rampant outgrowth of wickedness, and in a humble (gentle, modest) spirit receive and welcome the Word, which, implanted and rooted [in his/her heart), contains the power to save his/her soul (*mind, will, and emotions*).

In the name of Jesus, grace be to _____*on*_____ and peace from God our Father and from the Lord Jesus Christ, Who gave Himself for his/her sin so that He might deliver him/her from this present evil world, according to the will of God and our Father, to Whom be glory for ever and ever. Amen.

Scripture References

Hebrews 4:16 AMP	Ephesians 6:12
Psalm 50:15	~~Colossians 1:13~~
Psalm 56:13	Romans 8:2
Psalm 103:4 AMP	James 1:8,21 AMP
2 Timothy 1:7 AMP	Galatians 1:3-5
John 20:23 AMP	Ezekiel 22:30
2 Timothy 2:26 AMP	Matthew 12:29

$\mathcal{H}$edge of Protection

$\mathcal{F}$ather, in the name of Jesus, we lift up ____2____ to You and pray a hedge of protection around him/her. We thank You, Father, that You are a wall of fire round about ___1 0___ and that you set Your angels round about him/her.

We thank You, Father, that ____1 2____ dwells in the secret place of the Most High and abides under the shadow of the Almighty. We say of You, Lord, You are his/her refuge and fortress, in You will he/she trust. You cover ___1 0___ with Your feathers, and under Your wings shall he/she trust. ___2 0___ shall not be afraid of the terror by night or the arrow that flies by day. Only with his/her eyes will ____n 0____ behold and see the reward of the wicked.

Because ____e l____ has made You, Lord, his/her refuge and fortress, no evil shall befall him/her — no accident will overtake him/her ___a___ neither shall any plague or calamity come near him/her. For you give Your angels charge over ___c n t___, to keep him/her in all Your ways.

Father, because You have set Your love upon ___a n d___, therefore will You deliver him/her. ___a n___ shall call upon You, and You will answer him/her. You will be with him/her in trouble and will satisfy ___a s___ with a long life and show him/her Your salvation. Not a hair of his/her head shall perish. Amen.

Scripture References

Ezekiel 22:30

Zechariah 2:5

Psalm 34:7

Psalm 91:1,2 AMP

Psalm 91:4,5 AMP

Psalm 91:8-11 AMP

Psalm 91:14-16 AMP

Luke 21:18

$\mathcal{F}$inding Favor With Others

$\mathcal{F}$ather, in the name of Jesus, You make Your face to shine upon and enlighten _____ vou _____ and are gracious (kind, merciful, and giving favor) to him/her. _____ Love _____ is the head and not the tail. _____ ok _____ is above only and not beneath.

Thank You for favor for _____ Sorry _____ who seeks Your Kingdom and Your righteousness and diligently seeks good. _____ with _____ is a blessing to You, Lord, and is a blessing to _____ to _____ (name them: family, neighbors, business associates, etc.). Grace (favor) is with _____ Love _____, who loves the Lord Jesus in sincerity. _____ extends favor, honor, and love to _____ (names). _____ is flowing in Your love, Father. You are pouring out upon _____ the spirit of favor. You crown him/her with glory and honor, for he/she is Your child — Your workmanship.

_____ is a success today. _____ is someone very special with You, Lord. _____ is growing in the Lord — waxing strong in spirit. Father, You give _____ knowledge and skill in all learning and wisdom.

You bring _____ to find favor, compassion, and loving-kindness with _____ (names). _____ Love _____ obtains favor in the sight of all who look upon him/her this day in the

name of Jesus. _LUKE_ is filled with Your fullness —
rooted and grounded in love. You are doing exceeding abundantly
above all that _eat_ asks or thinks, for Your mighty power
is taking over in _at at_.

Thank You, Father, that _Psalm_ is well-favored by You
and by man, in Jesus' name! Amen.

Scripture References

Numbers 6:25 AMP	Psalm 8:5
Deuteronomy 28:13	Ephesians 2:10
Matthew 6:33	Luke 2:40
Proverbs 11:27	Daniel 1:17
Ephesians 6:24	Daniel 1:9 AMP
Luke 6:38	Esther 2:15,17
Zechariah 12:10 AMP	Ephesians 3:19,20

*I*mproving Communication

_____ is a disciple of Christ — taught of the Lord and obedient to His will. Great is his/her peace and undisturbed composure. _____ is constantly renewed in the spirit of his/her mind — having a fresh mental and spiritual attitude — and is putting on the new nature — the regenerate self — created in God's image, Godlike in true righteousness and holiness.

His/her life lovingly expresses truth in all things — speaking truly, dealing truly, living truly. _____ is enfolded in love, growing up in every way and in all things into Him, who is the Head, even Christ, the Messiah, the Anointed One. His/her mouth shall utter truth. _____ speaks excellent and princely things — the opening of his/her lips is for right things. All the words of his/her mouth are righteous. There is nothing contrary to truth or crooked in them.

_____ inclines his/her heart to Your testimonies, Father, and not to covetousness (robbery, sensuality, or unworthy riches). _____ does not love or cherish the world. The love of the Father is in him/her. _____ is set free from the lust of the flesh (craving for sensual gratification), the lust of the eyes (greedy longings of the mind), and the pride of life (assurance in his own resources or in the stability of earthly things).

_____ perceives and knows the truth and that nothing false is of the truth.

_____ prizes Your wisdom, Father, and exalts it, and it will exalt and promote him/her. _____ attends to God's Word, consents and submits to Your sayings. _____ keeps them in the center of his/her heart. For they are life to _____ and medicine to all his/her flesh. _____ keeps his/her heart with all diligence, for out of it flow the springs of life.

_____ will do nothing from factional motives, through contentiousness, strife, selfishness, or for unworthy ends — or prompted by conceit and empty arrogance. Instead, in the true spirit of humility, does _____ regard others as better than himself/herself. _____ esteems and looks upon and is concerned not merely for his/her own interests, but also for the interests of others.

_____ lets this same attitude and purpose and humble mind be in him/her that was in Christ Jesus. Thank You, Father, in Jesus' name. Amen.

Scripture References (AMP)

Isaiah 54:13	Psalm 119:36
Ephesians 4:23,24	1 John 2:15,16,21
Ephesians 4:15	Proverbs 4:8,20-23
Proverbs 8:6-8	Philippians 2:2-5

*E*mployment

*F*ather, in Jesus' name, we believe and confess Your Word over _____ today, knowing that You watch over Your Word to perform it. Your Word prospers in _____ whereto it is sent! Father, You are his/her Source of every consolation, comfort, and encouragement. _____ is courageous and grows in strength.

His/her desire is to owe no man anything but to love him. Therefore, _____ is strong and lets not his/her hands be weak or slack, for his/her work shall be rewarded. His/her wages are not counted as a favor or a gift, but as something owed to him. _____ makes it his/her ambition and definitely endeavors to live quietly and peacefully, minds his/her own affairs, and works with his/her hands. He/she is correct and honorable and commands the respect of the outside world, being self-supporting, dependent on nobody, and having need of nothing; for You, Father, supply to the full his/her every need.

He/she works in quietness, earns his/her own food and other necessities. He/she is not weary of doing right and continues in well-doing without weakening. _____ learns to apply himself/herself to good deeds — to honest labor and honorable employment — so that he/she is able to meet necessary demands whenever the occasion may require.

Father, You know the record of his/her works and what he/she is doing. You have set before _____ a door wide open, which no one is able to shut.

_____ does not fear and is not dismayed, for You, Father, strengthen him/her. You, Father, help _____ in Jesus' name; in Jesus, _____ has perfect peace and confidence and is of good cheer, for Jesus overcame the world and deprived it of its power to harm _____. He/she does not fret or have anxiety about anything, for Your peace, Father, mounts guard over his/her heart and mind. _____ knows the secret of facing every situation, for he/she is self-sufficient in Christ's sufficiency. _____ guards his/her mouth and his/her tongue, keeping himself/herself from trouble.

_____ prizes Your wisdom, Father, and acknowledges You. You direct, make straight and plain his/her path, and You promote him/her. Therefore, Father, _____ increases in Your wisdom (in broad and full understanding) and in stature and years and in favor with You, Father, and with man! Amen.

Scripture References

Jeremiah 1:12

Isaiah 55:11

2 Corinthians 1:3 AMP

1 Corinthians 16:13 AMP

Romans 13:8 AMP

2 Chronicles 15:7 AMP

Romans 4:4 AMP

1 Thessalonians 4:11,12 AMP

2 Thessalonians 3:12,13 AMP

Luke 2:52 AMP

Titus 3:14 AMP

Revelation 3:8 AMP

Isaiah 41:10 AMP

John 16:33 AMP

Philippians 4:6,7 AMP

Philippians 4:12,13 AMP

Proverbs 21:23 AMP

Proverbs 3:6 AMP

Proverbs 4:8 AMP

Overcoming Negative Work Attitudes

*T*hank You, Father, in Jesus' name, for watching over Your Word to perform it. _____ is obedient to his/her employers — bosses or supervisors — having respect for them and eager to please them, in singleness of motive and with all his/her heart, as service to Christ, not in the way of eye service — as if they were watching him/her — but as a servant (employee) of Christ, doing the will of God heartily and with his/her whole soul.

_____ readily renders service with goodwill, as to the Lord and not to men. He/she knows that for whatever good he/she does, he/she will receive his/her reward from the Lord.

_____ will do all things without grumbling, faultfinding, and complaining against God and questioning and doubting within himself/herself. He/she is blameless and harmless, a child of God without rebuke in the midst of a crooked and perverse nation, among whom he/she shines as a light in the world.

He/she reveres the Lord, and his/her work is a sincere expression of his/her devotion to Him. Whatever may be his/her task, he/she works at it heartily from the soul, as something done for God. The One Whom _____ is actually serving is the Lord. Amen.

Scripture References (AMP)

Jeremiah 1:12　　　　Colossians 3:22-24

Ephesians 6:5-8　　　Philippians 2:14,15

Comfort for a Person Who Has Lost a Christian Loved One

Father, I thank You that we have a High Priest Who is able to understand and sympathize and have a fellow feeling with_____'s weaknesses and infirmities (grief over the loss of his/her_____).

Father, I thank You that _____ does not sorrow, as one who has no hope, because he/she believes that Jesus died and rose again; even so his/her loved one also who sleeps in Jesus will God bring back with Him. I ask that You comfort _____, for You said, "Blessed are they that mourn: for they shall be comforted" (Matt. 5:4).

Jesus, You have come to heal the brokenhearted. It is in the name of Jesus that You, Father, comfort _____ because You have loved him/her and have given him/her everlasting consolation and good hope through grace.

Blessed be God, even the Father of our Lord Jesus Christ, the Father of mercies and the God of all comfort, Who comforts _____ in all his/her tribulation, that he/she may be able to comfort those who are in any trouble by the comfort wherewith he himself/she herself is comforted by God.

Father, thank You for appointing unto _____, who mourns in Zion, to give unto him/her beauty for ashes, the oil of joy for mourning, the garment of praise for the spirit of heaviness, that he/she might be called a tree of righteousness, the planting of the Lord, that You might be glorified.

In Jesus' name, amen.

Scripture References

Hebrews 4:15,16 AMP	2 Thessalonians 2:16
1 Thessalonians 4:13,14	2 Corinthians 1:3,4
Matthew 5:4	Isaiah 61:3
Luke 4:18	

Healing of the Handicapped

Father, we come before you boldly and confidently, knowing that You are not a man that You should lie and that You watch over Your Word to perform it. Therefore, Father, we bring before You those who are called handicapped and ill—mentally and physically. Father, by the authority of Your Word, we know without a doubt that it is Your will for these people—babies, children and adults—to be made completely whole and restored in the name of Jesus.

Although satan, the god of this world, comes against Your handiwork, we know You are the God of miracles, the God of love, power and might. Through Your redemptive plan, we are redeemed from the curse of the law. The law of the Spirit of life in Christ Jesus has made us free from the law of sin and death. We are seated with Christ in heavenly places far above all satanic forces. We bring those who have been attacked mercilessly—mentally and/or physically—before Your throne of grace. We intercede on their behalf, and for their families and loved ones.

We proclaim the victory Jesus won at Calvary when He disarmed the principalities and powers that were waged against us. We believe that everyone who has the opportunity this day to make Jesus their Lord and Savior will call upon His name and be saved. We bind their spirits, souls and bodies to the will of God, to the blood of Jesus, to mercy, grace and truth. We destroy strongholds of unforgiveness, fear, and distrust. In the name of Jesus, we loose unbelief, fear, discouragement, tradition, depression and oppression from the minds of the parents, children and individuals involved.

Father, we pray for born-again, Spirit-filled individuals in positions of authority—administrators, teachers, doctors, nurses, orderlies, attendants and volunteers. We pray that men and women of integrity, blameless and complete in Your sight, remain in these positions, but that the wicked be cut off and the treacherous be rooted out. Father, we pray for laborers of the harvest to go forth preaching the good news to the lost and to the Body of Christ.

We pray that You quicken these individuals to Your Word—that they may be filled with wisdom and revelation knowledge concerning the integrity of Your Word, speaking faith-filled words and doing faith-filled actions. We pray for the infilling of the Holy Spirit, divine health, the fruit of the recreated human spirit, the gifts of the Holy Spirit and deliverance. May they know that Jesus is their Source of every consolation, comfort and encouragement, and that they are to be sanctified—spirit, soul and body. We confess that they are redeemed from the curse of the law—redeemed from every sickness, disease, malady, affliction, defect, deficiency, deformity, injury and every demon.

We speak healing to unborn infants in the wombs of mothers for children are a heritage of the Lord and the fruit of the womb is their reward. (Ps. 127:3)

We speak restoration to damaged brain cells and activation of dormant brain cells. We speak normal intellect for one's age. We speak creative miracles to parts of the body and healing to all wounds. We speak words of life and say that they shall live in victory in this life and not die. We speak perfect soundness of mind and wholeness in body and spirit. We say that tongues are loosed and speech is distinct. We say ears, heart and eyes see in the name of Jesus. We say demons are cast out, bowing to the name of Jesus. We speak deliverance to bodies and minds, for You, Lord God, are the Help of their countenance and the Lifter of those bowed down—the joy of the Lord is their strength and stronghold!

We commission God's ministering spirits to go forth as they hearken to God's Word to provide the necessary help and assistance to those for whom we are praying! Father, no word of Yours is void of the power that it takes to cause itself to come to pass! We establish Your Word on this earth, for it is already forever settled in heaven. Nothing is too hard or impossible for You. All things are possible to us who believe. We pray for more intercessors to stand with us. Let our prayers be set forth as incense before You—a sweet fragrance to You! Praise the Lord! In Your name we pray, amen.

Scripture References

Romans 3:4	Mark 16:17
Mark 11:23,24	Jeremiah 1:12
Psalm 42:11	1 Peter 2:24
Acts 3:16	Psalm 146:8
Matthew 8:17	2 Corinthians 4:4
Nehemiah 8:10	Mark 7:35
John 10:10	Psalm 103:20

Proverbs 20:12

Matthew 9:37,38

Romans 8:2

Psalm 119:89

2 Corinthians 1:3

Matthew 18:18

Mark 9:23

Psalm 127:3

Galatians 3:13

Luke 1:37

Ephesians 1:17,18

Ephesians 2:6

Jeremiah 32:27

1 Thessalonians 5:23

Proverbs 2:21,22

Psalm 141:2

*T*hose Involved in Abortion

INTRODUCTION

*T*hrough our ministry, a dear child of God shared with us the following Scriptures, which continue to bring her through periods of grief and sorrow. God's grace and love have proven to be the balm necessary for healing the emotional pain incurred by an act that cannot be reversed. The memory of the decision will never be erased. Reminders are all around — at church, in the media, and in everyday life.

The prayer as written has a twofold application: (1) for a people — a nation — who have permitted the legalization of abortion on demand; (2) for both the man and woman involved in the decision-making process. During moments of intercession for women and men who are dealing with past mistakes, we have identified with them in their pain. God's Word is the medicine that heals and the salvation of souls.

PRAYER[1]

Father, in the name of Jesus, forgive us as a nation for disregarding the sanctity of life. We recognize that each person is

---

[1] This prayer can also be prayed in the singular "I" form by the individual person involved in abortion.

THOSE INVOLVED IN ABORTION

uniquely created by You, Lord — marvelously made! You know each one inside and out; You know every bone in the body. You know exactly how we are made, bit by bit, and how we are sculpted from nothing into something. All the stages of a life are spread out before You, and the days are prepared before a child even lives one day. Since we now see clearly, we value the life You give.

Father, each of us is an open book to You; even from a distance, You know what we are thinking. We are never out of Your sight. When we look back, we realize that You were there. You were present when we put to death the being/beings to whom You gave life.

Lord, we repent of our sin and the sin of our nation. Be merciful unto us, O Lord. We ask Your forgiveness, and You are faithful and just to forgive us and cleanse us from all unrighteousness.

Unless Your law had been our delight, we would have perished in our affliction. We will never forget Your precepts [how can we?], for it is by them You have quickened us (granted us life).

We are ready to halt and fall; our pain and sorrow are continually before us. For we do confess our guilt and iniquity; we are filled with sorrow for our sin.

So [instead of further rebuke, now] we desire rather to turn and be [graciously] forgiven and comforted and encouraged to keep us from being overwhelmed by excessive sorrow and despair.

We look to Jesus as our Savior and Consolation and welcome His peace and completeness to our souls. We cannot bring our child/children back again; we shall go to them; they will not return to us.

We are awaiting and looking for the [fulfillment, the realization of our] blessed hope, even the glorious appearing of our great God and Savior, Christ Jesus (the Messiah, the Anointed One).

In His name we pray, amen.

Scripture References

Psalm 139:14-16 MESSAGE	Psalm 119:92,93 AMP
Psalm 38:17,18 AMP	2 Corinthians 2:7 AMP
Psalm 139:2-5 MESSAGE	2 Samuel 12:23 AMP
1 John 1:9	Titus 2:13 AMP

$\mathscr{A}$n AIDS Patient

I.
PRAYER FOR THE CHILD OF GOD

$\mathscr{F}$ather, You sent Jesus to bind up _____'s heartaches and to heal his/her emotional and physical pain. The Bible says that You sent Your Word to heal him/her and to deliver _____ from all his/her destructions.

Lord, we believe; help our unbelief. We ask You to give _____ a spirit of wisdom and revelation [of insight into mysteries and secrets] in the [deep and intimate] knowledge of Jesus, the Messiah.

Father, as _____ grows in grace and the knowledge of the Lord Jesus Christ, help him/her to receive all the spiritual blessings given by You. Thank You for giving him/her peace that the world cannot take away.

Lord, Your Son, Jesus, gave His life for _____. He/she has received Him as his/her Lord and is born again, desiring to give the glory to You and to continue to fellowship with Your family. Jesus lives in his/her heart, and he/she loves You and loves others as he/she loves himself/herself. Thank You that _____ finds plenty of support from the Body of Christ so that he/she will find encouragement, edification, and comfort.

Heavenly Father, in Your mercy strengthen _____ and help him/her with his/her physical problems. Let him/her be aware that he/she is not alone, for there is nothing that can separate him/her from the love of Christ — not pain or stress or persecution. He/she will come to the top of every circumstance or trial through Jesus' love.

Father, _____ is trusting in You and doing good; so shall he/she dwell in the land and feed surely on Your faithfulness, and truly he/she shall be fed. _____ delights himself/herself also in You, and You will give him/her the desires and secret petitions of his/her heart. We ask You to give _____ the grace to commit his/her way to You, trusting in You, and You will bring it to pass.

Help _____ to enter into Your rest, Lord, and to wait for You without fretting himself/herself. May he/she cease from unrighteous anger and wrath.

Father, You have not given _____ a spirit of fear, but of power and of love and of a sound mind. Neither shall he/she be confounded and depressed. You have given him/her beauty for ashes, the oil of joy for mourning, and the garment of praise for the spirit of heaviness, that You might be glorified.

The chastisement [needful to obtain] _____'s peace and wellbeing was upon Jesus, and with the stripes [that wounded] Him, he/she was healed and made whole.

As Your child, Father, _____ has a joyful and confident hope of eternal salvation. This hope will never disappoint or delude him/her, for Your love has been poured out in his/her heart through the Holy Spirit Who has been given to him/her.

In the name of Jesus, amen.

Scripture References

Luke 4:18 AMP	Romans 8:35-37
Psalm 107:20	2 Corinthians 2:14
Mark 9:24	Psalm 37:3-5,7,8 AMP
Ephesians 1:17 AMP	2 Timothy 1:7
2 Peter 3:18	Isaiah 54:4 AMP
Ephesians 1:3	Isaiah 61:3
John 14:27	Isaiah 53:5 AMP
John 3:3	Romans 5:4,5 AMP
John 13:34	

II.
PRAYER FOR ONE WHO DOES NOT KNOW JESUS AS LORD

Thank You for calling us to be Your agents of intercession for _____. By the grace of God we will build up the wall and stand in the gap before You for _____ that he/she might be spared from eternal destruction.

Lord, we acknowledge Your Son, Jesus, as the Lamb of God Who takes away _____'s sins. Thank You for sending the Holy Spirit Who goes forth to convince and convict _____ of sin, righteousness, and judgment. Your kindness leads him/her to repent (to change his/her mind and inner man to accept Your will). You are the One Who delivers _____ and draws him/her to Yourself out of the control and dominion of darkness and transfers him/her into the Kingdom of the Son of Your love.

Lord of the harvest, we ask You to thrust the perfect laborer into _____'s path, a laborer to share Your Gospel in a special way so that he/she will listen and understand it. We believe that he/she will come to his/her senses — come out of the snare of the devil who has held him/her captive — and make Jesus the Lord of his/her life.

Father, as _____ grows in grace and the knowledge of the Lord Jesus Christ, help him/her to receive all the spiritual blessings given by You. Thank You for giving him/her peace that the world cannot take away.

Heavenly Father, in Your mercy strengthen _____ and help him/her with his/her physical problems. Let him/her be aware that he/she is not alone, for there is nothing that can separate him/her from the love of Christ — not pain or stress or persecution. He/she will come to the top of every circumstance or trial through Jesus' love.

Help _____ to enter into Your rest and to wait for You without fretting himself/herself. May he/she cease from unrighteous anger and wrath.

Father, You sent Jesus to bind up _____'s heartaches and to heal his/her emotional and physical pain. The Bible says that You sent Your Word to heal him/her and to deliver _____ from all his/her destructions. We ask You to give him/her a spirit of wisdom and revelation [of insight into mysteries, and secrets] in the [deep and intimate] knowledge of Jesus, the Messiah.

The chastisement [needful to obtain] _____'s peace and wellbeing was upon Jesus, and with the stripes that wounded Him, he/she was healed and made whole. As Your child, Father,

_____ has a joyful and confident hope of eternal salvation. This hope will never disappoint or delude him/her, for Your love has been poured out in his/her heart through the Holy Spirit Who has been given to him/her.

In the name of Jesus, amen.

Scripture References

Ezekiel 22:30 AMP	John 14:27
John 1:29	Romans 8:35-37
John 16:8-12 AMP	2 Corinthians 2:14
Romans 2:4 AMP	Psalm 37:7,8 AMP
Colossians 1:13 AMP	Luke 4:18 AMP
Matthew 9:38 AMP	Psalm 107:20
2 Timothy 2:26 NIV	Ephesians 1:17 AMP
2 Peter 3:18	Isaiah 53:5 AMP
Ephesians 1:3	Romans 5:5 AMP

$\mathcal{P}$rison Inmates

INTRODUCTION

$\mathcal{T}$he following prayers were written in response to letters from prisoners requesting prayers to be used by them in special circumstances. They may be prayed in agreement with a prayer partner or intercessor.

I.
PRAYER FOR AN INMATE'S
PROTECTION AND FUTURE

Father, I pray that I may become useful and helpful and kind to those around me, tenderhearted (compassionate, understanding, loving-hearted), forgiving others [readily and freely], as You, Father, in Christ forgave me my sins.

It is my desire to be an imitator of You, Lord. With the Holy Spirit as my Helper, I will [copy You and follow Your example], as a well-beloved child [imitates his/her father]. I purpose to walk in love [esteeming and delighting in others], as Christ loves me. As I attend to Your Word, I depend on Your Holy Spirit to teach me to live a life of victory in Christ Jesus my Lord.

In the name of Jesus, I am Your child. I am dwelling in the secret place of the Most High and abiding under the shadow of the Almighty. I say of You, Lord, that You are my Refuge and Fortress: my God; in You will I trust. You cover me with Your feathers, and under Your wings shall I trust: Your truth is my shield and buckler.

Because You are my Lord, my Refuge and Habitation, no evil shall befall me — no accident will overtake me — neither shall any plague or calamity come near me. You give Your angels [special] charge over me, to keep me in all of my ways [of obedience and service].

Thank You for hearing my prayer. You are with me in trouble; You deliver me and satisfy me with long life and show me Your salvation.

In Jesus' name, amen.

Scripture References

Ephesians 4:32 AMP	Psalm 91:9-11 AMP
Ephesians 5:1,2 AMP	Psalm 91:15,16
Psalm 91:1,2,4	

II.
PRAYER FOR AN INCARCERATED PARENT AND HIS/HER CHILDREN

Listen, God, I'm calling at the top of my lungs: "Be good to me! Answer me!"

When my heart whispered, "Seek God," my whole being replied, "I'm seeking Him!" Don't hide from me now.

I didn't know it before, but I know now that You've always been right here for me; don't turn Your back on me now. Don't throw me out and don't abandon me; You've always kept the door open.

Thank You for sending ministers to tell me about You and Your love for me.

My children say they hate me; they feel abandoned and alone. Even though their father/mother walked away from them, I ask You, Father, to take them in.

Lord of the harvest, I ask You to send laborers of the harvest and wise counselors to my children, who have been hurt by my actions.

Father, I have sinned against You, against my children, and against myself. I repent of the sins that have so easily beset me and ask You to forgive me.

Father, Your Word assures me that You forgive me and cleanse me from all unrighteousness. Thank You for forgiving me. I pray that my children will be willing to forgive me so that we may be a family again.

In the name of Jesus, I cast the care of my children on You and rest in the assurance that You will perfect that which concerns me. I put on the garment of praise and delight myself in You. Teach me Your ways, O Lord, that I may walk and live in Your truth.

In Jesus' name, amen.

Scripture References

Psalm 27:7-10 MESSAGE	Isaiah 61:3
Matthew 9:38	Psalm 37:4
1 John 1:9	Psalm 86:11 AMP
1 Peter 5:7	Hebrews 12:1
Psalm 138:8	

III.
PRAYER FOR AN INMATE TO PRAY
FOR HIS/HER FAMILY AND CAREGIVER

Father, I have sinned against You, against my children, and against myself. I repent of the sins that have so easily beset me and ask for Your forgiveness.

Father, Your Word assures me that You forgive me and cleanse me from all unrighteousness. Thank You for forgiving me. I pray that my children will be willing to forgive me so that we may be a family again.

Thank You for the one who has assumed responsibility for my children while I am away. I pray that You will strengthen him/her and fill him/her with Your Spirit Who gives him/her great wisdom, ability, and skill in rearing the children You gave to me. I repent for failing to assume my responsibility to my children, and I ask You to reward the one who is taking care of them.

His/her mouth shall speak of wisdom; and the meditation of his/her heart shall be understanding. I thank You that he/she is in Christ Jesus, Who has been made unto him/her wisdom from You — his/her righteousness, holiness, and redemption. He/she is filled with the knowledge of Your will in all spiritual wisdom and understanding so that he/she may live a life worthy of You and may please You in every way, bearing fruit in every good work.

Father, I am responsible for my own actions, and I recognize that what I have done has hurt my entire family. Forgive me for dishonoring You, my family, my friends, and my children. Give me the grace to pay my debt and do my assigned work as unto You.

Help me to develop diligence and patience, giving myself to prayer, study, and meditation in Your Word.

Lord, there is violence within these walls, but I look to You. Hide me in the secret place of Your presence from the plots of others. Keep me secretly in Your pavilion from the strife of tongues.

In the name of Jesus I pray, amen.

Scripture References

1 John 1:9	Colossians 1:9,10 AMP
Psalm 49:3	Colossians 3:23,24
1 Corinthians 1:30	Psalm 31:20

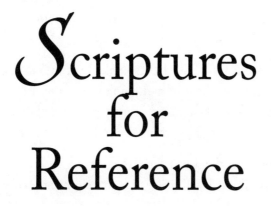

Scriptures for Reference

PART THREE

Genesis 1:1. In the beginning God created the heaven and the earth.

Genesis 1:2. And the earth was without form, and void; and darkness was upon the face of the deep. And the Spirit of God moved upon the face of the waters.

Genesis 1:26. And God said, Let us make man in our image, after our likeness: and let them have dominion over the fish of the sea, and over the fowl of the air, and over the cattle, and over all the earth, and over every creeping thing that creepeth upon the earth.

Genesis 2:18. And the Lord God said, It is not good that the man should be alone; I will make him an help meet for him.

Genesis 2:2. And on the seventh day God ended his work which he had made; and he rested on the seventh day from all his work which he had made.

Genesis 11:6. And the Lord said, Behold, the people is one, and they have all one language; and this they begin to do: and now nothing will be restrained from them, which they have imagined to do.

Genesis 15:1. After these things the word of the Lord came unto Abram in a vision, saying, Fear not, Abram: I am thy shield, and thy exceeding great reward.

Genesis 15:2. And Abram said, Lord God, what wilt thou give me, seeing I go childless, and the steward of my house is this Eliezer of Damascus?

Genesis 15:8. And he said, Lord God, whereby shall I know that I shall inherit it?

Genesis 22:14. And Abraham called the name of that place Jehovah-jireh: as it is said to this day, In the mount of the Lord it shall be seen.

SCRIPTURES FOR REFERENCE

Genesis 41:39. And Pharaoh said unto Joseph, Forasmuch as God hath shewed thee all this, there is none so discreet and wise as thou art:

Genesis 41:40. Thou shalt be over my house, and according unto thy word shall all my people be ruled: only in the throne will I be greater than thou.

Genesis 41:41. And Pharaoh said unto Joseph, See, I have set thee over all the land of Egypt.

Genesis 49:22. Joseph is a fruitful bough, even a fruitful bough by a well; whose branches run over the wall:

Genesis 49:23. The archers have sorely grieved him, and shot at him, and hated him:

Genesis 49:24. But his bow abode in strength, and the arms of his hands were made strong by the hands of the mighty God of Jacob; (from thence is the shepherd, the stone of Israel).

Genesis 49:25. Even by the God of thy father, who shall help thee; and by the Almighty, who shall bless thee with blessings of heaven above, blessings of the deep that lieth under, blessings of the breasts, and of the womb:

Genesis 49:26. The blessings of thy father have prevailed above the blessings of my progenitors unto the utmost bound of the everlasting hills: they shall be on the head of Joseph, and on the crown of the head of him that was separate from his brethren.

Genesis 50:20. But as for you, ye thought evil against me; but God meant it unto good, to bring to pass, as it is this day, to save much people alive.

Exodus 6:3. And I appeared unto Abraham, unto Isaac, and unto Jacob, by the name of God Almighty, but by my name Jehovah was I not known to them.

Exodus 6:4. And I have also established my covenant with them, to give them the land of Canaan, the land of their pilgrimage, wherein they were strangers.

Exodus 12:7. And they shall take of the blood, and strike it on the two side posts and on the upper door post of the houses, wherein they shall eat it.

Exodus 12:13. And the blood shall be to you for a token upon the houses where ye are: and when I see the blood, I will pass over you, and the plague shall not be upon you to destroy you, when I smite the land of Egypt.

Exodus 15:2. The Lord is my strength and song, and he is become my salvation: he is my God, and I will prepare him an habitation; my father's God, and I will exalt him.

Exodus 15:13. Thou in thy mercy hast led forth the people which thou hast redeemed: thou hast guided them in thy strength unto thy holy habitation.

Exodus 15:23. And when they came to Marah, they could not drink of the waters of Marah, for they were bitter: therefore the name of it was called Marah.

Exodus 15:24. And the people murmured against Moses, saying, What shall we drink?

Exodus 15:25. And he cried unto the Lord; and the Lord shewed him a tree, which when he had cast into the waters, the waters were made sweet: there he made for them a statute and an ordinance, and there he proved them.

Exodus 15:26. And said, If thou wilt diligently hearken to the voice of the Lord thy God, and wilt do that which is right in his sight, and wilt give ear to his commandments, and keep all his statutes, I will put none of these diseases upon thee, which I have brought upon the Egyptians: for I am the Lord that healeth thee.

Exodus 17:15. And Moses built an altar, and called the name of it Jehovah-nissi.

Exodus 31:3.And I have filled him with the spirit of God, in wisdom, and in understanding, and in knowledge, and in all manner of workmanship.

Exodus 31:4. To devise cunning works, to work in gold, and in silver, and in brass.

Exodus 33:14. And he said, My presence shall go with thee, and I will give thee rest.

Exodus 35:5. Take ye from among you an offering unto the Lord: whosoever is of a willing heart, let him bring it, an offering of the Lord; gold, and silver, and brass.

Exodus 35:33. And in the cutting of stones, to set them, and in carving of wood, to make any manner of cunning work.

Leviticus 17:11. For the life of the flesh is in the blood: and I have given it to you upon the altar to make an atonement for your souls: for it is the blood that maketh an atonement for the soul.

Leviticus 20:7. Sanctify yourselves therefore, and be ye holy: for I am the Lord your God.

Leviticus 20:8. And ye shall keep my statutes, and do them: I am the Lord which sanctify you.

Numbers 6:25. The Lord make his face shine upon thee, and be gracious unto thee.

Deuteronomy 6:1. Now these are the commandments, the statutes, and the judgments, which the Lord your God commanded to teach you, that ye might do them in the land whither ye go to possess it.

Deuteronomy 6:2. That thou mightest fear the Lord thy God, to keep all his statutes and his commandments, which I command thee, thou, and thy son, and thy son's son, all the days of thy life; and that thy days may be prolonged.

Deuteronomy 6:3. Hear therefore, O Israel, and observe to do it; that it may be well with thee, and that *ye may* increase mightily, as the Lord God of thy fathers hath promised thee, in the land that floweth with milk and honey.

Deuteronomy 6:4. Hear, O Israel: The Lord our God is one Lord.

Deuteronomy 6:5. And thou shalt love the Lord thy God with all thine heart, and with all thy soul, and with all thy might.

Deuteronomy 6:7. And thou shalt teach them diligently unto thy children, and shalt talk of them when thou sittest in thine house, and when thou walkest by the way, and when thou liest down, and when thou risest up.

Deuteronomy 8:17. And thou say in thine heart, My power and the might of mine hand hath gotten me this wealth.

Deuteronomy 8:18. But thou shalt remember the Lord thy God: for it is he that giveth thee power to get wealth, that he may establish his covenant which he sware unto thy fathers, as it is this day.

Deuteronomy 8:19. And it shall be, if thou do at all forget the Lord thy God, and walk after other gods, and serve them, and worship them, I testify against you this day that ye shall surely perish.

Deuteronomy 26:1. And it shall be, when thou art come in unto the land which the Lord thy God giveth thee for an inheritance, and possessest it, and dwellest therein.

Deuteronomy 26:3. And thou shalt go unto the priest that shall be in those days, and say unto him, I profess this day unto the Lord thy God, that I am come unto the country which the Lord sware unto our fathers for to give us.

Deuteronomy 26:8. And the Lord brought us forth out of Egypt with a mighty hand, and with an outstretched arm, and with great terribleness, and with signs, and with wonders.

Deuteronomy 26:10. And now, behold, I have brought the firstfruits of the land, which thou, O Lord, hast given me. And thou shalt set it before the Lord thy God, and worship before the Lord thy God:

Deuteronomy 26:11. And thou shalt rejoice in every good thing which the Lord thy God hath given unto thee, and unto thine house, thou, and the Levite, and the stranger that is among you.

Deuteronomy 26:14. I have not eaten thereof in my mourning, neither have I taken away ought thereof for any unclean use, nor given ought thereof for the dead: but I have hearkened to the voice of the Lord my God, and have done according to all that thou hast commanded me.

Deuteronomy 26:15. Look down from thy holy habitation, from heaven, and bless thy people Israel, and the land which thou hast given us, as thou swarest unto our fathers, a land that floweth with milk and honey.

Deuteronomy 28:3. Blessed shalt thou be in the city, and blessed shalt thou be in the field.

Deuteronomy 28:6. Blessed shalt thou be when thou comest in, and blessed shalt thou be when thou goest out.

Deuteronomy 28:10. And all people of the earth shall see that thou art called by the name of the Lord; and they shall be afraid of thee.

Deuteronomy 28:11. And the Lord shall make thee plenteous in goods, in the fruit of thy body, and in the fruit of thy cattle, and in the fruit of thy ground, in the land which the Lord sware unto thy fathers to give thee.

Deuteronomy 28:12. The Lord shall open unto thee his good treasure, the heaven to give the rain unto thy land in his season, and to bless all the work of thine hand: and thou shalt lend unto many nations, and thou shalt not borrow.

Deuteronomy 28:13. Then thou shalt say before the Lord thy God, I have brought away the hallowed things out of mine house, and also have given them unto the Levite, and unto the stranger, to the fatherless, and to the widow, according to all thy commandments which thou hast commanded me: I have not transgressed thy commandments, neither have I forgotten them.

Deuteronomy 28:32. Thy sons and thy daughters shall be given unto another people, and thine eyes shall look, and fail with longing for them all the day long: and there shall be no might in thine hand.

Deuteronomy 28:41. Thou shalt beget sons and daughters, but thou shalt not enjoy them; for they shall go into captivity.

SCRIPTURES FOR REFERENCE

Deuteronomy 30:19. I call heaven and earth to record this day against you, that I have set before you life and death, blessing and cursing: therefore choose life, that both thou and thy seed may live:

Deuteronomy 30:20. That thou mayest love the Lord thy God, and that thou mayest obey his voice, and that thou mayest cleave unto him: for he is thy life, and the length of thy days: that thou mayest dwell in the land which the Lord sware unto thy fathers, to Abraham, to Isaac, and to Jacob, to give them.

Joshua 1:5. There shall not any man be able to stand before thee all the days of thy life: as I was with Moses, so I will be with thee: I will not fail thee, nor forsake thee.

Joshua 1:7. Only be thou strong and very courageous, that thou mayest observe to do according to all the law, which Moses my servant commanded thee: turn not from it to the right hand or to the left, that thou mayest prosper whithersoever thou goest.

Joshua 1:8. This book of the law shall not depart out of thy mouth; but thou shalt meditate therein day and night, that thou mayest observe to do according to all that is written therein: for then thou shalt make thy way prosperous, and then thou shalt have good success.

Joshua 24:15. And if it seem evil unto you to serve the Lord, choose you this day whom ye will serve; whether the gods which your fathers served that were on the other side of the flood, or the gods of the Amorites, in whose land ye dwell: but as for me and my house, we will serve the Lord.

Judges 6:24. Then Gideon built an altar there unto the Lord, and called it Jehovah-shalom: unto this day it is yet in Ophrah of the Abi-ezrites.

1 Samuel 15:22. And Samuel said, Hath the Lord as great delight in burnt offerings and sacrifices, as in obeying the voice of the Lord? Behold, to obey is better than sacrifice, and to hearken than the fat of rams.

1 Samuel 15:23. For rebellion is as the sin of witchcraft, and stubbornness is as iniquity and idolatry. Because thou hast rejected the word of the Lord, he hath also rejected thee from being king.

2 Samuel 12:23. But now he is dead, wherefore should I fast? can I bring him back again? I shall go to him, but he shall not return to me.

1 Kings 3:9. Give therefore thy servant an understanding heart to judge thy people, that I may discern between good and bad: for who is able to judge this thy so great a people?

1 Kings 4:29. And God gave Solomon wisdom and understanding exceeding much, and largeness of heart, even as the sand that is on the sea shore.

1 Kings 8:56. Blessed be the Lord, that hath given rest unto his people Israel, according to all that he promised: there hath not failed one word of all his good promise, which he promised by the hand of Moses his servant.

1 Kings 8:59. And let these my words, wherewith I have made supplication before the Lord, be nigh unto the Lord our God day and night, that he maintain the cause of his servant, and the cause of his people Israel at all times, as the matter shall require:

1 Kings 8:60. That all the people of the earth may know that the Lord is God, and that there is none else.

1 Kings 18:25. And Elijah said unto the prophets of Baal, Choose you one bullock for yourselves, and dress it first; for ye are many; and call on the name of your gods, but put no fire under.

1 Kings 18:26. And they took the bullock which was given them, and they dressed it, and called on the name of Baal from morning even until noon, saying, O Baal, hear us. But there was no voice, nor any that answered. And they leaped upon the altar which was made.

1 Kings 18:27. And it came to pass at noon, that Elijah mocked them, and said, Cry aloud: for he is a god; either he is talking, or he is pursuing, or he is in a journey, or peradventure he sleepeth, and must be awaked.

1 Kings 18:28. And they cried aloud, and cut themselves after their manner with knives and lancets, till the blood gushed out upon them.

1 Kings 18:29. And it came to pass, when midday was past, and they prophesied until the time of the offering of the evening sacrifice, that there was neither voice, nor any to answer, nor any that regarded.

1 Chronicles 16:11. Seek the Lord and his strength, seek his face continually.

1 Chronicles 29:11. Thine, O Lord, is the greatness, and the power, and the glory, and the victory, and the majesty: for all that is in the heaven and in the earth is thine; thine is the kingdom, O Lord, and thou art exalted as head above all.

2 Chronicles 15:7. Be ye strong therefore, and let not your hands be weak: for your work shall be rewarded.

2 Chronicles 16:9. For the eyes of the Lord run to and fro throughout the whole earth, to shew himself strong in the behalf of them whose heart is perfect toward him. Herein thou hast done foolishly: therefore from henceforth thou shalt have wars.

Nehemiah 2:3. And said unto the king, Let the king live for ever: why should not my countenance be sad, when the city, the place of my fathers' sepulchres, lieth waste, and the gates thereof are consumed with fire?

Nehemiah 8:10. Then he said unto them, Go your way, eat the fat, and drink the sweet, and send portions unto them for whom nothing is prepared: for this day is holy unto our Lord: neither be ye sorry; for the joy of the Lord is your strength.

Esther 2:15. Now when the turn of Esther, the daughter of Abihail the uncle of Mordecai, who had taken her for his daughter, was come to go in unto the king, she required nothing but what Hegai the king's chamberlain, the keeper of the women, appointed. And Esther obtained favour in the sight of all them that looked upon her.

Esther 2:17. And the king loved Esther above all the women, and she obtained grace and favour in his sight more than all the virgins; so that he set the royal crown upon her head, and made her queen instead of Vashti.

Esther 4:14. For if thou altogether holdest thy peace at this time, then shall there enlargement and deliverance arise to the Jews from another place; but thou and thy father's house shall be destroyed: and who knoweth whether thou art come to the kingdom for such a time as this?

Job 22:30. He shall deliver the island of the innocent: and it is delivered by the pureness of thine hands.

Job 38:36. Who hath put wisdom in the inward parts? or who hath given understanding to the heart?

SCRIPTURES FOR REFERENCE

Psalm 1:1. Blessed is the man that walketh not in the counsel of the ungodly, nor standeth in the way of sinners, nor sitteth in the seat of the scornful.

Psalm 1:2. But his delight is in the law of the Lord; and in his law doth he meditate day and night.

Psalm 1:3. And he shall be like a tree planted by the rivers of water, that bringeth forth his fruit in his season; his leaf also shall not wither; and whatsoever he doeth shall prosper.

Psalm 1:4. The ungodly are not so: but are like the chaff which the wind driveth away.

Psalm 1:5. Therefore the ungodly shall not stand in the judgment, nor sinners in the congregation of the righteous.

Psalm 1:6. For the Lord knoweth the way of the righteous: way of the ungodly shall perish.

Psalm 2:8. Ask of me, and I shall give thee the heathen for thine inheritance, and the uttermost parts of the earth for thy possession.

Psalm 3:3. But thou, O Lord, art a shield for me; my glory, and the lifter up of mine head.

Psalm 3:4. I cried unto the Lord with my voice, and he heard me out of his holy hill. Selah.

Psalm 3:5. I laid me down and slept; I awaked; for the Lord sustained me.

Psalm 4:8. I will both lay me down in peace, and sleep: for thou, Lord, only makest me dwell in safety.

Psalm 5:12. For thou, Lord, wilt bless the righteous; with favour wilt thou compass him as with a shield.

Psalm 8:1. O Lord our Lord, how excellent is thy name in all the earth! who hast set thy glory above the heavens.

Psalm 8:2. Out of the mouth of babes and sucklings hast thou ordained strength because of thine enemies, that thou mightest still the enemy and the avenger.

Psalm 8:5. For thou hast made him a little lower than the angels, and hast crowned him with glory and honour.

Psalm 9:1. I will praise thee, O Lord, with my whole heart; I will shew forth all thy marvellous works.

Psalm 9:2. I will be glad and rejoice in thee: I will sing praise to thy name, O thou most High.

Psalm 9:3. When mine enemies are turned back, they shall fall and perish at thy presence.

Psalm 9:9. The Lord also will be a refuge for the oppressed, a refuge in times of trouble.

Psalm 9:10. And they that know thy name will put their trust in thee: for thou, Lord, hast not forsaken them that seek thee.

Psalm 16:11. Thou wilt shew me the path of life: in thy presence is fulness of joy; at thy right hand there are pleasures for evermore.

Psalm 18:30. As for God, his way is perfect: the word of the Lord is tried: he is a buckler to all those that trust in him.

Psalm 19:14. Let the words of my mouth, and the meditation of my heart, be acceptable in thy sight, O Lord, my strength, and my redeemer.

Psalm 22:2. O my God, I cry in the daytime, but thou hearest not; and in the night season, and am not silent.

SCRIPTURES FOR REFERENCE

Psalm 23:1. The Lord is my shepherd; I shall not want.

Psalm 23:2. He maketh me to lie down in green pastures: he leadeth me beside the still waters.

Psalm 23:3. He restoreth my soul: he leadeth me in the paths of righteousness for his name's sake.

Psalm 23:4. Yea, though I walk through the valley of the shadow of death, I will fear no evil: for thou art with me; thy rod and thy staff they comfort me.

Psalm 23:5. Thou preparest a table before me in the presence of mine enemies: thou anointest my head with oil; my cup runneth over.

Psalm 23:6. Surely goodness and mercy shall follow me all the days of my life: and I will dwell in the house of the Lord for ever.

Psalm 25:1. Unto thee, O Lord, do I lift up my soul.

Psalm 25:2. O my God, I trust in thee: let me not be ashamed, let not mine enemies triumph over me.

Psalm 27:1. The Lord is my light and my salvation; whom shall I fear? the Lord is the strength of my life; of whom shall I be afraid?

Psalm 27:2. When the wicked, even mine enemies and my foes, came upon me to eat up my flesh, they stumbled and fell.

Psalm 27:3. Though an host should encamp against me, my heart shall not fear: though war should rise against me, in this will I be confident.

Psalm 27:4. One thing have I desired of the Lord, that will I seek after; that I may dwell in the house of the Lord all the days of my life, to behold the beauty of the Lord, and to inquire in his temple.

Psalm 27:5. For in the time of trouble he shall hide me in his pavilion: in the secret of his tabernacle shall he hide me; he shall set me up upon a rock.

Psalm 27:6. And now shall mine head be lifted up above mine enemies round about me: therefore will I offer in his tabernacle sacrifices of joy; I will sing, yea, I will sing praises unto the Lord.

Psalm 27:7. Hear, O Lord, when I cry with my voice: have mercy also upon me, and answer me.

Psalm 27:8. When thou saidst, Seek ye my face; my heart said unto thee, Thy face, Lord, will I seek.

Psalm 27:9. Hide not thy face far from me; put not thy servant away in anger: thou hast been my help; leave me not, neither forsake me, O God of my salvation.

Psalm 27:10. When my father and my mother forsake me, then the Lord will take me up.

Psalm 27:13. I had fainted, unless I had believed to see the goodness of the Lord in the land of the living.

Psalm 27:14. Wait on the Lord: be of good courage, and he shall strengthen thine heart: wait, I say, on the Lord.

Psalm 30:4. Sing unto the Lord, O ye saints of his, and give thanks at the remembrance of his holiness.

Psalm 30:5. For his anger endureth but a moment; in his favour is life: weeping may endure for a night, but joy cometh in the morning.

Psalm 31:20. Thou shalt hide them in the secret of thy presence from the pride of man: thou shalt keep them secretly in a pavilion from the strife of tongues.

Psalm 31:22. For I said in my haste, I am cut off from before thine eyes: nevertheless thou heardest the voice of my supplications when I cried unto thee.

Psalm 31:23. O love the Lord, all ye his saints: for the Lord preserveth the faithful, and plentifully rewardeth the proud doer.

Psalm 31:24. Be of good courage, and he shall strengthen your heart, all ye that hope in the Lord.

Psalm 32:1. Blessed is he whose transgression is forgiven, whose sin is covered.

Psalm 32:2. Blessed is the man unto whom the Lord imputeth not iniquity, and in whose spirit there is no guile.

Psalm 32:3. When I kept silence, my bones waxed old through my roaring all the day long.

Psalm 32:4. For day and night thy hand was heavy upon me: my moisture is turned into the drought of summer. Selah.

Psalm 32:5. I acknowledged my sin unto thee, and mine iniquity have I not hid. I said, I will confess my transgressions unto the Lord; and thou forgavest the iniquity of my sin. Selah.

Psalm 32:6. For this shall every one that is godly pray unto thee in a time when thou mayest be found: surely in the floods of great waters they shall not come nigh unto him.

Psalm 32:7. Thou art my hiding place; thou shalt preserve me from trouble; thou shalt compass me about with songs of deliverance. Selah.

Psalm 32:8. I will instruct thee and teach thee in the way which thou shalt go: I will guide thee with mine eye.

Psalm 33:11. The counsel of the Lord standeth for ever, the thoughts of his heart to all generations.

Psalm 33:12. Blessed is the nation whose God is the Lord; and the people whom he hath chosen for his own inheritance.

Psalm 34:3. O magnify the Lord with me, and let us exalt his name together.

Psalm 34:7. The angel of the Lord encampeth round about them that fear him, and delivereth them.

Psalm 34:10. The young lions do lack, and suffer hunger: but they that seek the Lord shall not want any good thing.

Psalm 34:14. Depart from evil, and do good; seek peace, and pursue it.

Psalm 34:17. The righteous cry, and the Lord heareth, and delivereth them out of all their troubles.

Psalm 34:18. The Lord is nigh unto them that are of a broken heart; and saveth such as be of a contrite spirit.

Psalm 34:19. Many are the afflictions of the righteous: but the Lord delivereth him out of them all.

Psalm 34:20. He keepeth all his bones: not one of them is broken.

Psalm 35:27. Let them shout for joy, and be glad, that favour my righteous cause: yea, let them say continually, Let the Lord be magnified, which hath pleasure in the prosperity of his servant.

Psalm 35:28. And my tongue shall speak of thy righteousness and of thy praise all the day long.

Psalm 37:4. Delight thyself also in the Lord; and he shall give thee the desires of thine heart.

Psalm 37:5. Commit thy way unto the Lord; trust also in him; and he shall bring it to pass.

Psalm 37:6. And he shall bring forth thy righteousness as the light, and thy judgment as the noonday.

Psalm 37:7. Rest in the Lord, and wait patiently for him: fret not thyself because of him who prospereth in his way, because of the man who bringeth wicked devices to pass.

Psalm 37:23. The steps of a good man are ordered by the Lord: and he delighteth in his way.

Psalm 37:24. Though he fall, he shall not be utterly cast down: for the Lord upholdeth him with his hand.

Psalm 37:25. I have been young, and now am old; yet have I not seen the righteous forsaken, nor his seed begging bread.

Psalm 38:17. For the arms of the wicked shall be broken: but the Lord upholdeth the righteous.

Psalm 38:18. The Lord knoweth the days of the upright: and their inheritance shall be for ever.

Psalm 40:3. And he hath put a new song in my mouth, even praise unto our God: many shall see it, and fear, and shall trust in the Lord.

Psalm 42:5. Why art thou cast down, O my soul? and why art thou disquieted in me? hope thou in God: for I shall yet praise him for the help of his countenance.

Psalm 42:11. Why art thou cast down, O my soul? and why art thou disquieted within me? hope thou in God: for I shall yet praise him, who is the health of my countenance, and my God.

Psalm 43:4. Then will I go unto the altar of God, unto God my exceeding joy: yea, upon the harp will I praise thee, O God my God.

Psalm 45:1. My heart is inditing a good matter: I speak of the things which I have made touching the king: my tongue is the pen of a ready writer.

Psalm 46:1. God is our refuge and strength, a very present help in trouble.

Psalm 49:3. My mouth shall speak of wisdom; and the meditation of my heart shall be of understanding.

Psalm 50:15. And call upon me in the day of trouble: I will deliver thee, and thou shalt glorify me.

Psalm 50:23. Whoso offereth praise glorifieth me: and to him that ordereth his conversation aright will I shew the salvation of God.

Psalm 51:6. Behold, thou desirest truth in the inward parts: and in the hidden part thou shalt make me to know wisdom.

Psalm 51:7. Purge me with hyssop, and I shall be clean: wash me, and I shall be whiter than snow.

Psalm 51:10. Create in me a clean heart, O God; and renew a right spirit within me.

Psalm 51:12. Restore unto me the joy of thy salvation; and uphold me with thy free spirit.

Psalm 51:13. Then will I teach transgressors thy ways; and sinners shall be converted unto thee.

Psalm 55:1. Give ear to my prayer, O God; and hide not thyself from my supplication.

SCRIPTURES FOR REFERENCE

Psalm 55:2. Attend unto me, and hear me: I mourn in my complaint, and make a noise.

Psalm 55:5. Fearfulness and trembling are come upon me, and horror hath overwhelmed me.

Psalm 55:6. And I said, Oh that I had wings like a dove! for then would I fly away, and be at rest.

Psalm 55:7. Lo, then would I wander far off, and remain in the wilderness. Selah.

Psalm 55:8. I would hasten my escape from the windy storm and tempest.

Psalm 55:9. Destroy, O Lord, and divide their tongues: for I have seen violence and strife in the city.

Psalm 55:10. Day and night they go about it upon the walls thereof: mischief also and sorrow are in the midst of it.

Psalm 55:11. Wickedness is in the midst thereof: deceit and guile depart not from her streets.

Psalm 55:12. For it was not an enemy that reproached me; then I could have borne it: neither was it he that hated me that did magnify himself against me; then I would have hid myself from him:

Psalm 55:13. But it was thou, a man mine equal, my guide, and mine acquaintance.

Psalm 55:14. We took sweet counsel together, and walked unto the house of God in company.

Psalm 55:16. As for me, I will call upon God; and the Lord shall save me.

Psalm 55:18. He hath delivered my soul in peace from the battle that was against me: for there were many with me.

Psalm 55:22. Cast thy burden upon the Lord, and he shall sustain thee: he shall never suffer the righteous to be moved.

Psalm 56:1. Be merciful unto me, O God: for man would swallow me up; he fighting daily oppresseth me.

Psalm 56:2. Mine enemies would daily swallow me up: for they be many that fight against me, O thou most High.

Psalm 56:3. What time I am afraid, I will trust in thee.

Psalm 56:4. In God I will praise his word, in God I have put my trust; I will not fear what flesh can do unto me.

Psalm 56:5. Every day they wrest my words: all their thoughts are against me for evil.

Psalm 56:8. Thou tellest my wanderings: put thou my tears into thy bottle: are they not in thy book?

Psalm 56:9. When I cry unto thee, then shall mine enemies turn back: this I know; for God is for me.

Psalm 56:13. For thou hast delivered my soul from death: wilt not thou deliver my feet from falling, that I may walk before God in the light of the living?

Psalm 57:1. Be merciful unto me, O God, be merciful unto me: for my soul trusteth in thee: yea, in the shadow of thy wings will I make my refuge, until these calamities be overpast.

Psalm 57:2. I will cry unto God most high; unto God that performeth all things for me.

Psalm 59:9. Because of his strength will I wait upon thee: for God is my defence.

SCRIPTURES FOR REFERENCE

Psalm 59:17. Unto thee, O my strength, will I sing: for God is my defence, and the God of my mercy.

Psalm 63:3. Because thy lovingkindness is better than life, my lips shall praise thee.

Psalm 63:4. Thus will I bless thee while I live: I will lift up my hands in thy name.

Psalm 63:5. My soul shall be satisfied as with marrow and fatness; and my mouth shall praise thee with joyful lips:

Psalm 68:11. The Lord gave the word: great was the company of those that published it.

Psalm 71:8. Let my mouth be filled with thy praise and with thy honour all the day.

Psalm 72:11. Yea, all kings shall fall down before him: all nations shall serve him.

Psalm 74:20. Have respect unto the covenant: for the dark places of the earth are full of the habitations of cruelty.

Psalm 84:11. For the Lord God is a sun and shield: the Lord will give grace and glory: no good thing will he withhold from them that walk uprightly.

Psalm 85:6. Wilt thou not revive us again: that thy people may rejoice in thee?

Psalm 85:7. Shew us thy mercy, O Lord, and grant us thy salvation.

Psalm 86:11. Teach me thy way, O Lord; I will walk in thy truth: unite my heart to fear thy name.

Psalm 86:12. I will praise thee, O Lord my God, with all my heart: and I will glorify thy name for evermore.

Psalm 91:1. He that dwelleth in the secret place of the most High shall abide under the shadow of the Almighty.

Psalm 91:2. I will say of the Lord, He is my refuge and my fortress: my God; in him will I trust.

Psalm 91:3. Surely he shall deliver thee from the snare of the fowler, and from the noisome pestilence.

Psalm 91:4. He shall cover thee with his feathers, and under his wings shalt thou trust: his truth shall be thy shield and buckler.

Psalm 91:5. Thou shalt not be afraid for the terror by night; nor for the arrow that flieth by day;

Psalm 91:6. Nor for the pestilence that walketh in darkness; nor for the destruction that wasteth at noonday.

Psalm 91:7. A thousand shall fall at thy side, and ten thousand at thy right hand; but it shall not come nigh thee.

Psalm 91:8. Only with thine eyes shalt thou behold and see the reward of the wicked.

Psalm 91:9. Because thou hast made the Lord, which is my refuge, even the most High, thy habitation;

Psalm 91:10. There shall no evil befall thee, neither shall any plague come nigh thy dwelling.

Psalm 91:11. For he shall give his angels charge over thee, to keep thee in all thy ways.

Psalm 91:12. They shall bear thee up in their hands, lest thou dash thy foot against a stone.

Psalm 91:13. Thou shalt tread upon the lion and adder: the young lion and the dragon shalt thou trample under feet.

Psalm 91:14. Because he hath set his love upon me, therefore will I deliver him: I will set him on high, because he hath known my name.

Psalm 91:15. He shall call upon me, and I will answer him: I will be with him in trouble; I will deliver him, and honour him.

Psalm 91:16. With long life will I satisfy him, and shew him my salvation.

Psalm 92:1. It is a good thing to give thanks unto the Lord, and to sing praises unto thy name, O most High.

Psalm 94:14. For the Lord will not cast off his people, neither will he forsake his inheritance.

Psalm 96:1. O sing unto the Lord a new song: sing unto the Lord, all the earth.

Psalm 98:1. O sing unto the Lord a new song; for he hath done marvellous things: his right hand, and his holy arm, hath gotten him the victory.

Psalm 98:2. The Lord hath made known his salvation: his righteousness hath he openly shewed in the sight of the heathen.

Psalm 100:1. Make a joyful noise unto the Lord, all ye lands.

Psalm 100:2. Serve the Lord with gladness: come before his presence with singing.

Psalm 100:3. Know ye that the Lord he is God: it is he that hath made us, and not we ourselves; we are his people, and the sheep of his pasture.

Psalm 100:4. Enter into his gates with thanksgiving, and into his courts with praise: be thankful unto him, and bless his name.

Psalm 100:5. For the Lord is good; his mercy is everlasting; and his truth endureth to all generations.

Psalm 101:3. I will set no wicked thing before mine eyes: I hate the work of them that turn aside; it shall not cleave to me.

Psalm 101:8. I will early destroy all the wicked of the land; that I may cut off all wicked doers from the city of the Lord.

Psalm 103:1. Bless the Lord, O my soul: and all that is within me, bless his holy name.

Psalm 103:2. Bless the Lord, O my soul, and forget not all his benefits.

Psalm 103:3. Who forgiveth all thine iniquities; who healeth all thy diseases.

Psalm 103:4. Who redeemeth thy life from destruction; who crowneth thee with lovingkindness and tender mercies.

Psalm 103:5. Who satisfieth thy mouth with good things; so that thy youth is renewed like the eagle's.

Psalm 103:20. Bless the Lord, ye his angels, that excel in strength, that do his commandments, hearkening unto the voice of his word.

Psalm 105:14. He suffered no man to do them wrong: yea, he reproved kings for their sakes.

Psalm 106:47. Save us, O Lord our God, and gather us from among the heathen, to give thanks unto thy holy name, and to triumph in thy praise.

Psalm 106:48. Blessed be the Lord God of Israel from everlasting to everlasting: and let all the people say, Amen. Praise ye the Lord.

Psalm 107:20. He sent his word, and healed them, and delivered them from their destructions.

Psalm 112:1. Praise ye the Lord. Blessed is the man that feareth the Lord, that delighteth greatly in his commandments.

Psalm 112:2. His seed shall be mighty upon earth: the generation of the upright shall be blessed.

Psalm 112:3. Wealth and riches shall be in his house: and his righteousness endureth for ever.

Psalm 112:4. Unto the upright there ariseth light in the darkness: he is gracious, and full of compassion, and righteous.

Psalm 112:5. A good man sheweth favour, and lendeth: he will guide his affairs with discretion.

Psalm 112:6. Surely he shall not be moved for ever: the righteous shall be in everlasting remembrance.

Psalm 112:7. He shall not be afraid of evil tidings: his heart is fixed, trusting in the Lord.

Psalm 112:8. His heart is established, he shall not be afraid, until he see his desire upon his enemies.

Psalm 112:9. He hath dispersed, he hath given to the poor; his righteousness endureth for ever; his horn shall be exalted with honour.

Psalm 112:10. The wicked shall see it, and be grieved; he shall gnash with his teeth, and melt away: the desire of the wicked shall perish.

Psalm 113:9. He maketh the barren woman to keep house, and to be a joyful mother of children. Praise ye the Lord.

Psalm 117:2. For his merciful kindness is great toward us: and the truth of the Lord endureth for ever. Praise ye the Lord.

Psalm 118:6. The Lord is on my side; I will not fear: what can man do unto me?

Psalm 118:24. This is the day which the Lord hath made; we will rejoice and be glad in it.

Psalm 119:9. Wherewithal shall a young man cleanse his way? by taking heed thereto according to thy word.

Psalm 119:10. With my whole heart have I sought thee: O let me not wander from thy commandments.

Psalm 119:11. Thy word have I hid in mine heart, that I might not sin against thee.

Psalm 119:16. I will delight myself in thy statutes: I will not forget thy word.

Psalm 119:17. Deal bountifully with thy servant, that I may live, and keep thy word.

Psalm 119:24. Thy testimonies also are my delight and my counsellors.

Psalm 119:25. My soul cleaveth unto the dust: quicken thou me according to thy word.

Psalm 119:28. My soul melteth for heaviness: strengthen thou me according unto thy word.

Psalm 119:36. Incline my heart unto thy testimonies, and not to covetousness.

Psalm 119:37. Turn away mine eyes from beholding vanity; and quicken thou me in thy way.

SCRIPTURES FOR REFERENCE

Psalm 119:40. Behold, I have longed after thy precepts: quicken me in thy righteousness.

Psalm 119:50. This is my comfort in my affliction: for thy word hath quickened me.

Psalm 119:66. Teach me good judgment and knowledge: for I have believed thy commandments.

Psalm 119:89. For ever, O Lord, thy word is settled in heaven.

Psalm 119:92. Unless thy law had been my delights, I should then have perished in mine affliction.

Psalm 119:93. I will never forget thy precepts: for with them thou hast quickened me.

Psalm 119:104. Through thy precepts I get understanding: therefore I hate every false way.

Psalm 119:105. Thy word is a lamp unto my feet, and a light unto my path.

Psalm 119:130. The entrance of thy words giveth light; it giveth understanding unto the simple.

Psalm 119:160. Thy word is true from the beginning: and every one of thy righteous judgments endureth for ever.

Psalm 119:165. Great peace have they which love thy law: and nothing shall offend them.

Psalm 121:1. I will lift up mine eyes unto the hills, from whence cometh my help.

Psalm 121:2. My help cometh from the Lord, which made heaven and earth.

Psalm 121:3. He will not suffer thy foot to be moved: he that keepeth thee will not slumber.

Psalm 121:4. Behold, he that keepeth Israel shall neither slumber nor sleep.

Psalm 121:5. The Lord is thy keeper: the Lord is thy shade upon thy right hand.

Psalm 121:6. The sun shall not smite thee by day, nor the moon by night.

Psalm 121:7. The Lord shall preserve thee from all evil: he shall preserve thy soul.

Psalm 121:8. The Lord shall preserve thy going out and thy coming in from this time forth, and even for evermore.

Psalm 122:6. Pray for the peace of Jerusalem: they shall prosper that love thee.

Psalm 122:7. Peace be within thy walls, and prosperity within thy palaces.

Psalm 122:8. For my brethren and companions' sakes, I will now say, Peace be within thee.

Psalm 122:9. Because of the house of the Lord our God I will seek thy good.

Psalm 123:4. Our soul is exceedingly filled with the scorning of those that are at ease, and with the contempt of the proud.

Psalm 127:1. Except the Lord build the house, they labour in vain that build it: except the Lord keep the city, the watchman waketh but in vain.

Psalm 127:2. It is vain for you to rise up early, to sit up late, to eat the bread of sorrows: for so he giveth his beloved sleep.

Psalm 127:3. Lo, children are an heritage of the Lord: and the fruit of the womb is his reward.

Psalm 128:3. Thy wife shall be as a fruitful vine by the sides of thine house: thy children like olive plants round about thy table.

Psalm 128:4. Behold, that thus shall the man be blessed that feareth the Lord.

Psalm 136:1. O give thanks unto the Lord; for he is good: for his mercy endureth for ever.

Psalm 136:25. Who giveth food to all flesh: for his mercy endureth for ever.

Psalm 138:2. I will worship toward thy holy temple, and praise thy name for thy lovingkindness and for thy truth: for thou hast magnified thy word above all thy name.

Psalm 138:8. The Lord will perfect that which concerneth me: thy mercy, O Lord, endureth for ever: forsake not the works of thine own hands.

Psalm 139:1. O Lord, thou hast searched me, and known me.

Psalm 139:2. Thou knowest my downsitting and mine uprising, thou understandest my thought afar off.

Psalm 139:3. Thou compassest my path and my lying down, and art acquainted with all my ways.

Psalm 139:4. For there is not a word in my tongue, but, lo, O Lord, thou knowest it altogether.

Psalm 139:5. Thou hast beset me behind and before, and laid thine hand upon me.

Psalm 139:6. Such knowledge is too wonderful for me; it is high, I cannot attain unto it.

Psalm 139:7. Whither shall I go from thy spirit? or whither shall I flee from thy presence?

Psalm 139:8. If I ascend up into heaven, thou art there: if I make my bed in hell, behold, thou art there.

Psalm 139:9. If I take the wings of the morning, and dwell in the uttermost parts of the sea;

Psalm 139:10. Even there shall thy hand lead me, and thy right hand shall hold me.

Psalm 139:11. If I say, Surely the darkness shall cover me; even the night shall be light about me.

Psalm 139:12. Yea, the darkness hideth not from thee; but the night shineth as the day: the darkness and the light are both alike to thee.

Psalm 139:13. For thou hast possessed my reins: thou hast covered me in my mother's womb.

Psalm 139:14. I will praise thee; for I am fearfully and wonderfully made: marvellous are thy works; and that my soul knoweth right well.

Psalm 139:15. My substance was not hid from thee, when I was made in secret, and curiously wrought in the lowest parts of the earth.

Psalm 139:16. Thine eyes did see my substance, yet being unperfect; and in thy book all my members were written, which in continuance were fashioned, when as yet there was none of them.

Psalm 139:17. How precious also are thy thoughts unto me, O God! how great is the sum of them!

Psalm 139:18. If I should count them, they are more in number than the sand: when I awake, I am still with thee.

Psalm 139:19. Surely thou wilt slay the wicked, O God: depart from me therefore, ye bloody men.

Psalm 139:20. For they speak against thee wickedly, and thine enemies take thy name in vain.

Psalm 139:21. Do not I hate them, O Lord, that hate thee? and am not I grieved with those that rise up against thee?

Psalm 139:22. I hate them with perfect hatred: I count them mine enemies.

Psalm 139:23. Search me, O God, and know my heart: try me, and know my thoughts:

Psalm 139:24. And see if there be any wicked way in me, and lead me in the way everlasting.

Psalm 141:2. Let my prayer be set forth before thee as incense; and the lifting up of my hands as the evening sacrifice.

Psalm 141:3. Set a watch, O Lord, before my mouth; keep the door of my lips.

Psalm 143:10. Teach me to do thy will; for thou art my God: thy spirit is good; lead me into the land of uprightness.

Psalm 144:7. Send thine hand from above; rid me, and deliver me out of great waters, from the hand of strange children;

Psalm 144:8. Whose mouth speaketh vanity, and their right hand is a right hand of falsehood.

Psalm 144:15. Happy is that people, that is in such a case: yea, happy is that people, whose God is the Lord.

Psalm 146:7. Which executeth judgment for the oppressed: which giveth food to the hungry. The Lord looseth the prisoners:

Psalm 146:8. The Lord openeth the eyes of the blind: the Lord raiseth them that are bowed down: the Lord loveth the righteous.

Psalm 147:1. Praise ye the Lord: for it is good to sing praises unto our God; for it is pleasant; and praise is comely.

Psalm 147:3. He healeth the broken in heart, and bindeth up their wounds.

Psalm 147:4. He telleth the number of the stars; he calleth them all by their names.

Psalm 147:5. Great is our Lord, and of great power: his understanding is infinite.

Psalm 147:6. The Lord lifteth up the meek: he casteth the wicked down to the ground.

Psalm 147:15. He sendeth forth his commandment upon earth: his word runneth very swiftly.

Psalm 149:1. Praise ye the Lord. Sing unto the Lord a new song, and his praise in the congregation of saints.

Psalm 149:5. Let the saints be joyful in glory: let them sing aloud upon their beds.

Psalm 150:1. Praise ye the Lord. Praise God in his sanctuary: praise him in the firmament of his power.

Psalm 150:2. Praise him for his mighty acts: praise him according to his excellent greatness.

Psalm 150:3. Praise him with the sound of the trumpet: praise him with the psaltery and harp.

Psalm 150:4. Praise him with the timbrel and dance: praise him with stringed instruments and organs.

Psalm 150:5. Praise him upon the loud cymbals: praise him upon the high sounding cymbals.

Psalm 150:6. Let every thing that hath breath praise the Lord. Praise ye the Lord.

Proverbs 1:2. To know wisdom and instruction; to perceive the words of understanding;

Proverbs 1:3. To receive the instruction of wisdom, justice, and judgment, and equity;

Proverbs 1:4. To give subtilty to the simple, to the young man knowledge and discretion.

Proverbs 1:5. A wise man will hear, and will increase learning; and a man of understanding shall attain unto wise counsels.

Proverbs 2:2. So that thou incline thine ear unto wisdom, and apply thine heart to understanding;

Proverbs 2:3. Yea, if thou criest after knowledge, and liftest up thy voice for understanding.

Proverbs 2:6. For the Lord giveth wisdom: out of his mouth cometh knowledge and understanding.

Proverbs 2:7. He layeth up sound wisdom for the righteous: he is a buckler to them that walk uprightly.

Proverbs 2:8. He keepeth the paths of judgment, and preserveth the way of his saints.

Proverbs 2:9. Then shalt thou understand righteousness, and judgment, and equity; yea, every good path.

Proverbs 2:10. When wisdom entereth into thine heart, and knowledge is pleasant unto thy soul;

Proverbs 2:11. Discretion shall preserve thee, understanding shall keep thee:

Proverbs 2:12. To deliver thee from the way of the evil man, from the man that speaketh froward things;

Proverbs 2:13. Who leave the paths of uprightness, to walk in the ways of darkness;

Proverbs 2:14. Who rejoice to do evil, and delight in the frowardness of the wicked;

Proverbs 2:15. Whose ways are crooked, and they froward in their paths.

Proverbs 2:21. For the upright shall dwell in the land, and the perfect shall remain in it.

Proverbs 2:22. But the wicked shall be cut off from the earth, and the transgressors shall be rooted out of it.

Proverbs 3:1. My son, forget not my law; but let thine heart keep my commandments:

Proverbs 3:2. For length of days, and long life, and peace, shall they add to thee.

Proverbs 3:3. Let not mercy and truth forsake thee: bind them about thy neck; write them upon the table of thine heart:

Proverbs 3:4. So shalt thou find favour and good understanding in the sight of God and man.

Proverbs 3:5. Trust in the Lord with all thine heart; and lean not unto thine own understanding.

Proverbs 3:6. In all thy ways acknowledge him, and he shall direct thy paths.

Proverbs 3:7. Be not wise in thine own eyes: fear the Lord, and depart from evil.

Proverbs 3:8. It shall be health to thy navel, and marrow to thy bones.

Proverbs 3:16. Length of days is in her right hand; and in her left hand riches and honour.

Proverbs 3:23. Then shalt thou walk in thy way safely, and thy foot shall not stumble.

Proverbs 3:24. When thou liest down, thou shalt not be afraid: yea, thou shalt lie down, and thy sleep shall be sweet.

Proverbs 3:25. Be not afraid of sudden fear, neither of the desolation of the wicked, when it cometh.

Proverbs 3:26. For the Lord shall be thy confidence, and shall keep thy foot from being taken.

Proverbs 3:27. Withhold not good from them to whom it is due, when it is in the power of thine hand to do it.

Proverbs 3:30. Strive not with a man without cause, if he have done thee no harm.

Proverbs 4:6. Forsake her not, and she shall preserve thee: love her, and she shall keep thee.

Proverbs 4:7. Wisdom is the principal thing; therefore get wisdom: and with all thy getting get understanding.

Proverbs 4:8. Exalt her, and she shall promote thee: he shall bring thee to honour, when thou dost embrace her.

Proverbs 4:9. She shall give to thine head an ornament of grace: a crown of glory shall she deliver to thee.

Proverbs 4:11. I have taught thee in the way of wisdom; I have led thee in right paths.

Proverbs 4:12. When thou goest, thy steps shall not be straitened; and when thou runnest, thou shalt not stumble.

Proverbs 4:13. Take fast hold of instruction; let her not go: keep her; for she is thy life.

Proverbs 4:18. But the path of the just is as the shining light, that shineth more and more unto the perfect day.

Proverbs 4:20. My son, attend to my words; incline thine ear unto my sayings.

Proverbs 4:21. Let them not depart from thine eyes; keep them in the midst of thine heart.

Proverbs 4:22. For they are life unto those that find them, and health to all their flesh.

Proverbs 4:23. Keep thy heart with all diligence; for out of it are the issues of life.

Proverbs 4:24. Put away from thee a froward mouth, and perverse lips put far from thee.

Proverbs 4:25. Let thine eyes look right on, and let thine eyelids look straight before thee.

Proverbs 4:26. Ponder the path of thy feet, and let all thy ways be established.

Proverbs 5:15. Drink waters out of thine own cistern, and running waters out of thine own well.

Proverbs 5:16. Let thy fountains be dispersed abroad, and rivers of waters in the streets.

Proverbs 5:17. Let them be only thine own, and not strangers' with thee.

Proverbs 5:18. Let thy fountain be blessed: and rejoice with the wife of thy youth.

Proverbs 5:19. Let her be as the loving hind and pleasant roe; let her breasts satisfy thee at all times; and be thou ravished always with her love.

Proverbs 6:16. These six things doth the Lord hate: yea, seven are an abomination unto him:

Proverbs 6:17. A proud look, a lying tongue, and hands that shed innocent blood,

Proverbs 6:18. An heart that deviseth wicked imaginations, feet that be swift in running to mischief.

Proverbs 6:19. A false witness that speaketh lies, and he that soweth discord among brethren.

Proverbs 8:6. Hear; for I will speak of excellent things; and the opening of my lips shall be right things.

Proverbs 8:7. For my mouth shall speak truth; and wickedness is an abomination to my lips.

Proverbs 8:8. All the words of my mouth are in righteousness; there is nothing froward or perverse in them.

Proverbs 8:17. I love them that love me; and those that seek me early shall find me.

Proverbs 8:32. Now therefore hearken unto me, O ye children: for blessed are they that keep my ways.

Proverbs 10:1. The proverbs of Solomon. A wise son maketh a glad father: but a foolish son is the heaviness of his mother.

Proverbs 10:20. The tongue of the just is as choice silver: the heart of the wicked is little worth.

Proverbs 10:21. The lips of the righteous feed many: but fools die for want of wisdom.

Proverbs 11:2. When pride cometh, then cometh shame: but with the lowly is wisdom.

Proverbs 11:6. The righteousness of the upright shall deliver them: but transgressors shall be taken in their own naughtiness.

Proverbs 11:11. By the blessing of the upright the city is exalted: but it is overthrown by the mouth of the wicked.

Proverbs 11:14. Where no counsel is, the people fall: but in the multitude of counsellors there is safety.

Proverbs 11:27. He that diligently seeketh good procureth favour: but he that seeketh mischief, it shall come unto him.

Proverbs 12:4. A virtuous woman is a crown to her husband: but she that maketh ashamed is as rottenness in his bones.

Proverbs 12:7. The wicked are overthrown, and are not: but the house of the righteous shall stand.

Proverbs 13:1 .A wise son heareth his father's instruction: but a scorner heareth not rebuke.

Proverbs 13:11. Wealth gotten by vanity shall be diminished: but he that gathereth by labour shall increase.

Proverbs 13:20. He that walketh with wise men shall be wise: but a companion of fools shall be destroyed.

Proverbs 14:1. Every wise woman buildeth her house: but the foolish plucketh it down with her hands.

Proverbs 14:15. The simple believeth every word: but the prudent man looketh well to his going.

Proverbs 14:25. A true witness delivereth souls: but a deceitful witness speaketh lies.

Proverbs 15:1. A soft answer turneth away wrath: but grievous words stir up anger.

Proverbs 15:6. In the house of the righteous is much treasure: but in the revenues of the wicked is trouble.

Proverbs 15:8. The sacrifice of the wicked is an abomination to the Lord: but the prayer of the upright is his delight.

Proverbs 15:13. A merry heart maketh a cheerful countenance: but by sorrow of the heart the spirit is broken.

Proverbs 15:30. The light of the eyes rejoiceth the heart: and a good report maketh the bones fat.

Proverbs 15:31. The ear that heareth the reproof of life abideth among the wise.

Proverbs 16:2. All the ways of a man are clean in his own eyes; but the Lord weigheth the spirits.

Proverbs 16:3. Commit thy works unto the Lord, and thy thoughts shall be established.

Proverbs 16:7. When a man's ways please the Lord, he maketh even his enemies to be at peace with him.

Proverbs 16:9. A man's heart deviseth his way: but the Lord directeth his steps.

Proverbs 16:10. A divine sentence is in the lips of the king: his mouth transgresseth not in judgment.

Proverbs 16:12. It is an abomination to kings to commit wickedness: for the throne is established by righteousness.

Proverbs 16:13. Righteous lips are the delight of kings; and they love him that speaketh right.

Proverbs 17:17. A friend loveth at all times, and a brother is born for adversity.

Proverbs 17:22. A merry heart doeth good like a medicine: but a broken spirit drieth the bones.

Proverbs 18:10. The name of the Lord is a strong tower: the righteous runneth into it, and is safe.

Proverbs 18:20. A man's belly shall be satisfied with the fruit of his mouth; and with the increase of his lips shall he be filled.

Proverbs 18:21. Death and life are in the power of the tongue: and they that love it shall eat the fruit thereof.

Proverbs 18:22. Whoso findeth a wife findeth a good thing, and obtaineth favour of the Lord.

Proverbs 18:24. A man that hath friends must shew himself friendly: and there is a friend that sticketh closer than a brother.

Proverbs 19:14. House and riches are the inheritance of fathers: and a prudent wife is from the Lord.

Proverbs 19:17. He that hath pity upon the poor lendeth unto the Lord; and that which he hath given will he pay him again.

Proverbs 20:12. The hearing ear, and the seeing eye, the Lord hath made even both of them.

Proverbs 20:13. Love not sleep, lest thou come to poverty; open thine eyes, and thou shalt be satisfied with bread.

Proverbs 20:26. A wise king scattereth the wicked, and bringeth the wheel over them.

Proverbs 20:27. The spirit of man is the candle of the Lord, searching all the inward parts of the belly.

Proverbs 20:28. Mercy and truth preserve the king: and his throne is upholden by mercy.

Proverbs 21:1. The king's heart is in the hand of the Lord, as the rivers of water: he turneth it whithersoever he will.

Proverbs 21:4. An high look, and a proud heart, and the plowing of the wicked, is sin.

Proverbs 21:5. The thoughts of the diligent tend only to plenteousness; but of every one that is hasty only to want.

Proverbs 21:23. Whoso keepeth his mouth and his tongue keepeth his soul from troubles.

Proverbs 21:29. A wicked man hardeneth his face: but as for the upright, he directeth his way.

Proverbs 22:4. By humility and the fear of the Lord are riches, and honour, and life.

Proverbs 22:6. Train up a child in the way he should go: and when he is old, he will not depart from it.

Proverbs 22:29. A wicked man hardeneth his face: but as for the upright, he directeth his way.

Proverbs 23:1. When thou sittest to eat with a ruler, consider diligently what is before thee.

Proverbs 23:2. And put a knife to thy throat, if thou be a man given to appetite.

Proverbs 23:3. Be not desirous of his dainties: for they are deceitful meat.

Proverbs 24:3. Through wisdom is an house builded; and by understanding it is established:

Proverbs 24:4. And by knowledge shall the chambers be filled with all precious and pleasant riches.

Proverbs 25:15. By long forbearing is a prince persuaded, and a soft tongue breaketh the bone.

Proverbs 25:16. Hast thou found honey? eat so much as is sufficient for thee, lest thou be filled therewith, and vomit it.

Proverbs 28:1. The wicked flee when no man pursueth: but the righteous are bold as a lion.

Proverbs 28:2. For the transgression of a land many are the princes thereof: but by a man of understanding and knowledge the state thereof shall be prolonged.

Proverbs 28:7. Whoso keepeth the law is a wise son: but he that is a companion of riotous men shameth his father.

Proverbs 29:2. When the righteous are in authority, the people rejoice: but when the wicked beareth rule, the people mourn.

Proverbs 29:25. The fear of man bringeth a snare: but whoso putteth his trust in the Lord shall be safe.

Proverbs 31:11. The heart of her husband doth safely trust in her, so that he shall have no need of spoil.

Proverbs 31:12. She will do him good and not evil all the days of her life.

Proverbs 31:25. Strength and honour are her clothing; and she shall rejoice in time to come.

Proverbs 31:26. She openeth her mouth with wisdom; and in her tongue is the law of kindness.

Proverbs 31:27. She looketh well to the ways of her household, and eateth not the bread of idleness.

Proverbs 31:28. Her children arise up, and call her blessed; her husband also, and he praiseth her.

Proverbs 31:29. Many daughters have done virtuously, but thou excellest them all.

Proverbs 31:30. Favour is deceitful, and beauty is vain: but a woman that feareth the Lord, she shall be praised.

Proverbs 31:31. Give her of the fruit of her hands; and let her own works praise her in the gates.

Ecclesiastes 4:9. Two are better than one; because they have a good reward for their labour.

Ecclesiastes 4:10. For if they fall, the one will lift up his fellow: but woe to him that is alone when he falleth; for he hath not another to help him up.

Song of Solomon 2:4. He brought me to the banqueting house, and his banner over me was love.

Isaiah 1:16. Wash you, make you clean; put away the evil of your doings from before mine eyes; cease to do evil;

Isaiah 1:17. Learn to do well; seek judgment, relieve the oppressed, judge the fatherless, plead for the widow.

Isaiah 1:19. If ye be willing and obedient, ye shall eat the good of the land.

Isaiah 6:6. Then flew one of the seraphims unto me, having a live coal in his hand, which he had taken with the tongs from off the altar:

Isaiah 6:7. And he laid it upon my mouth, and said, Lo, this hath touched thy lips; and thine iniquity is taken away, and thy sin purged.

Isaiah 9:6. For unto us a child is born, unto us a son is given: and the government shall be upon his shoulder: and his name shall be called Wonderful, Counsellor, The mighty God, The everlasting Father, The Prince of Peace.

Isaiah 10:27. And it shall come to pass in that day, that his burden shall be taken away from off thy shoulder, and his yoke from off thy neck, and the yoke shall be destroyed because of the anointing.

SCRIPTURES FOR REFERENCE

Isaiah 11:2. And the spirit of the Lord shall rest upon him, the spirit of wisdom and understanding, the spirit of counsel and might, the spirit of knowledge and of the fear of the Lord;

Isaiah 11:3. And shall make him of quick understanding in the fear of the Lord: and he shall not judge after the sight of his eyes, neither reprove after the hearing of his ears.

Isaiah 11:9. They shall not hurt nor destroy in all my holy mountain: for the earth shall be full of the knowledge of the Lord, as the waters cover the sea.

Isaiah 26:3. Thou wilt keep him in perfect peace, whose mind is stayed on thee: because he trusteth in thee.

Isaiah 29:23. But when he seeth his children, the work of mine hands, in the midst of him, they shall sanctify my name, and sanctify the Holy One of Jacob, and shall fear the God of Israel.

Isaiah 29:24. They also that erred in spirit shall come to understanding, and they that murmured shall learn doctrine.

Isaiah 32:15. Until the spirit be poured upon us from on high, and the wilderness be a fruitful field, and the fruitful field be counted for a forest.

Isaiah 32:16. Then judgment shall dwell in the wilderness, and righteousness remain in the fruitful field.

Isaiah 32:17. And the work of righteousness shall be peace; and the effect of righteousness quietness and assurance for ever.

Isaiah 32:18. And my people shall dwell in a peaceable habitation, and in sure dwellings, and in quiet resting places.

Isaiah 33:2. O Lord, be gracious unto us; we have waited for thee: be thou their arm every morning, our salvation also in the time of trouble.

Isaiah 33:6. And wisdom and knowledge shall be the stability of thy times, and strength of salvation: the fear of the Lord is his treasure.

Isaiah 35:3. Strengthen ye the weak hands, and confirm the feeble knees.

Isaiah 35:4. Say to them that are of a fearful heart, Be strong, fear not: behold, your God will come with vengeance, even God with a recompence; he will come and save you.

Isaiah 40:29. He giveth power to the faint; and to them that have no might he increaseth strength.

Isaiah 40:30. Even the youths shall faint and be weary, and the young men shall utterly fall:

Isaiah 40:31. But they that wait upon the Lord shall renew their strength; they shall mount up with wings as eagles; they shall run, and not be weary; and they shall walk, and not faint.

Isaiah 41:10. Fear thou not; for I am with thee: be not dismayed; for I am thy God: I will strengthen thee; yea, I will help thee; yea, I will uphold thee with the right hand of my righteousness.

Isaiah 42:10. Sing unto the Lord a new song, and his praise from the end of the earth, ye that go down to the sea, and all that is therein; the isles, and the inhabitants thereof.

Isaiah 43:1. But now thus saith the Lord that created thee, O Jacob, and he that formed thee, O Israel, Fear not: for I have redeemed thee, I have called thee by thy name; thou art mine.

Isaiah 43:2. When thou passest through the waters, I will be with thee; and through the rivers, they shall not overflow thee: when thou walkest through the fire, thou shalt not be burned; neither shall the flame kindle upon thee.

Isaiah 43:3. For I am the Lord thy God, the Holy One of Israel, thy Saviour: I gave Egypt for thy ransom, Ethiopia and Seba for thee.

Isaiah 43:5. Fear not: for I am with thee: I will bring thy seed from the east, and gather thee from the west;

Isaiah 43:6. I will say to the north, Give up; and to the south, Keep not back: bring my sons from far, and my daughters from the ends of the earth.

Isaiah 43:26. Put me in remembrance: let us plead together: declare thou, that thou mayest be justified.

Isaiah 45:2. I will go before thee, and make the crooked places straight: I will break in pieces the gates of brass, and cut in sunder the bars of iron.

Isaiah 45:17. But Israel shall be saved in the Lord with an everlasting salvation: ye shall not be ashamed nor confounded world without end.

Isaiah 48:17. Thus saith the Lord, thy Redeemer, the Holy One of Israel; I am the Lord thy God which teacheth thee to profit, which leadeth thee by the way that thou shouldest go.

Isaiah 49:25. But thus saith the Lord, Even the captives of the mighty shall be taken away, and the prey of the terrible shall be delivered: for I will contend with him that contendeth with thee, and I will save thy children.

Isaiah 50:4. The Lord God hath given me the tongue of the learned, that I should know how to speak a word in season to him that is weary: he wakeneth morning by morning, he wakeneth mine ear to hear as the learned.

Isaiah 50:10. Who is among you that feareth the Lord, that obeyeth the voice of his servant, that walketh in darkness, and hath no light? let him trust in the name of the Lord, and stay upon his God.

Isaiah 51:7. Hearken unto me, ye that know righteousness, the people in whose heart is my law; fear ye not the reproach of men, neither be ye afraid of their revilings.

Isaiah 51:8. For the moth shall eat them up like a garment, and the worm shall eat them like wool: but my righteousness shall be for ever, and my salvation from generation to generation.

Isaiah 51:11. Therefore the redeemed of the Lord shall return, and come with singing unto Zion; and everlasting joy shall be upon their head: they shall obtain gladness and joy; and sorrow and mourning shall flee away.

Isaiah 53:3. He is despised and rejected of men; a man of sorrows, and acquainted with grief: and we hid as it were our faces from him; he was despised, and we esteemed him not.

Isaiah 53:4. Surely he hath borne our griefs, and carried our sorrows: yet we did esteem him stricken, smitten of God, and afflicted.

Isaiah 53:5. But he was wounded for our transgressions, he was bruised for our iniquities: the chastisement of our peace was upon him; and with his stripes we are healed.

Isaiah 54:4. Fear not; for thou shalt not be ashamed: neither be thou confounded; for thou shalt not be put to shame: for thou shalt forget the shame of thy youth, and shalt not remember the reproach of thy widowhood any more.

Isaiah 54:13. And all thy children shall be taught of the Lord; and great shall be the peace of thy children.

Isaiah 54:14. In righteousness shalt thou be established: thou shalt be far from oppression; for thou shalt not fear: and from terror; for it shall not come near thee.

Isaiah 54:15. Behold, they shall surely gather together, but not by me: whosoever shall gather together against thee shall fall for thy sake.

Isaiah 54:16. Behold, I have created the smith that bloweth the coals in the fire, and that bringeth forth an instrument for his work; and I have created the waster to destroy.

Isaiah 54:17. No weapon that is formed against thee shall prosper; and every tongue that shall rise against thee in judgment thou shalt condemn. This is the heritage of the servants of the Lord, and their righteousness is of me, saith the Lord.

Isaiah 55:8. For my thoughts are not your thoughts, neither are your ways my ways, saith the Lord.

Isaiah 55:11. So shall my word be that goeth forth out of my mouth: it shall not return unto me void, but it shall accomplish that which I please, and it shall prosper in the thing whereto I sent it.

Isaiah 57:8. Behind the doors also and the posts hast thou set up thy remembrance: for thou hast discovered thyself to another than me, and art gone up; thou hast enlarged thy bed, and made thee a covenant with them; thou lovedst their bed where thou sawest it.

Isaiah 57:15. For thus saith the high and lofty One that inhabiteth eternity, whose name is Holy; I dwell in the high and holy place, with him also that is of a contrite and humble spirit, to revive the spirit of the humble, and to revive the heart of the contrite ones.

Isaiah 57:18. I have seen his ways, and will heal him: I will lead him also, and restore comforts unto him and to his mourners.

Isaiah 58:6. Is not this the fast that I have chosen? to loose the bands of wickedness, to undo the heavy burdens, and to let the oppressed go free, and that ye break every yoke?

Isaiah 59:19. So shall they fear the name of the Lord from the west, and his glory from the rising of the sun. When the enemy shall come in like a flood, the Spirit of the Lord shall lift up a standard against him.

Isaiah 60:1. Arise, shine; for thy light is come, and the glory of the Lord is risen upon thee.

Isaiah 61:1. The Spirit of the Lord God is upon me; because the Lord hath anointed me to preach good tidings unto the meek; he hath sent me to bind up the brokenhearted, to proclaim liberty to the captives, and the opening of the prison to them that are bound.

Isaiah 61:3. To appoint unto them that mourn in Zion, to give unto them beauty for ashes, the oil of joy for mourning, the garment of praise for the spirit of heaviness; that they might be called trees of righteousness, the planting of the Lord, that he might be glorified.

Isaiah 61:6. But ye shall be named the Priests of the Lord: men shall call you the Ministers of our God: ye shall eat the riches of the Gentiles, and in their glory shall ye boast yourselves.

Isaiah 62:5. For as a young man marrieth a virgin, so shall thy sons marry thee: and as the bridegroom rejoiceth over the bride, so shall thy God rejoice over thee.

SCRIPTURES FOR REFERENCE

Jeremiah 1:5. Before I formed thee in the belly I knew thee; and before thou camest forth out of the womb I sanctified thee, and I ordained thee a prophet unto the nations.

Jeremiah 1:12. Then said the Lord unto me, Thou hast well seen: for I will hasten my word to perform it.

Jeremiah 15:16. Thy words were found, and I did eat them; and thy word was unto me the joy and rejoicing of mine heart: for I am called by thy name, O Lord God of hosts.

Jeremiah 23:5. Behold, the days come, saith the Lord, that I will raise unto David a righteous Branch, and a King shall reign and prosper, and shall execute judgment and justice in the earth.

Jeremiah 23:6. In his days Judah shall be saved, and Israel shall dwell safely: and this is his name whereby he shall be called, The Lord Our Righteousness.

Jeremiah 29:7. And seek the peace of the city whither I have caused you to be carried away captives, and pray unto the Lord for it: for in the peace thereof shall ye have peace.

Jeremiah 29:8. For thus saith the Lord of hosts, the God of Israel; Let not your prophets and your diviners, that be in the midst of you, deceive you, neither hearken to your dreams which ye cause to be dreamed.

Jeremiah 29:11. For I know the thoughts that I think toward you, saith the Lord, thoughts of peace, and not of evil, to give you an expected end.

Jeremiah 29:12. Then shall ye call upon me, and ye shall go and pray unto me, and I will hearken unto you.

Jeremiah 29:13. And ye shall seek me, and find me, when ye shall search for me with all your heart.

Jeremiah 31:16. Thus saith the Lord; Refrain thy voice from weeping, and thine eyes from tears: for thy work shall be rewarded, saith the Lord; and they shall come again from the land of the enemy.

Jeremiah 31:17. And there is hope in thine end, saith the Lord, that thy children shall come again to their own border.

Jeremiah 32:27. Behold, I am the Lord, the God of all flesh: is there any thing too hard for me?

Jeremiah 33:3. Call unto me, and I will answer thee, and shew thee great and mighty things, which thou knowest not.

Jeremiah 46:27. But fear not thou, O my servant Jacob, and be not dismayed, O Israel: for, behold, I will save thee from afar off, and thy seed from the land of their captivity; and Jacob shall return, and be in rest and at ease, and none shall make him afraid.

Ezekiel 11:19. And I will give them one heart, and I will put a new spirit within you; and I will take the stony heart out of their flesh, and will give them an heart of flesh.

Ezekiel 22:30. And I sought for a man among them, that should make up the hedge, and stand in the gap before me for the land, that I should not destroy it: but I found none.

Ezekiel 48:35. It was round about eighteen thousand measures: and the name of the city from that day shall be, The Lord is there.

Daniel 1:4. Children in whom was no blemish, but well favoured, and skilful in all wisdom, and cunning in knowledge, and understanding science, and such as had ability in them to stand in the king's palace, and whom they might teach the learning and the tongue of the Chaldeans.

Daniel 1:9. Now God had brought Daniel into favour and tender love with the prince of the eunuchs.

Daniel 1:17. As for these four children, God gave them knowledge and skill in all learning and wisdom: and Daniel had understanding in all visions and dreams.

Daniel 1:20. And in all matters of wisdom and understanding, that the king inquired of them, he found them ten times better than all the magicians and astrologers that were in all his realm.

Daniel 9:18. O my God, incline thine ear, and hear; open thine eyes, and behold our desolations, and the city which is called by thy name: for we do not present our supplications before thee for our righteousnesses, but for thy great mercies.

Daniel 10:20. Then said he, Knowest thou wherefore I come unto thee? and now will I return to fight with the prince of Persia: and when I am gone forth, lo, the prince of Grecia shall come.

Daniel 10:21. But I will shew thee that which is noted in the scripture of truth: and there is none that holdeth with me in these things, but Michael your prince.

Hosea 2:18. And in that day will I make a covenant for them with the beasts of the field, and with the fowls of heaven, and with the creeping things of the ground: and I will break the bow and the sword and the battle out of the earth, and will make them to lie down safely.

Joel 3:14. Multitudes, multitudes in the valley of decision: for the day of the Lord is near in the valley of decision.

Zechariah 2:5. For I, saith the Lord, will be unto her a wall of fire round about, and will be the glory in the midst of her.

Zephaniah 3:17. The Lord thy God in the midst of thee is mighty; he will save, he will rejoice over thee with joy; he will rest in his love, he will joy over thee with singing.

Zechariah 10:6. And I will strengthen the house of Judah, and I will save the house of Joseph, and I will bring them again to place them; for I have mercy upon them: and they shall be as though I had not cast them off: for I am the Lord their God, and will hear them.

Zechariah 10:12. And I will strengthen them in the Lord; and they shall walk up and down in his name, saith the Lord.

Zechariah 12:10. And I will pour upon the house of David, and upon the inhabitants of Jerusalem, the spirit of grace and of supplications: and they shall look upon me whom they have pierced, and they shall mourn for him, as one mourneth for his only son, and shall be in bitterness for him, as one that is in bitterness for his firstborn.

Zechariah 14:5. And ye shall flee to the valley of the mountains; for the valley of the mountains shall reach unto Azal: yea, ye shall flee, like as ye fled from before the earthquake in the days of Uzziah king of Judah: and the Lord my God shall come, and all the saints with thee.

Zechariah 14:9. And the Lord shall be king over all the earth: in that day shall there be one Lord, and his name one.

Malachi 3:8. Will a man rob God? Yet ye have robbed me. But ye say, Wherein have we robbed thee? In tithes and offerings.

SCRIPTURES FOR REFERENCE

Malachi 3:9. Ye are cursed with a curse: for ye have robbed me, even this whole nation.

Malachi 3:10. Bring ye all the tithes into the storehouse, that there may be meat in mine house, and prove me now herewith, saith the Lord of hosts, if I will not open you the windows of heaven, and pour you out a blessing, that there shall not be room enough to receive it.

Malachi 3:11. And I will rebuke the devourer for your sakes, and he shall not destroy the fruits of your ground; neither shall your vine cast her fruit before the time in the field, saith the Lord of hosts.

Malachi 3:12. And all nations shall call you blessed: for ye shall be a delightsome land, saith the Lord of hosts.

Matthew 4:4. But he answered and said, It is written, Man shall not live by bread alone, but by every word that proceedeth out of the mouth of God.

Malachi 4:6. And he shall turn the heart of the fathers to the children, and the heart of the children to their fathers, lest I come and smite the earth with a curse.

Matthew 5:4. Blessed are they that mourn: for they shall be comforted.

Matthew 5:5. Blessed are the meek: for they shall inherit the earth.

Matthew 5:14. Ye are the light of the world. A city that is set on an hill cannot be hid.

Matthew 5:16. Let your light so shine before men, that they may see your good works, and glorify your Father which is in heaven.

Matthew 5:37. But let your communication be, Yea, yea; Nay, nay: for whatsoever is more than these cometh of evil.

Matthew 5:44. But I say unto you, Love your enemies, bless them that curse you, do good to them that hate you, and pray for them which despitefully use you, and persecute you.

Matthew 6:6. But thou, when thou prayest, enter into thy closet, and when thou hast shut thy door, pray to thy Father which is in secret; and thy Father which seeth in secret shall reward thee openly.

Matthew 6:7. But when ye pray, use not vain repetitions, as the heathen do: for they think that they shall be heard for their much speaking.

Matthew 6:8. Be not ye therefore like unto them: for your Father knoweth what things ye have need of, before ye ask him.

Matthew 6:9. After this manner therefore pray ye: Our Father which art in heaven, Hallowed be thy name.

Matthew 6:10. Thy kingdom come. Thy will be done in earth, as it is in heaven.

Matthew 6:11. Give us this day our daily bread.

Matthew 6:12. And forgive us our debts, as we forgive our debtors.

Matthew 6:13. And lead us not into temptation, but deliver us from evil: For thine is the kingdom, and the power, and the glory, for ever. Amen.

Matthew 6:14. For if ye forgive men their trespasses, your heavenly Father will also forgive you:

Matthew 6:15. But if ye forgive not men their trespasses, neither will your Father forgive your trespasses.

Matthew 6:25. Therefore I say unto you, Take no thought for your life, what ye shall eat, or what ye shall drink; nor yet for your body, what ye shall put on. Is not the life more than meat, and the body than raiment?

Matthew 6:31. Therefore take no thought, saying, What shall we eat? or, What shall we drink? or, Wherewithal shall we be clothed?

Matthew 6:32. (For after all these things do the Gentiles seek:) for your heavenly Father knoweth that ye have need of all these things.

Matthew 6:33. But seek ye first the kingdom of God, and his righteousness; and all these things shall be added unto you.

Matthew 6:34. Take therefore no thought for the morrow: for the morrow shall take thought for the things of itself. Sufficient unto the day is the evil thereof.

Matthew 7:1. Judge not, that ye be not judged.

Matthew 7:12. Therefore all things whatsoever ye would that men should do to you, do ye even so to them: for this is the law and the prophets.

Matthew 7:14. Because strait is the gate, and narrow is the way, which leadeth unto life, and few there be that find it.

Matthew 8:16. When the even was come, they brought unto him many that were possessed with devils: and he cast out the spirits with his word, and healed all that were sick:

Matthew 8:17. That it might be fulfilled which was spoken by Esaias the prophet, saying, Himself took our infirmities, and bare our sicknesses.

Matthew 9:37. Then saith he unto his disciples, The harvest truly is plenteous, but the labourers are few;

Matthew 9:38. Pray ye therefore the Lord of the harvest, that he will send forth labourers into his harvest.

Matthew 10:38. And he that taketh not his cross, and followeth after me, is not worthy of me.

Matthew 10:39. He that findeth his life shall lose it: and he that loseth his life for my sake shall find it.

Matthew 11:28. Come unto me, all ye that labour and are heavy laden, and I will give you rest.

Matthew 11:29. Take my yoke upon you, and learn of me; for I am meek and lowly in heart: and ye shall find rest unto your souls.

Matthew 11:30. For my yoke is easy, and my burden is light.

Matthew 12:29. Or else how can one enter into a strong man's house, and spoil his goods, except he first bind the strong man? and then he will spoil his house.

Matthew 12:34. O generation of vipers, how can ye, being evil, speak good things? for out of the abundance of the heart the mouth speaketh.

Matthew 12:35. A good man out of the good treasure of the heart bringeth forth good things: and an evil man out of the evil treasure bringeth forth evil things.

Matthew 12:36. But I say unto you, That every idle word that men shall speak, they shall give account thereof in the day of judgment.

Matthew 12:37. For by thy words thou shalt be justified, and by thy words thou shalt be condemned.

Matthew 12:43. When the unclean spirit is gone out of a man, he walketh through dry places, seeking rest, and findeth none.

Matthew 12:44. Then he saith, I will return into my house from whence I came out; and when he is come, he findeth it empty, swept, and garnished.

Matthew 12:45. Then goeth he, and taketh with himself seven other spirits more wicked than himself, and they enter in and dwell there: and the last state of that man is worse than the first. Even so shall it be also unto this wicked generation.

Matthew 13:23. But he that received seed into the good ground is he that heareth the word, and understandeth it; which also beareth fruit, and bringeth forth, some an hundredfold, some sixty, some thirty.

Matthew 15:4. For God commanded, saying, Honour thy father and mother: and, He that curseth father or mother, let him die the death.

Matthew 16:3. And in the morning, It will be foul weather to day: for the sky is red and lowring. O ye hypocrites, ye can discern the face of the sky; but can ye not discern the signs of the times?

Matthew 16:19. And I will give unto thee the keys of the kingdom of heaven: and whatsoever thou shalt bind on earth shall be bound in heaven: and whatsoever thou shalt loose on earth shall be loosed in heaven.

Matthew 18:18. Verily I say unto you, Whatsoever ye shall bind on earth shall be bound in heaven: and whatsoever ye shall loose on earth shall be loosed in heaven.

Matthew 18:19. Again I say unto you, That if two of you shall agree on earth as touching any thing that they shall ask, it shall be done for them of my Father which is in heaven.

Matthew 19:5. And said, For this cause shall a man leave father and mother, and shall cleave to his wife: and they twain shall be one flesh?

Matthew 19:6. Wherefore they are no more twain, but one flesh. What therefore God hath joined together, let not man put asunder.

Matthew 21:22. And all things, whatsoever ye shall ask in prayer, believing, ye shall receive.

Matthew 22:39. And the second is like unto it, Thou shalt love thy neighbour as thyself.

Matthew 23:11. But he that is greatest among you shall be your servant.

Matthew 25:21. His lord said unto him, Well done, thou good and faithful servant: thou hast been faithful over a few things, I will make thee ruler over many things: enter thou into the joy of thy lord.

Matthew 26:41. Watch and pray, that ye enter not into temptation: the spirit indeed is willing, but the flesh is weak.

Mark 4:35. And the same day, when the even was come, he saith unto them, Let us pass over unto the other side.

Mark 7:35. And straightway his ears were opened, and the string of his tongue was loosed, and he spake plain.

Mark 9:23. Jesus said unto him, If thou canst believe, all things are possible to him that believeth.

Mark 9:24. And straightway the father of the child cried out, and said with tears, Lord, I believe; help thou mine unbelief.

Mark 10:29. And Jesus answered and said, Verily I say unto you, There is no man that hath left house, or brethren, or sisters, or father, or mother, or wife, or children, or lands, for my sake, and the gospel's.

Mark 10:30. But he shall receive an hundredfold now in this time, houses, and brethren, and sisters, and mothers, and children, and lands, with persecutions; and in the world to come eternal life.

Mark 11:23. For verily I say unto you, That whosoever shall say unto this mountain, Be thou removed, and be thou cast into the sea;

and shall not doubt in his heart, but shall believe that those things which he saith shall come to pass; he shall have whatsoever he saith.

Mark 11:24. Therefore I say unto you, What things soever ye desire, when ye pray, believe that ye receive them, and ye shall have them.

Mark 11:25. And when ye stand praying, forgive, if ye have ought against any: that your Father also which is in heaven may forgive you your trespasses.

Mark 16:17. And these signs shall follow them that believe; In my name shall they cast out devils; they shall speak with new tongues;

Mark 16:18. They shall take up serpents; and if they drink any deadly thing, it shall not hurt them; they shall lay hands on the sick, and they shall recover.

Mark 16:20. And they went forth, and preached every where, the Lord working with them, and confirming the word with signs following. Amen.

Luke 1:17. And he shall go before him in the spirit and power of Elias, to turn the hearts of the fathers to the children, and the disobedient to the wisdom of the just; to make ready a people prepared for the Lord.

Luke 1:37. For with God nothing shall be impossible.

Luke 1:50. And his mercy is on them that fear him from generation to generation.

Luke 1:80. And the child grew, and waxed strong in spirit, and was in the deserts till the day of his shewing unto Israel.

Luke 2:30. For mine eyes have seen thy salvation,

Luke 2:31. Which thou hast prepared before the face of all people;

Luke 2:32. A light to lighten the Gentiles, and the glory of thy people Israel.

Luke 2:40. And the child grew, and waxed strong in spirit, filled with wisdom: and the grace of God was upon him.

Luke 2:52. And Jesus increased in wisdom and stature, and in favour with God and man.

Luke 4:18. The Spirit of the Lord is upon me, because he hath anointed me to preach the gospel to the poor; he hath sent me to heal the brokenhearted, to preach deliverance to the captives, and recovering of sight to the blind, to set at liberty them that are bruised,

Luke 4:19. To preach the acceptable year of the Lord.

Luke 6:27. But I say unto you which hear, Love your enemies, do good to them which hate you,

Luke 6:28. Bless them that curse you, and pray for them which despitefully use you.

Luke 6:30. Give to every man that asketh of thee; and of him that taketh away thy goods ask them not again.

Luke 6:31. And as ye would that men should do to you, do ye also to them likewise.

Luke 6:35. But love ye your enemies, and do good, and lend, hoping for nothing again; and your reward shall be great, and ye shall be the children of the Highest: for he is kind unto the unthankful and to the evil.

Luke 6:36. Be ye therefore merciful, as your Father also is merciful.

Luke 6:37. Judge not, and ye shall not be judged: condemn not, and ye shall not be condemned: forgive, and ye shall be forgiven:

Luke 6:38. Give, and it shall be given unto you; good measure, pressed down, and shaken together, and running over, shall men give into your bosom. For with the same measure that ye mete withal it shall be measured to you again.

Luke 6:48. He is like a man which built an house, and digged deep, and laid the foundation on a rock: and when the flood arose, the stream beat vehemently upon that house, and could not shake it: for it was founded upon a rock.

Luke 7:23. And blessed is he, whosoever shall not be offended in me.

Luke 7:37. And, behold, a woman in the city, which was a sinner, when she knew that Jesus sat at meat in the Pharisee's house, brought an alabaster box of ointment.

Luke 7:38. And stood at his feet behind him weeping, and began to wash his feet with tears, and did wipe them with the hairs of her head, and kissed his feet, and anointed them with the ointment.

Luke 7:39. Now when the Pharisee which had bidden him saw it, he spake within himself, saying, This man, if he were a prophet, would have known who and what manner of woman this is that toucheth him: for she is a sinner.

Luke 10:19. Behold, I give unto you power to tread on serpents and scorpions, and over all the power of the enemy: and nothing shall by any means hurt you.

Luke 10:27. And he answering said, Thou shalt love the Lord thy God with all thy heart, and with all thy soul, and with all thy strength, and with all thy mind; and thy neighbour as thyself.

Luke 10:28. And he said unto him, Thou hast answered right: this do, and thou shalt live.

Luke 11:13. If ye then, being evil, know how to give good gifts unto your children: how much more shall your heavenly Father give the Holy Spirit to them that ask him?

Luke 12:11. And when they bring you unto the synagogues, and unto magistrates, and powers, take ye no thought how or what thing ye shall answer, or what ye shall say:

Luke 12:12. For the Holy Ghost shall teach you in the same hour what ye ought to say.

Luke 13:11. And, behold, there was a woman which had a spirit of infirmity eighteen years, and was bowed together, and could in no wise lift up herself.

Luke 13:12. And when Jesus saw her, he called her to him, and said unto her, Woman, thou art loosed from thine infirmity.

Luke 17:21. Neither shall they say, Lo here! or, lo there! for, behold, the kingdom of God is within you.

Luke 18:1. And he spake a parable unto them to this end, that men ought always to pray, and not to faint.

Luke 18:27. And he said, The things which are impossible with men are possible with God.

Luke 19:10. For the Son of man is come to seek and to save that which was lost.

Luke 21:11. And great earthquakes shall be in divers places, and famines, and pestilences; and fearful sights and great signs shall there be from heaven.

Luke 21:18. But there shall not an hair of your head perish.

Luke 21:25. And there shall be signs in the sun, and in the moon, and in the stars; and upon the earth distress of nations, with perplexity; the sea and the waves roaring;

Luke 21:26. Men's hearts failing them for fear, and for looking after those things which are coming on the earth: for the powers of heaven shall be shaken.

Luke 21:34. And take heed to yourselves, lest at any time your hearts be overcharged with surfeiting, and drunkenness, and cares of this life, and so that day come upon you unawares.

Luke 23:34. Then said Jesus, Father, forgive them; for they know not what they do. And they parted his raiment, and cast lots.

John 1:9. That was the true Light, which lighteth every man that cometh into the world.

John 1:12. But as many as received him, to them gave he power to become the sons of God, even to them that believe on his name.

John 1:14. And the Word was made flesh, and dwelt among us, (and we beheld his glory, the glory as of the only begotten of the Father,) full of grace and truth.

John 3:6. That which is born of the flesh is flesh; and that which is born of the Spirit is spirit.

John 3:7. Marvel not that I said unto thee, Ye must be born again.

John 3:15. That whosoever believeth in him should not perish, but have eternal life.

John 3:16. For God so loved the world, that he gave his only begotten Son, that whosoever believeth in him should not perish, but have everlasting life.

John 4:13. Jesus answered and said unto her, Whosoever drinketh of this water shall thirst again.

John 6:37. All that the Father giveth me shall come to me; and him that cometh to me I will in no wise cast out.

John 6:38. For I came down from heaven, not to do mine own will, but the will of him that sent me.

John 6:45. It is written in the prophets, And they shall be all taught of God. Every man therefore that hath heard, and hath learned of the Father, cometh unto me.

John 6:48. I am that bread of life.

John 6:49. Your fathers did eat manna in the wilderness, and are dead.

John 6:50. This is the bread which cometh down from heaven, that a man may eat thereof, and not die.

John 6:51. I am the living bread which came down from heaven: if any man eat of this bread, he shall live for ever: and the bread that I will give is my flesh, which I will give for the life of the world.

John 6:63. It is the spirit that quickeneth; the flesh profiteth nothing: the words that I speak unto you, they are spirit, and they are life.

John 7:36. What manner of saying is this that he said, Ye shall seek me, and shall not find me: and where I am, thither ye cannot come?

John 7:37. In the last day, that great day of the feast, Jesus stood and cried, saying, If any man thirst, let him come unto me, and drink.

John 7:38. He that believeth on me, as the scripture hath said, out of his belly shall flow rivers of living water.

John 7:39. (But this spake he of the Spirit, which they that believe on him should receive: for the Holy Ghost was not yet given; because that Jesus was not yet glorified.)

John 8:29. And he that sent me is with me: the Father hath not left me alone; for I do always those things that please him.

John 8:32. And ye shall know the truth, and the truth shall make you free.

John 8:36. If the Son therefore shall make you free, ye shall be free indeed.

John 10:3. To him the porter openeth; and the sheep hear his voice: and he calleth his own sheep by name, and leadeth them out.

John 10:4. And when he putteth forth his own sheep, he goeth before them, and the sheep follow him: for they know his voice.

John 10:5. And a stranger will they not follow, but will flee from him: for they know not; the voice of strangers.

John 10:10. The thief cometh not, but for to steal, and to kill, and to destroy: I am come that they might have life, and that they might have it more abundantly.

John 10:27. My sheep hear my voice, and I know them, and they follow me.

John 10:28. And I give unto them eternal life; and they shall never perish, neither shall any man pluck them out of my hand.

John 10:29. My Father, which gave them me, is greater than all; and no man is able to pluck them out of my Father's hand.

John 12:24. Verily, verily, I say unto you, Except a corn of wheat fall into the ground and die, it abideth alone: but if it die, it bringeth forth much fruit.

John 12:43. For they loved the praise of men more than the praise of God.

John 13:34. A new commandment I give unto you, That ye love one another; as I have loved you, that ye also love one another.

John 14:1. Let not your heart be troubled: ye believe in God, believe also in me.

John 14:6. Jesus saith unto him, I am the way, the truth, and the life: no man cometh unto the Father, but by me.

John 14:13. And whatsoever ye shall ask in my name, that will I do, that the Father may be glorified in the Son.

John 14:16. And I will pray the Father, and he shall give you another Comforter, that he may abide with you for ever;

John 14:17. Even the Spirit of truth; whom the world cannot receive, because it seeth him not, neither knoweth him: but ye know him; for he dwelleth with you, and shall be in you.

John 14:26. But the Comforter, which is the Holy Ghost, whom the Father will send in my name, he shall teach you all things, and bring all things to your remembrance, whatsoever I have said unto you.

John 14:27. Peace I leave with you, my peace I give unto you: not as the world giveth, give I unto you. Let not your heart be troubled, neither let it be afraid.

John 15:1. I am the true vine, and my Father is the husbandman.

John 15:2. Every branch in me that beareth not fruit he taketh away: and every branch that beareth fruit, he purgeth it, that it may bring forth more fruit.

John 15:3. Now ye are clean through the word which I have spoken unto you.

John 15:4. Abide in me, and I in you. As the branch cannot bear fruit of itself, except it abide in the vine; no more can ye, except ye abide in me.

John 15:5. I am the vine, ye are the branches: He that abideth in me, and I in him, the same bringeth forth much fruit: for without me ye can do nothing.

John 15:6. If a man abide not in me, he is cast forth as a branch, and is withered; and men gather them, and cast them into the fire, and they are burned.

John 15:7. If ye abide in me, and my words abide in you, ye shall ask what ye will, and it shall be done unto you.

John 15:8. Herein is my Father glorified, that ye bear much fruit; so shall ye be my disciples.

John 15:13. Greater love hath no man than this, that a man lay down his life for his friends.

John 15:14. Ye are my friends, if ye do whatsoever I command you.

John 15:15. Henceforth I call you not servants; for the servant knoweth not what his lord doeth: but I have called you friends; for all things that I have heard of my Father I have made known unto you.

John 15:16. Ye have not chosen me, but I have chosen you, and ordained you, that ye should go and bring forth fruit, and that your fruit should remain: that whatsoever ye shall ask of the Father in my name, he may give it you.

John 15:26. But when the Comforter is come, whom I will send unto you from the Father, even the Spirit of truth, which proceedeth from the Father, he shall testify of me.

John 16:8. And when he is come, he will reprove the world of sin, and of righteousness, and of judgment:

John 16:9. Of sin, because they believe not on me.

John 16:13. Howbeit when he, the Spirit of truth, is come, he will guide you into all truth: for he shall not speak of himself; but whatsoever he shall hear, that shall he speak: and he will shew you things to come.

John 16:14. He shall glorify me: for he shall receive of mine, and shall shew it unto you.

John 16:15. All things that the Father hath are mine: therefore said I, that he shall take of mine, and shall shew it unto you.

John 16:23. And in that day ye shall ask me nothing. Verily, verily, I say unto you, Whatsoever ye shall ask the Father in my name, he will give it you.

John 16:33. These things I have spoken unto you, that in me ye might have peace. In the world ye shall have tribulation: but be of good cheer; I have overcome the world.

John 17:17. Sanctify them through thy truth: thy word is truth.

John 17:18. As thou hast sent me into the world, even so have I also sent them into the world.

John 17:19. And for their sakes I sanctify myself, that they also might be sanctified through the truth.

John 17:21. That they all may be one; as thou, Father, art in me, and I in thee, that they also may be one in us: that the world may believe that thou hast sent me.

John 17:22. And the glory which thou gavest me I have given them; that they may be one, even as we are one:

John 17:23. I in them, and thou in me, that they may be made perfect in one; and that the world may know that thou hast sent me, and hast loved them, as thou hast loved me.

John 20:23. Whosesoever sins ye remit, they are remitted unto them; and whosesoever sins ye retain, they are retained.

Acts 1:8. But ye shall receive power, after that the Holy Ghost is come upon you: and ye shall be witnesses unto me both in Jerusalem, and in all Judaea, and in Samaria, and unto the uttermost part of the earth.

Acts 2:1. And when the day of Pentecost was fully come, they were all with one accord in one place.

Acts 2:4. And they were all filled with the Holy Ghost, and began to speak with other tongues, as the Spirit gave them utterance.

Acts 2:17. And it shall come to pass in the last days, saith God, I will pour out of my Spirit upon all flesh: and your sons and your daughters shall prophesy, and your young men shall see visions, and your old men shall dream dreams:

Acts 2:18. And on my servants and on my handmaidens I will pour out in those days of my Spirit; and they shall prophesy.

Acts 2:21. And it shall come to pass, that whosoever shall call on the name of the Lord shall be saved.

Acts 2:32. This Jesus hath God raised up, whereof we all are witnesses.

Acts 2:33. Therefore being by the right hand of God exalted, and having received of the Father the promise of the Holy Ghost, he hath shed forth this, which ye now see and hear.

Acts 2:39. For the promise is unto you, and to your children, and to all that are afar off, even as many as the Lord our God shall call.

Acts 2:46. And they, continuing daily with one accord in the temple, and breaking bread from house to house, did eat their meat with gladness and singleness of heart.

Acts 3:16. And his name through faith in his name hath made this man strong, whom ye see and know: yea, the faith which is by him hath given him this perfect soundness in the presence of you all.

Acts 4:10. Be it known unto you all, and to all the people of Israel, that by the name of Jesus Christ of Nazareth, whom ye crucified, whom God raised from the dead, even by him doth this man stand here before you whole.

Acts 4:11. This is the stone which was set at nought of you builders, which is become the head of the corner.

Acts 4:13. Now when they saw the boldness of Peter and John, and perceived that they were unlearned and ignorant men, they marvelled; and they took knowledge of them, that they had been with Jesus.

Acts 4:21. So when they had further threatened them, they let them go, finding nothing how they might punish them, because of the people: for all men glorified God for that which was done.

SCRIPTURES FOR REFERENCE

Acts 4:24. And when they heard that, they lifted up their voice to God with one accord, and said, Lord, thou art God, which hast made heaven, and earth, and the sea, and all that in them is.

Acts 4:29. And now, Lord, behold their threatenings: and grant unto thy servants, that with all boldness they may speak thy word.

Acts 4:30. By stretching forth thine hand to heal; and that signs and wonders may be done by the name of thy holy child Jesus.

Acts 4:31. And when they had prayed, the place was shaken where they were assembled together; and they were all filled with the Holy Ghost, and they spake the word of God with boldness.

Acts 4:34. Neither was there any among them that lacked: for as many as were possessors of lands or houses sold them, and brought the prices of the things that were sold.

Acts 5:12. And by the hands of the apostles were many signs and wonders wrought among the people; (and they were all with one accord in Solomon's porch).

Acts 5:13. And of the rest durst no man join himself to them: but the people magnified them.

Acts 5:16. There came also a multitude out of the cities round about unto Jerusalem, bringing sick folks, and them which were vexed with unclean spirits: and they were healed every one.

Acts 6:3. Wherefore, brethren, look ye out among you seven men of honest report, full of the Holy Ghost and wisdom, whom we may appoint over this business.

Acts 6:10. And they were not able to resist the wisdom and the spirit by which he spake.

Acts 8:12. But when they believed Philip preaching the things concerning the kingdom of God, and the name of Jesus Christ, they were baptized, both men and women.

Acts 8:13. Then Simon himself believed also: and when he was baptized, he continued with Philip, and wondered, beholding the miracles and signs which were done.

Acts 8:14. Now when the apostles which were at Jerusalem heard that Samaria had received the word of God, they sent unto them Peter and John:

Acts 8:15. Who, when they were come down, prayed for them, that they might receive the Holy Ghost:

Acts 8:16. (For as yet he was fallen upon none of them: only they were baptized in the name of the Lord Jesus.)

Acts 8:17. Then laid they their hands on them, and they received the Holy Ghost.

Acts 10:38. How God anointed Jesus of Nazareth with the Holy Ghost and with power: who went about doing good, and healing all that were oppressed of the devil; for God was with him.

Acts 10:44. While Peter yet spake these words, the Holy Ghost fell on all them which heard the word.

Acts 10:45. And they of the circumcision which believed were astonished, as many as came with Peter, because that on the Gentiles also was poured out the gift of the Holy Ghost.

Acts 10:46. For they heard them speak with tongues, and magnify God.

Acts 12:24. But the word of God grew and multiplied.

Acts 16:31. And they said, Believe on the Lord Jesus Christ, and thou shalt be saved, and thy house.

Acts 17:28. For in him we live, and move, and have our being; as certain also of your own poets have said, For we are also his offspring.

Acts 17:29. Forasmuch then as we are the offspring of God, we ought not to think that the Godhead is like unto gold, or silver, or stone, graven by art and man's device.

Acts 19:2. He said unto them, Have ye received the Holy Ghost since ye believed? And they said unto him, We have not so much as heard whether there be any Holy Ghost.

Acts 19:5. When they heard this, they were baptized in the name of the Lord Jesus.

Acts 19:6. And when Paul had laid his hands upon them, the Holy Ghost came on them; and they spake with tongues, and prophesied.

Acts 20:28. Take heed therefore unto yourselves, and to all the flock, over the which the Holy Ghost hath made you overseers, to feed the church of God, which he hath purchased with his own blood.

Acts 20:32. And now, brethren, I commend you to God, and to the word of his grace, which is able to build you up, and to give you an inheritance among all them which are sanctified.

Acts 22:14. And he said, The God of our fathers hath chosen thee, that thou shouldest know his will, and see that Just One, and shouldest hear the voice of his mouth.

Acts 26:18. To open their eyes, and to turn them from darkness to light, and from the power of Satan unto God, that they may receive forgiveness of sins, and inheritance among them which are sanctified by faith that is in me.

Romans 2:4. Or despisest thou the riches of his goodness and forbearance and longsuffering; not knowing that the goodness of God leadeth thee to repentance?

Romans 3:4. God forbid: yea, let God be true, but every man a liar; as it is written, That thou mightest be justified in thy sayings, and mightest overcome when thou art judged.

Romans 3:23. For all have sinned, and come short of the glory of God.

Romans 3:31. Do we then make void the law through faith? God forbid: yea, we establish the law.

Romans 4:4. Now to him that worketh is the reward not reckoned of grace, but of debt.

Romans 4:7. Saying, Blessed are they whose iniquities are forgiven, and whose sins are covered.

Romans 4:8. Blessed is the man to whom the Lord will not impute sin.

Romans 4:17. (As it is written, I have made thee a father of many nations,) before him whom he believed, even God, who quickeneth the dead, and calleth those things which be not as though they were.

Romans 4:24. But for us also, to whom it shall be imputed, if we believe on him that raised up Jesus our Lord from the dead;

Romans 4:25. Who was delivered for our offences, and was raised again for our justification.

Romans 5:3. And not only so, but we glory in tribulations also: knowing that tribulation worketh patience;

Romans 5:4. And patience, experience; and experience, hope:

Romans 5:5. And hope maketh not ashamed; because the love of God is shed abroad in our hearts by the Holy Ghost which is given unto us.

Romans 5:8. But God commendeth his love toward us, in that, while we were yet sinners, Christ died for us.

Romans 5:20. Moreover the law entered, that the offence might abound. But where sin abounded, grace did much more abound.

Romans 6:4. Therefore we are buried with him by baptism into death: that like as Christ was raised up from the dead by the glory of the Father, even so we also should walk in newness of life.

Romans 6:13. Neither yield ye your members as instruments of unrighteousness unto sin: but yield yourselves unto members as instruments of righteousness unto God.

Romans 6:18. Being then made free from sin, ye became the servants of righteousness.

Romans 7:21. I find then a law, that, when I would do good, evil is present with me.

Romans 7:22. For I delight in the law of God after the inward man:

Romans 7:23. But I see another law in my members, warring against the law of my mind, and bringing me into captivity to the law of sin which is in my members.

Romans 7:24. O wretched man that I am! who shall deliver me from the body of this death?

Romans 7:25. I thank God through Jesus Christ our Lord. So then with the mind I myself serve the law of God; but with the flesh the law of sin.

Romans 8:1. There is therefore now no condemnation to them which are in Christ Jesus, who walk not after the flesh, but after the Spirit.

Romans 8:2. For the law of the Spirit of life in Christ Jesus hath made me free from the law of sin and death.

Romans 8:3. For what the law could not do, in that it was weak through the flesh, God sending his own Son in the likeness of sinful flesh, and for sin, condemned sin in the flesh.

Romans 8:4. That the righteousness of the law might be fulfilled in us, who walk not after the flesh, but after the Spirit.

Romans 8:9. But ye are not in the flesh, but in the Spirit, if so be that the Spirit of God dwell in you. Now if any man have not the Spirit of Christ, he is none of his.

Romans 8:10. And if Christ be in you, the body is dead because of sin; but the Spirit is life because of righteousness.

Romans 8:11. But if the Spirit of him that raised up Jesus from the dead dwell in you, he that raised up Christ from the dead shall also quicken your mortal bodies by his Spirit that dwelleth in you.

Romans 8:14. For as many as are led by the Spirit of God, they are the sons of God.

Romans 8:15. For ye have not received the spirit of bondage again to fear; but ye have received the Spirit of adoption, whereby we cry, Abba, Father.

Romans 8:16. The Spirit itself beareth witness with our spirit, that we are the children of God:

Romans 8:17. And if children, then heirs; heirs of God, and joint-heirs with Christ; if so be that we suffer with him, that we may be also glorified together.

Romans 8:18. For I reckon that the sufferings of this present time are not worthy to be compared with the glory which shall be revealed in us.

Romans 8:26. Likewise the Spirit also helpeth our infirmities: for we know not what we should pray for as we ought: but the Spirit itself maketh intercession for us with groanings which cannot be uttered.

Romans 8:27. And he that searcheth the hearts knoweth what is the mind of the Spirit, because he maketh intercession for the saints according to the will of God.

Romans 8:28. And we know that all things work together for good to them that love God, to them who are the called according to his purpose.

Romans 8:29. For whom he did foreknow, he also did predestinate to be conformed to the image of his Son, that he might be the firstborn among many brethren.

Romans 8:30. Moreover whom he did predestinate, them he also called: and whom he called, them he also justified: and whom he justified, them he also glorified.

Romans 8:31. What shall we then say to these things? If God be for us, who can be against us?

Romans 8:32. He that spared not his own Son, but delivered him up for us all, how shall he not with him also freely give us all things?

Romans 8:33. Who shall lay any thing to the charge of God's elect? It is God that justifieth.

Romans 8:34. Who is he that condemneth? It is Christ that died, yea rather, that is risen again, who is even at the right hand of God, who also maketh intercession for us.

Romans 8:35. Who shall separate us from the love of Christ? shall tribulation, or distress, or persecution, or famine, or nakedness, or peril, or sword?

Romans 8:36. As it is written, For thy sake we are killed all the day long; we are accounted as sheep for the slaughter.

Romans 8:37. Nay, in all these things we are more than conquerors through him that loved us.

Romans 8:38. For I am persuaded, that neither death, nor life, nor angels, nor principalities, nor powers, nor things present, nor things to come,

Romans 8:39. Nor height, nor depth, nor any other creature, shall be able to separate us from the love of God, which is in Christ Jesus our Lord.

Romans 9:1. I say the truth in Christ, I lie not, my conscience also bearing me witness in the Holy Ghost.

Romans 10:9. That if thou shalt confess with thy mouth the Lord Jesus, and shalt believe in thine heart that God hath raised him from the dead, thou shalt be saved.

Romans 10:10. For with the heart man believeth unto righteousness; and with the mouth confession is made unto salvation.

Romans 10:13. For whosoever shall call upon the name of the Lord shall be saved.

Romans 10:14. How then shall they call on him in whom they have not believed? and how shall they believe in him of whom they have not heard? and how shall they hear without a preacher?

Romans 10:17. So then faith cometh by hearing, and hearing by the word of God.

Romans 11:7. What then? Israel hath not obtained that which he seeketh for; but the election hath obtained it, and the rest were blinded.

Romans 11:11. I say then, Have they stumbled that they should fall? God forbid: but rather through their fall salvation is come unto the Gentiles, for to provoke them to jealousy.

Romans 11:29. For the gifts and calling of God are without repentance.

Romans 12:1. I beseech you therefore, brethren, by the mercies of God, that ye present your bodies a living sacrifice, holy, acceptable unto God, which is your reasonable service.

Romans 12:2. And be not conformed to this world: but be ye transformed by the renewing of your mind, that ye may prove what is that good, and acceptable, and perfect, will of God.

Romans 12:3. For I say, through the grace given unto me, to every man that is among you, not to think of himself more highly than he ought to think; but to think soberly, according as God hath dealt to every man the measure of faith.

Romans 12:5. So we, being many, are one body in Christ, and every one members one of another.

Romans 12:6. Having then gifts differing according to the grace that is given to us, whether prophecy, let us prophesy according to the proportion of faith.

Romans 12:7. Or ministry, let us wait on our ministering: or he that teacheth, on teaching.

Romans 12:10. Be kindly affectioned one to another with brotherly love; in honour preferring one another;

Romans 12:11. Not slothful in business; fervent in spirit; serving the Lord.

Romans 12:14. Bless them which persecute you: bless, and curse not.

Romans 12:15. Rejoice with them that do rejoice, and weep with them that weep.

Romans 12:16. Be of the same mind one toward another. Mind not high things, but condescend to men of low estate.

Romans 12:17. Be not wise in your own conceits. Recompense to no man evil for evil.

Romans 12:18. Provide things honest in the sight of all men. If it be possible, as much as lieth in you, live peaceably with all men.

Romans 12:21. Be not overcome of evil, but overcome evil with good.

Romans 13:1. Let every soul be subject unto the higher powers. For there is no power but of God: the powers that be are ordained of God.

Romans 13:2. Whosoever therefore resisteth the power, resisteth the ordinance of God: and they that resist shall receive to themselves damnation.

Romans 13:3. For rulers are not a terror to good works, but to the evil. Wilt thou then not be afraid of the power? do that which is good, and thou shalt have praise of the same:

Romans 13:4. For he is the minister of God to thee for good. But if thou do that which is evil, be afraid; for he beareth not the sword in vain: for he is the minister of God, a revenger to execute wrath upon him that doeth evil.

Romans 13:5. Wherefore ye must needs be subject, not only for wrath, but also for conscience sake.

Romans 13:7. Render therefore to all their dues: tribute to whom tribute is due; custom to whom custom; fear to whom fear; honour to whom honour.

Romans 13:8. Owe no man any thing, but to love one another: for he that loveth another hath fulfilled the law.

Romans 13:9. For this, Thou shalt not commit adultery, Thou shalt not kill, Thou shalt not steal, Thou shalt not bear false witness, Thou shalt not covet; and if there be any other commandment, it is briefly comprehended in this saying, namely, Thou shalt love thy neighbour as thyself.

Romans 13:12. The night is far spent, the day is at hand: let us therefore cast off the works of darkness, and let us put on the armour of light.

Romans 13:13. Let us walk honestly, as in the day; not in rioting and drunkenness, not in chambering and wantonness, not in strife and envying.

Romans 13:14. But put ye on the Lord Jesus Christ, and make not provision for the flesh, to fulfil the lusts thereof.

Romans 14:17. For the kingdom of God is not meat and drink; but righteousness, and peace, and joy in the Holy Ghost.

Romans 14:21. It is good neither to eat flesh, nor to drink wine, nor any thing whereby thy brother stumbleth, or is offended, or is made weak.

Romans 15:2. Let every one of us please his neighbour for his good to edification.

Romans 15:18. For I will not dare to speak of any of those things which Christ hath not wrought by me, to make the Gentiles obedient, by word and deed.

Romans 15:21. But as it is written, To whom he was not spoken of, they shall see: and they that have not heard shall understand.

1 Corinthians 1:3. Grace be unto you, and peace, from God our Father, and from the Lord Jesus Christ.

1 Corinthians 1:4. I thank my God always on your behalf, for the grace of God which is given you by Jesus Christ.

1 Corinthians 1:8. Who shall also confirm you unto the end, that ye may be blameless in the day of our Lord Jesus Christ.

1 Corinthians 1:10. Now I beseech you, brethren, by the name of our Lord Jesus Christ, that ye all speak the same thing, and that there be no divisions among you; but that ye be perfectly joined together in the same mind and in the same judgment.

1 Corinthians 1:30. But of him are ye in Christ Jesus, who of God is made unto us wisdom, and righteousness, and sanctification, and redemption.

1 Corinthians 2:7. But we speak the wisdom of God in a mystery, even the hidden wisdom, which God ordained before the world unto our glory.

1 Corinthians 2:8. Which none of the princes of this world knew: for had they known it, they would not have crucified the Lord of glory.

1 Corinthians 2:9. But as it is written, Eye hath not seen, nor ear heard, neither have entered into the heart of man, the things which God hath prepared for them that love him.

1 Corinthians 2:10. But God hath revealed them unto us by his Spirit: for the Spirit searcheth all things, yea, the deep things of God.

1 Corinthians 2:11. For what man knoweth the things of a man, save the spirit of man which is in him? even so the things of God knoweth no man, but the Spirit of God.

1 Corinthians 2:12. Now we have received, not the spirit of the world, but the spirit which is of God; that we might know the things that are freely given to us of God.

1 Corinthians 2:13. Which things also we speak, not in the words which man's wisdom teacheth, but which the Holy Ghost teacheth; comparing spiritual things with spiritual.

1 Corinthians 2:14. But the natural man receiveth not the things of the Spirit of God: for they are foolishness unto him: neither can he know them, because they are spiritually discerned.

1 Corinthians 2:15. But he that is spiritual judgeth all things, yet he himself is judged of no man.

1 Corinthians 2:16. For who hath known the mind of the Lord, that he may instruct him? But we have the mind of Christ.

1 Corinthians 3:6. I have planted, Apollos watered; but God gave the increase.

1 Corinthians 3:9. For we are labourers together with God: ye are God's husbandry, ye are God's building.

1 Corinthians 4:5. Therefore judge nothing before the time, until the Lord come, who both will bring to light the hidden things of darkness, and will make manifest the counsels of the hearts: and then shall every man have praise of God.

1 Corinthians 6:12. All things are lawful unto me, but all things are not expedient: all things are lawful for me, but I will not be brought under the power of any.

1 Corinthians 6:13. Meats for the belly, and the belly for meats: but God shall destroy both it and them. Now the body is not for fornication, but for the Lord; and the Lord for the body.

1 Corinthians 6:17. But he that is joined unto the Lord is one spirit.

1 Corinthians 6:18. Flee fornication. Every sin that a man doeth is without the body; but he that committeth fornication sinneth against his own body.

1 Corinthians 6:19. What? know ye not that your body is the temple of the Holy Ghost which is in you, which ye have of God, and ye are not your own?

1 Corinthians 6:20. For ye are bought with a price: therefore glorify God in your body, and in your spirit, which are God's.

1 Corinthians 7:1. Now concerning the things whereof ye wrote unto me: It is good for a man not to touch a woman.

1 Corinthians 7:2. Nevertheless, to avoid fornication, let every man have his own wife, and let every woman have her own husband.

1 Corinthians 7:3. Let the husband render unto the wife due benevolence: and likewise also the wife unto the husband.

SCRIPTURES FOR REFERENCE

1 Corinthians 7:4. The wife hath not power of her own body, but the husband: and likewise also the husband hath not power of his own body, but the wife.

1 Corinthians 7:5. Defraud ye not one the other, except it be with consent for a time, that ye may give yourselves to fasting and prayer; and come together again, that Satan tempt you not for your incontinency.

1 Corinthians 9:11. If we have sown unto you spiritual things, is it a great thing if we shall reap your carnal things?

1 Corinthians 9:12. If others be partakers of this power over you, are not we rather? Nevertheless we have not used this power; but suffer all things, lest we should hinder the gospel of Christ. Do ye not know that they which minister about holy things live of the things of the temple? and they which wait at the altar are partakers with the altar?

1 Corinthians 9:14. Even so hath the Lord ordained that they which preach the gospel should live of the gospel.

1 Corinthians 9:27. But I keep under my body, and bring it into subjection: lest that by any means, when I have preached to others, I myself should be a castaway.

1 Corinthians 10:13. There hath no temptation taken you but such as is common to man: but God is faithful, who will not suffer you to be tempted above that ye are able; but will with the temptation also make a way to escape, that ye may be able to bear it.

1 Corinthians 11:3. But I would have you know, that the head of every man is Christ; and the head of the woman is the man; and the head of Christ is God.

1 Corinthians 11:7. Now in this that I declare unto you I praise you not, that ye come together not for the better, but for the worse.

1 Corinthians 11:31. For if we would judge ourselves, we should not be judged.

1 Corinthians 12:3. Wherefore I give you to understand, that no man speaking by the Spirit of God calleth Jesus accursed: and that no man can say that Jesus is the Lord, but by the Holy Ghost.

1 Corinthians 12:27. Now ye are the body of Christ, and members in particular.

1 Corinthians 13:4. Charity suffereth long, and is kind; charity envieth not; charity vaunteth not itself, is not puffed up.

1 Corinthians 13:5. Doth not behave itself unseemly, seeketh not her own, is not easily provoked, thinketh no evil.

1 Corinthians 13:6. Rejoiceth not in iniquity, but rejoiceth in the truth.

1 Corinthians 13:7. Beareth all things, believeth all things, hopeth all things, endureth all things.

1 Corinthians 13:8. Charity never faileth: but whether there be prophecies, they shall fail; whether there be tongues, they shall cease; whether there be knowledge, it shall vanish away.

1 Corinthians 13:11. When I was a child, I spake as a child, I understood as a child, I thought as a child: but when I became a man, I put away childish things.

1 Corinthians 14:1. Follow after charity, and desire spiritual gifts, but rather that ye may prophesy.

1 Corinthians 14:18. I thank my God, I speak with tongues more than ye all.

SCRIPTURES FOR REFERENCE

1 Corinthians 14:27. If any man speak in an unknown tongue, let it be by two, or at the most by three, and that by course; and let one interpret.

1 Corinthians 14:33. For God is not the author of confusion, but of peace, as in all churches of the saints.

1 Corinthians 15:33. Be not deceived: evil communications corrupt good manners.

1 Corinthians 15:34. Awake to righteousness, and sin not; for some have not the knowledge of God: I speak this to your shame.

1 Corinthians 16:13. Watch ye, stand fast in the faith, quit you like men, be strong.

2 Corinthians 1:3. Blessed be God, even the Father of our Lord Jesus Christ, the Father of mercies, and the God of all comfort;

2 Corinthians 1:4. Who comforteth us in all our tribulation, that we may be able to comfort them which are in any trouble, by the comfort wherewith we ourselves are comforted of God.

2 Corinthians 1:11. Ye also helping together by prayer for us, that for the gift bestowed upon us by the means of many persons thanks may be given by many on our behalf.

2 Corinthians 1:12. For our rejoicing is this, the testimony of our conscience, that in simplicity and godly sincerity, not with fleshly wisdom, but by the grace of God, we have had our conversation in the world, and more abundantly to you-ward.

2 Corinthians 1:13. For we write none other things unto you, than what ye read or acknowledge; and I trust ye shall acknowledge even to the end.

2 Corinthians 1:24. Not for that we have dominion over your faith, but are helpers of your joy: for by faith ye stand.

2 Corinthians 2:7. So that contrariwise ye ought rather to forgive him, and comfort him, lest perhaps such a one should be swallowed up with overmuch sorrow.

2 Corinthians 2:11. Lest Satan should get an advantage of us: for we are not ignorant of his devices.

2 Corinthians 2:14. Now thanks be unto God, which always causeth us to triumph in Christ, and maketh manifest the savour of his knowledge by us in every place.

2 Corinthians 3:5. Not that we are sufficient of ourselves to think any thing as of ourselves; but our sufficiency is of God;

2 Corinthians 3:6. Who also hath made us able ministers of the new testament; not of the letter, but of the spirit: for the letter killeth, but the spirit giveth life.

2 Corinthians 3:17. Now the Lord is that Spirit: and where the Spirit of the Lord is, there is liberty.

2 Corinthians 3:18. But we all, with open face beholding as in a glass the glory of the Lord, are changed into the same image from glory to glory, even as by the Spirit of the Lord.

2 Corinthians 4:4. In whom the god of this world hath blinded the minds of them which believe not, lest the light of the glorious gospel of Christ, who is the image of God, should shine unto them.

2 Corinthians 4:6. For God, who commanded the light to shine out of darkness, hath shined in our hearts, to give the light of the knowledge of the glory of God in the face of Jesus Christ.

SCRIPTURES FOR REFERENCE

2 Corinthians 4:16. For which cause we faint not; but though our outward man perish, yet the inward man is renewed day by day.

2 Corinthians 4:18. While we look not at the things which are seen, but at the things which are not seen: for the things which are seen are temporal; but the things which are not seen are eternal.

2 Corinthians 5:7. (For we walk by faith, not by sight.)

2 Corinthians 5:17. Therefore if any man be in Christ, he is a new creature: old things are passed away; behold, all things are become new.

2 Corinthians 5:18. And all things are of God, who hath reconciled us to himself by Jesus Christ, and hath given to us the ministry of reconciliation;

2 Corinthians 5:19. To wit, that God was in Christ, reconciling the world unto himself, not imputing their trespasses unto them; and hath committed unto us the word of reconciliation.

2 Corinthians 5:20. Now then we are ambassadors for Christ, as though God did beseech you by us: we pray you in Christ's stead, be ye reconciled to God.

2 Corinthians 5:21. For he hath made him to be sin for us, who knew no sin; that we might be made the righteousness of God in him.

2 Corinthians 6:14. Be ye not unequally yoked together with unbelievers: for what fellowship hath righteousness with unrighteousness? and what communion hath light with darkness?

2 Corinthians 6:17. Wherefore come out from among them, and be ye separate, saith the Lord, and touch not the unclean thing; and I will receive you.

2 Corinthians 7:1. Having therefore these promises, dearly beloved, let us cleanse ourselves from all filthiness of the flesh and spirit, perfecting holiness in the fear of God.

2 Corinthians 9:6. But this I say, He which soweth sparingly shall reap also sparingly; and he which soweth bountifully shall reap also bountifully.

2 Corinthians 9:7. Every man according as he purposeth in his heart, so let him give; not grudgingly, or of necessity: for God loveth a cheerful giver.

2 Corinthians 9:8. And God is able to make all grace abound toward you; that ye, always having all sufficiency in all things, may abound to every good work:

2 Corinthians 9:9. (As it is written, He hath dispersed abroad; he hath given to the poor: his righteousness remaineth for ever.

2 Corinthians 9:10. Now he that ministereth seed to the sower both minister bread for your food, and multiply your seed sown, and increase the fruits of your righteousness;)

2 Corinthians 9:11. Being enriched in every thing to all bountifulness, which causeth through us thanksgiving to God.

2 Corinthians 9:12. For the administration of this service not only supplieth the want of the saints, but is abundant also by many thanksgivings unto God;

2 Corinthians 9:13. Whiles by the experiment of this ministration they glorify God for your professed subjection unto the gospel of Christ, and for your liberal distribution unto them, and unto all men;

2 Corinthians 9:14. And by their prayer for you, which long after you for the exceeding grace of God in you.

2 Corinthians 9:15. Thanks be unto God for his unspeakable gift.

2 Corinthians 10:3. For though we walk in the flesh, we do not war after the flesh:

2 Corinthians 10:4. (For the weapons of our warfare are not carnal, but mighty through God to the pulling down of strong holds;)

2 Corinthians 10:5. Casting down imaginations, and every high thing that exalteth itself against the knowledge of God, and bringing into captivity every thought to the obedience of Christ;

2 Corinthians 10:6. And having in a readiness to revenge all disobedience, when your obedience is fulfilled.

2 Corinthians 12:9. And he said unto me, My grace is sufficient for thee: for my strength is made perfect in weakness. Most gladly therefore will I rather glory in my infirmities, that the power of Christ may rest upon me.

Galatians 1:3. Grace be to you and peace from God the Father, and from our Lord Jesus Christ,

Galatians 1:4. Who gave himself for our sins, that he might deliver us from this present evil world, according to the will of God and our Father:

Galatians 1:5. To whom be glory for ever and ever. Amen.

Galatians 2:20. I am crucified with Christ: nevertheless I live; yet not I, but Christ liveth in me: and the life which I now live in the flesh I live by the faith of the Son of God, who loved me, and gave himself for me.

Galatians 3:13. Christ hath redeemed us from the curse of the law, being made a curse for us: for it is written, Cursed is every one that hangeth on a tree.

Galatians 3:14. That the blessing of Abraham might come on the Gentiles through Jesus Christ; that we might receive the promise of the Spirit through faith.

Galatians 3:27. For as many of you as have been baptized into Christ have put on Christ.

Galatians 3:28. There is neither Jew nor Greek, there is neither bond nor free, there is neither male nor female: for ye are all one in Christ Jesus.

Galatians 5:6. For in Jesus Christ neither circumcision availeth any thing, nor uncircumcision; but faith which worketh by love.

Galatians 5:13. For, brethren, ye have been called unto liberty; only use not liberty for an occasion to the flesh, but by love serve one another.

Galatians 5:22. But the fruit of the Spirit is love, joy, peace, longsuffering, gentleness, goodness, faith,

Galatians 5:23. Meekness, temperance: against such there is no law.

Galatians 5:24. And they that are Christ's have crucified the flesh with the affections and lusts.

Galatians 5:25. If we live in the Spirit, let us also walk in the Spirit.

Galatians 6:4 But let every man prove his own work, and then shall he have rejoicing in himself alone, and not in another.

Galatians 6:5. For every man shall bear his own burden.

Galatians 6:6. Let him that is taught in the word communicate unto him that teacheth in all good things.

Galatians 6:7. Be not deceived; God is not mocked: for whatsoever a man soweth, that shall he also reap.

Galatians 6:8. For he that soweth to his flesh shall of the flesh reap corruption; but he that soweth to the Spirit shall of the Spirit reap life everlasting.

Galatians 6:9. And let us not be weary in well doing: for in due season we shall reap, if we faint not.

Galatians 6:10. As we have therefore opportunity, let us do good unto all men, especially unto them who are of the household of faith.

Ephesians 1:3. Blessed be the God and Father of our Lord Jesus Christ, who hath blessed us with all spiritual blessings in heavenly places in Christ:

Ephesians 1:4. According as he hath chosen us in him before the foundation of the world, that we should be holy and without blame before him in love:

Ephesians 1:5. Having predestinated us unto the adoption of children by Jesus Christ to himself, according to the good pleasure of his will,

Ephesians 1:6. To the praise of the glory of his grace, wherein he hath made us accepted in the beloved.

Ephesians 1:7. In whom we have redemption through his blood, the forgiveness of sins, according to the riches of his grace;

Ephesians 1:8. Wherein he hath abounded toward us in all wisdom and prudence.

Ephesians 1:16. Cease not to give thanks for you, making mention of you in my prayers;

Ephesians 1:17. That the God of our Lord Jesus Christ, the Father of glory, may give unto you the spirit of wisdom and revelation in the knowledge of him:

Ephesians 1:18. The eyes of your understanding being enlightened; that ye may know what is the hope of his calling, and what the riches of the glory of his inheritance in the saints,

Ephesians 1:19. And what is the exceeding greatness of his power to us-ward who believe, according to the working of his mighty power,

Ephesians 1:20. Which he wrought in Christ, when he raised him from the dead, and set him at his own right hand in the heavenly places,

Ephesians 1:22. And hath put all things under his feet, and gave him to be the head over all things to the church,

Ephesians 1:23. Which is his body, the fulness of him that filleth all in all.

Ephesians 2:1. And you hath he quickened, who were dead in trespasses and sins.

Ephesians 2:2. Wherein in time past ye walked according to the course of this world, according to the prince of the power of the air, the spirit that now worketh in the children of disobedience.

Ephesians 2:3. Among whom also we all had our conversation in times past in the lusts of our flesh, fulfilling the desires of the flesh and of the mind; and were by nature the children of wrath, even as others.

Ephesians 2:4. But God, who is rich in mercy, for his great love wherewith he loved us.

Ephesians 2:5. Even when we were dead in sins, hath quickened us together with Christ, (by grace ye are saved).

Ephesians 2:6. And hath raised us up together, and made us sit together in heavenly places in Christ Jesus.

Ephesians 2:7. That in the ages to come he might shew the exceeding riches of his grace in his kindness toward us through Christ Jesus.

Ephesians 2:8. For by grace are ye saved through faith; and that not of yourselves: it is the gift of God.

Ephesians 2:9. Not of works, lest any man should boast.

Ephesians 2:10. For we are his workmanship, created in Christ Jesus unto good works, which God hath before ordained that we should walk in them.

Ephesians 2:13. But now in Christ Jesus ye who sometimes were far off are made nigh by the blood of Christ.

Ephesians 2:14. For he is our peace, who hath made both one, and hath broken down the middle wall of partition between us;

Ephesians 2:15. Having abolished in his flesh the enmity, even the law of commandments contained in ordinances; for to make in himself of twain one new man, so making peace;

Ephesians 2:16. And that he might reconcile both unto God in one body by the cross, having slain the enmity thereby:

Ephesians 2:17. And came and preached peace to you which were afar off, and to them that were nigh.

Ephesians 2:18. For through him we both have access by one Spirit unto the Father.

Ephesians 2:19. Now therefore ye are no more strangers and foreigners, but fellowcitizens with the saints, and of the household of God;

Ephesians 2:20. And are built upon the foundation of the apostles and prophets, Jesus Christ himself being the chief corner stone;

Ephesians 2:21. In whom all the building fitly framed together groweth unto an holy temple in the Lord:

Ephesians 2:22. In whom ye also are builded together for an habitation of God through the Spirit.

Ephesians 3:12. In whom we have boldness and access with confidence by the faith of him.

Ephesians 3:14. For this cause I bow my knees unto the Father of our Lord Jesus Christ,

Ephesians 3:15. Of whom the whole family in heaven and earth is named,

Ephesians 3:16. That he would grant you, according to the riches of his glory, to be strengthened with might by his Spirit in the inner man.

Ephesians 3:17. That Christ may dwell in your hearts by faith; that ye, being rooted and grounded in love.

Ephesians 3:18. May be able to comprehend with all saints what is the breadth, and length, and depth, and height.

Ephesians 3:19. And to know the love of Christ, which passeth knowledge, that ye might be filled with all the fulness of God.

Ephesians 3:20. Now unto him that is able to do exceeding abundantly above all that we ask or think, according to the power that worketh in us.

Ephesians 4:2. With all lowliness and meekness, with longsuffering, forbearing one another in love.

Ephesians 4:3. Endeavouring to keep the unity of the Spirit in the bond of peace.

Ephesians 4:4. There is one body, and one Spirit, even as ye are called in one hope of your calling;

Ephesians 4:5. One Lord, one faith, one baptism,

Ephesians 4:6. One God and Father of all, who is above all, and through all, and in you all.

Ephesians 4:11. And he gave some, apostles; and some, prophets; and some, evangelists; and some, pastors and teachers.

Ephesians 4:12. For the perfecting of the saints, for the work of the ministry, for the edifying of the body of Christ.

Ephesians 4:13. Till we all come in the unity of the faith, and of the knowledge of the Son of God, unto a perfect man, unto the measure of the stature of the fulness of Christ.

Ephesians 4:14. That we henceforth be no more children, tossed to and fro, and carried about with every wind of doctrine, by the sleight of men, and cunning craftiness, whereby they lie in wait to deceive;

Ephesians 4:15. But speaking the truth in love, may grow up into him in all things, which is the head, even Christ:

Ephesians 4:16. From whom the whole body fitly joined together and compacted by that which every joint supplieth, according to the effectual working in the measure of every part, maketh increase of the body unto the edifying of itself in love.

Ephesians 4:20. But ye have not so learned Christ;

Ephesians 4:21. If so be that ye have heard him, and have been taught by him, as the truth is in Jesus:

Ephesians 4:22. That ye put off concerning the former conversation the old man, which is corrupt according to the deceitful lusts.

Ephesians 4:23. And be renewed in the spirit of your mind;

Ephesians 4:24. And that ye put on the new man, which after God is created in righteousness and true holiness.

Ephesians 4:26. Be ye angry, and sin not: let not the sun go down upon your wrath:

Ephesians 4:27. Neither give place to the devil.

Ephesians 4:28. Let him that stole steal no more: but rather let him labour, working with his hands the thing which is good, that he may have to give to him that needeth.

Ephesians 4:29. Let no corrupt communication proceed out of your mouth, but that which is good to the use of edifying, that it may minister grace unto the hearers.

Ephesians 4:30. And grieve not the holy Spirit of God, whereby ye are sealed unto the day of redemption.

Ephesians 4:31. Let all bitterness, and wrath, and anger, and clamour, and evil speaking, be put away from you, with all malice.

Ephesians 4:32. And be ye kind one to another, tenderhearted, forgiving one another, even as God for Christ's sake hath forgiven you.

Ephesians 5:1. Be ye therefore followers of God, as dear children.

Ephesians 5:2. And walk in love, as Christ also hath loved us, and hath given himself for us an offering and a sacrifice to God for a sweetsmelling savour.

Ephesians 5:3. But fornication, and all uncleanness, or covetousness, let it not be once named among you, as becometh saints.

Ephesians 5:4. Neither filthiness, nor foolish talking, nor jesting, which are not convenient: but rather giving of thanks.

Ephesians 5:8. For ye were sometimes darkness, but now are ye light in the Lord: walk as children of light:

Ephesians 5:9. (For the fruit of the Spirit is in all goodness and righteousness and truth.)

Ephesians 5:13. But all things that are reproved are made manifest by the light: for whatsoever doth make manifest is light.

Ephesians 5:15. See then that ye walk circumspectly, not as fools, but as wise.

Ephesians 5:16. Redeeming the time, because the days are evil.

Ephesians 5:17. Wherefore be ye not unwise, but understanding what the will of the Lord is.

Ephesians 5:18. And be not drunk with wine, wherein is excess; but be filled with the Spirit.

Ephesians 5:19. Speaking to yourselves in psalms and hymns and spiritual songs, singing and making melody in your heart to the Lord.

Ephesians 5:20. Giving thanks always for all things unto God and the Father in the name of our Lord Jesus Christ;

Ephesians 5:21. Submitting yourselves one to another in the fear of God.

Ephesians 5:22. Wives, submit yourselves unto your own husbands, as unto the Lord.

Ephesians 5:23. For the husband is the head of the wife, even as Christ is the head of the church: and he is the saviour of the body.

Ephesians 5:24. Therefore as the church is subject unto Christ, so let the wives be to their own husbands in every thing.

Ephesians 5:25. Husbands, love your wives, even as Christ also loved the church, and gave himself for it.

Ephesians 5:26. That he might sanctify and cleanse it with the washing of water by the word.

Ephesians 5:27. That he might present it to himself a glorious church, not having spot, or wrinkle, or any such thing; but that it should be holy and without blemish.

Ephesians 5:28. So ought men to love their wives as their own bodies. He that loveth his wife loveth himself.

Ephesians 5:29. For no man ever yet hated his own flesh; but nourisheth and cherisheth it, even as the Lord the church.

Ephesians 5:30. For we are members of his body, of his flesh, and of his bones.

Ephesians 5:30. For we are members of his body, of his flesh, and of his bones.

Ephesians 5:33. Nevertheless let every one of you in particular so love his wife even as himself; and the wife see that she reverence her husband.

Ephesians 6:1. Children, obey your parents in the Lord: for this is right.

Ephesians 6:2. Honour thy father and mother; which is the first commandment with promise.

Ephesians 6:3. That it may be well with thee, and thou mayest live long on the earth.

Ephesians 6:4. And, ye fathers, provoke not your children to wrath: but bring them up in the nurture and admonition of the Lord.

Ephesians 6:5. Servants, be obedient to them that are your masters according to the flesh, with fear and trembling, in singleness of your heart, as unto Christ;

Ephesians 6:6. Not with eyeservice, as menpleasers; but as the servants of Christ, doing the will of God from the heart;

Ephesians 6:7. With good will doing service, as to the Lord, and not to men:

Ephesians 6:8. Knowing that whatsoever good thing any man doeth, the same shall he receive of the Lord, whether he be bond or free.

Ephesians 6:10. Finally, my brethren, be strong in the Lord, and in the power of his might.

Ephesians 6:11. Put on the whole armour of God, that ye may be able to stand against the wiles of the devil.

Ephesians 6:12. For we wrestle not against flesh and blood, but against principalities, against powers, against the rulers of the darkness of this world, against spiritual wickedness in high places.

Ephesians 6:13. Wherefore take unto you the whole armour of God, that ye may be able to withstand in the evil day, and having done all, to stand.

Ephesians 6:14. Stand therefore, having your loins girt about with truth, and having on the breastplate of righteousness;

Ephesians 6:15. And your feet shod with the preparation of the gospel of peace.

Ephesians 6:16. Above all, taking the shield of faith, wherewith ye shall be able to quench all the fiery darts of the wicked.

Ephesians 6:17. And take the helmet of salvation, and the sword of the Spirit, which is the word of God.

Ephesians 6:18. Praying always with all prayer and supplication in the Spirit, and watching thereunto with all perseverance and supplication for all saints;

Ephesians 6:19. And for me, that utterance may be given unto me, that I may open my mouth boldly, to make known the mystery of the gospel,

Ephesians 6:20. For which I am an ambassador in bonds: that therein I may speak boldly, as I ought to speak.

Ephesians 6:24. Grace be with all them that love our Lord Jesus Christ in sincerity. Amen.

Philippians 1:4. Always in every prayer of mine for you all making request with joy,

Philippians 1:5. For your fellowship in the gospel from the first day until now;

Philippians 1:6. Being confident of this very thing, that he which hath begun a good work in you will perform it until the day of Jesus Christ:

Philippians 1:7. Even as it is meet for me to think this of you all, because I have you in my heart; inasmuch as both in my bonds, and in the defence and confirmation of the gospel, ye all are partakers of my grace.

Philippians 1:8. For God is my record, how greatly I long after you all in the bowels of Jesus Christ.

Philippians 1:9. And this I pray, that your love may abound yet more and more in knowledge and in all judgment.

Philippians 1:10. That ye may approve things that are excellent; that ye may be sincere and without offence till the day of Christ.

Philippians 1:11. Being filled with the fruits of righteousness, which are by Jesus Christ, unto the glory and praise of God.

Philippians 1:20. According to my earnest expectation and my hope, that in nothing I shall be ashamed, but that with all boldness, as always, so now also Christ shall be magnified in my body, whether it be by life, or by death.

Philippians 1:25. And having this confidence, I know that I shall abide and continue with you all for your furtherance and joy of faith;

Philippians 1:26. That your rejoicing may be more abundant in Jesus Christ for me by my coming to you again.

Philippians 1:27. Only let your conversation be as it becometh the gospel of Christ: that whether I come and see you, or else be absent, I may hear of your affairs, that ye stand fast in one spirit, with one mind striving together for the faith of the gospel;

Philippians 1:28. And in nothing terrified by your adversaries: which is to them an evident token of perdition, but to you of salvation, and that of God.

Philippians 2:2. Fulfil ye my joy, that ye be likeminded, having the same love, being of one accord, of one mind.

Philippians 2:3. Let nothing be done through strife or vainglory; but in lowliness of mind let each esteem other better than themselves.

Philippians 2:4. Look not every man on his own things, but every man also on the things of others.

Philippians 2:5. Let this mind be in you, which was also in Christ Jesus.

Philippians 2:9. Wherefore God also hath highly exalted him, and given him a name which is above every name.

Philippians 2:10. That at the name of Jesus every knee should bow, of things in heaven, and things in earth, and things under the earth;

Philippians 2:11. And that every tongue should confess that Jesus Christ is Lord, to the glory of God the Father.

Philippians 2:12. Wherefore, my beloved, as ye have always obeyed, not as in my presence only, but now much more in my absence, work out your own salvation with fear and trembling.

Philippians 2:13. For it is God which worketh in you both to will and to do of his good pleasure.

Philippians 2:14. Do all things without murmurings and disputings.

Philippians 2:15. That ye may be blameless and harmless, the sons of God, without rebuke, in the midst of a crooked and perverse nation, among whom ye shine as lights in the world.

Philippians 2:16. Holding forth the word of life; that I may rejoice in the day of Christ, that I have not run in vain, neither laboured in vain.

Philippians 3:1. Finally, my brethren, rejoice in the Lord. To write the same things to you, to me indeed is not grievous, but for you it is safe.

Philippians 3:7. But what things were gain to me, those I counted loss for Christ.

Philippians 3:8. Yea doubtless, and I count all things but loss for the excellency of the knowledge of Christ Jesus my Lord: for whom I have suffered the loss of all things, and do count them but dung, that I may win Christ,

Philippians 3:9. And be found in him, not having mine own righteousness, which is of the law, but that which is through the faith of Christ, the righteousness which is of God by faith:

Philippians 3:10. That I may know him, and the power of his resurrection, and the fellowship of his sufferings, being made conformable unto his death;

Philippians 3:11. If by any means I might attain unto the resurrection of the dead.

Philippians 3:12. Not as though I had already attained, either were already perfect: but I follow after, if that I may apprehend that for which also I am apprehended of Christ Jesus.

Philippians 3:13. Brethren, I count not myself to have apprehended: but this one thing I do, forgetting those things which are behind, and reaching forth unto those things which are before,

Philippians 3:14. I press toward the mark for the prize of the high calling of God in Christ Jesus.

Philippians 3:15. Let us therefore, as many as be perfect, be thus minded: and if in any thing ye be otherwise minded, God shall reveal even this unto you.

Philippians 3:16. Nevertheless, whereto we have already attained, let us walk by the same rule, let us mind the same thing.

Philippians 3:17. Brethren, be followers together of me, and mark them which walk so as ye have us for an ensample.

Philippians 4:4. Rejoice in the Lord alway: and again I say, Rejoice.

Philippians 4:5. Let your moderation be known unto all men. The Lord is at hand.

Philippians 4:6. Be careful for nothing; but in every thing by prayer and supplication with thanksgiving let your requests be made known unto God.

Philippians 4:7. And the peace of God, which passeth all understanding, shall keep your hearts and minds through Christ Jesus.

Philippians 4:8. Finally, brethren, whatsoever things are true, whatsoever things are honest, whatsoever things are just, whatsoever things are pure, whatsoever things are lovely, whatsoever things are of good report; if there be any virtue, and if there be any praise, think on these things.

Philippians 4:9. Those things, which ye have both learned, and received, and heard, and seen in me, do: and the God of peace shall be with you.

Philippians 4:11. Not that I speak in respect of want: for I have learned, in whatsoever state I am, therewith to be content.

Philippians 4:12. I know both how to be abased, and I know how to abound: every where and in all things I am instructed both to be full and to be hungry, both to abound and to suffer need.

Philippians 4:13. I can do all things through Christ which strengtheneth me.

Philippians 4:17. Not because I desire a gift: but I desire fruit that may abound to your account.

Philippians 4:18. But I have all, and abound: I am full, having received of Epaphroditus the things which were sent from you, an odour of a sweet smell, a sacrifice acceptable, wellpleasing to God.

Philippians 4:19. But my God shall supply all your need according to his riches in glory by Christ Jesus.

Colossians 1:9. For this cause we also, since the day we heard it, do not cease to pray for you, and to desire that ye might be filled with the knowledge of his will in all wisdom and spiritual understanding.

Colossians 1:10. That ye might walk worthy of the Lord unto all pleasing, being fruitful in every good work, and increasing in the knowledge of God;

Colossians 1:11. Strengthened with all might, according to his glorious power, unto all patience and longsuffering with joyfulness;

Colossians 1:12. Giving thanks unto the Father, which hath made us meet to be partakers of the inheritance of the saints in light:

Colossians 1:13. Who hath delivered us from the power of darkness, and hath translated us into the kingdom of his dear Son:

Colossians 1:14. In whom we have redemption through his blood, even the forgiveness of sins.

Colossians 1:29. Whereunto I also labour, striving according to his working, which worketh in me mightily.

Colossians 2:3. In whom are hid all the treasures of wisdom and knowledge.

Colossians 2:5. For though I be absent in the flesh, yet am I with you in the spirit, joying and beholding your order, and the stedfastness of your faith in Christ.

Colossians 2:6. As ye have therefore received Christ Jesus the Lord, so walk ye in him.

Colossians 2:7. Rooted and built up in him, and stablished in the faith, as ye have been taught, abounding therein with thanksgiving.

Colossians 2:9. For in him dwelleth all the fulness of the Godhead bodily.

Colossians 2:10. And ye are complete in him, which is the head of all principality and power.

Colossians 2:14. Blotting out the handwriting of ordinances that was against us, which was contrary to us, and took it out of the way, nailing it to his cross.

Colossians 2:15. And having spoiled principalities and powers, he made a shew of them openly, triumphing over them in it.

Colossians 3:2. Set your affection on things above, not on things on the earth.

Colossians 3:12. Put on therefore, as the elect of God, holy and beloved, bowels of mercies, kindness, humbleness of mind, meekness, longsuffering;

Colossians 3:13. Forbearing one another, and forgiving one another, if any man have a quarrel against any: even as Christ forgave you, so also do ye.

Colossians 3:14. And above all these things put on charity, which is the bond of perfectness.

Colossians 3:15. And let the peace of God rule in your hearts, to the which also ye are called in one body; and be ye thankful.

Colossians 3:16. Let the word of Christ dwell in you richly in all wisdom; teaching and admonishing one another in Psalm and hymns and spiritual songs, singing with grace in your hearts to the Lord.

Colossians 3:17. And whatsoever ye do in word or deed, do all in the name of the Lord Jesus, giving thanks to God and the Father by him.

Colossians 3:21. Fathers, provoke not your children to anger, lest they be discouraged.

Colossians 3:22. Servants, obey in all things your masters according to the flesh; not with eyeservice, as menpleasers; but in singleness of heart, fearing God:

Colossians 3:23. And whatsoever ye do, do it heartily, as to the Lord, and not unto men.

Colossians 3:24. Knowing that of the Lord ye shall receive the reward of the inheritance: for ye serve the Lord Christ.

Colossians 4:2. Continue in prayer, and watch in the same with thanksgiving.

Colossians 4:6. Let your speech be alway with grace, seasoned with salt, that ye may know how ye ought to answer every man.

Colossians 4:12. Epaphras, who is one of you, a servant of Christ, saluteth you, always labouring fervently for you in prayers, that ye may stand perfect and complete in all the will of God.

1 Thessalonians 4:3. For this is the will of God, even your sanctification, that ye should abstain from fornication:

1 Thessalonians 4:4. That every one of you should know how to possess his vessel in sanctification and honour;

1 Thessalonians 4:5. Not in the lust of concupiscence, even as the Gentiles which know not God.

1 Thessalonians 4:8. He therefore that despiseth, despiseth not man, but God, who hath also given unto us his holy Spirit.

1 Thessalonians 4:11. And that ye study to be quiet, and to do your own business, and to work with your own hands, as we commanded you;

1 Thessalonians 4:12. That ye may walk honestly toward them that are without, and that ye may have lack of nothing.

1 Thessalonians 4:13. But I would not have you to be ignorant, brethren, concerning them which are asleep, that ye sorrow not, even as others which have no hope.

1 Thessalonians 4:16. For the Lord himself shall descend from heaven with a shout, with the voice of the archangel, and with the trump of God: and the dead in Christ shall rise first:

1 Thessalonians 4:17. Then we which are alive and remain shall be caught up together with them in the clouds, to meet the Lord in the air: and so shall we ever be with the Lord.

1 Thessalonians 5:8. But let us, who are of the day, be sober, putting on the breastplate of faith and love; and for an helmet, the hope of salvation.

1 Thessalonians 5:11. Wherefore comfort yourselves together, and edify one another, even as also ye do.

1 Thessalonians 5:18. In every thing give thanks: for this is the will of God in Christ Jesus concerning you.

1 Thessalonians 5:22. Abstain from all appearance of evil.

1 Thessalonians 5:23. And the very God of peace sanctify you wholly; and I pray God your whole spirit and soul and body be preserved blameless unto the coming of our Lord Jesus Christ.

1 Thessalonians 5:24. Faithful is he that calleth you, who also will do it.

2 Thessalonians 2:16. Now our Lord Jesus Christ himself, and God, even our Father, which hath loved us, and hath given us everlasting consolation and good hope through grace.

2 Thessalonians 3:3. But the Lord is faithful, who shall stablish you, and keep you from evil.

2 Thessalonians 3:12. Now them that are such we command and exhort by our Lord Jesus Christ, that with quietness they work, and eat their own bread.

2 Thessalonians 3:13. But ye, brethren, be not weary in well doing.

1 Timothy 2:1. I exhort therefore, that, first of all, supplications, prayers, intercessions, and giving of thanks, be made for all men;

1 Timothy 2:2. For kings, and for all that are in authority; that we may lead a quiet and peaceable life in all godliness and honesty.

1 Timothy 2:3. For this is good and acceptable in the sight of God our Saviour.

1 Timothy 4:4. For every creature of God is good, and nothing to be refused, if it be received with thanksgiving:

1 Timothy 4:5. For it is sanctified by the word of God and prayer.

1 Timothy 4:8. For bodily exercise profiteth little: but godliness is profitable unto all things, having promise of the life that now is, and of that which is to come.

1 Timothy 5:8. But if any provide not for his own, and specially for those of his own house, he hath denied the faith, and is worse than an infidel.

1 Timothy 6:12. Fight the good fight of faith, lay hold on eternal life, whereunto thou art also called, and hast professed a good profession before many witnesses.

2 Timothy 1:7. For God hath not given us the spirit of fear; but of power, and of love, and of a sound mind.

2 Timothy 1:8. Be not thou therefore ashamed of the testimony of our Lord, nor of me his prisoner: but be thou partaker of the afflictions of the gospel according to the power of God.

2 Timothy 1:12. For the which cause I also suffer these things: nevertheless I am not ashamed: for I know whom I have believed, and am persuaded that he is able to keep that which I have committed unto him against that day.

2 Timothy 1:13. Hold fast the form of sound words, which thou hast heard of me, in faith and love which is in Christ Jesus.

2 Timothy 1:14. That good thing which was committed unto thee keep by the Holy Ghost which dwelleth in us.

2 Timothy 2:9. Wherein I suffer trouble, as an evil doer, even unto bonds; but the word of God is not bound.

2 Timothy 2:15. Study to shew thyself approved unto God, a workman that needeth not to be ashamed, rightly dividing the word of truth.

2 Timothy 2:16. But shun profane and vain babblings: for they will increase unto more ungodliness.

2 Timothy 2:21. If a man therefore purge himself from these, he shall be a vessel unto honour, sanctified, and meet for the master's use, and prepared unto every good work.

2 Timothy 2:22. Flee also youthful lusts: but follow righteousness, faith, charity, peace, with them that call on the Lord out of a pure heart.

2 Timothy 2:23. But foolish and unlearned questions avoid, knowing that they do gender strifes.

2 Timothy 2:24. And the servant of the Lord must not strive; but be gentle unto all men, apt to teach, patient,

2 Timothy 2:25. In meekness instructing those that oppose themselves; if God peradventure will give them repentance to the acknowledging of the truth;

2 Timothy 2:26. And that they may recover themselves out of the snare of the devil, who are taken captive by him at his will.

2 Timothy 3:2. For men shall be lovers of their own selves, covetous, boasters, proud, blasphemers, disobedient to parents, unthankful, unholy,

2 Timothy 3:3. Without natural affection, trucebreakers, false accusers, incontinent, fierce, despisers of those that are good,

2 Timothy 3:4. Traitors, heady, highminded, lovers of pleasures more than lovers of God;

2 Timothy 3:5. Having a form of godliness, but denying the power thereof: from such turn away.

2 Timothy 3:6. For of this sort are they which creep into houses, and lead captive silly women laden with sins, led away with divers lusts,

2 Timothy 3:7. Ever learning, and never able to come to the knowledge of the truth.

2 Timothy 3:8. Now as Jannes and Jambres withstood Moses, so do these also resist the truth: men of corrupt minds, reprobate concerning the faith.

2 Timothy 3:9. But they shall proceed no further: for their folly shall be manifest unto all men, as theirs also was.

2 Timothy 3:14. But continue thou in the things which thou hast learned and hast been assured of, knowing of whom thou hast learned them;

2 Timothy 3:15. And that from a child thou hast known the holy scriptures, which are able to make thee wise unto salvation through faith which is in Christ Jesus.

2 Timothy 4:18. And the Lord shall deliver me from every evil work, and will preserve me unto his heavenly kingdom: to whom be glory for ever and ever. Amen.

Titus 1:11. Whose mouths must be stopped, who subvert whole houses, teaching things which they ought not, for filthy lucre's sake.

Titus 2:4. That they may teach the young women to be sober, to love their husbands, to love their children,

Titus 2:5. To be discreet, chaste, keepers at home, good, obedient to their own husbands, that the word of God be not blasphemed.

Titus 2:6. Young men likewise exhort to be sober minded.

Titus 2:11. For the grace of God that bringeth salvation hath appeared to all men,

Titus 2:12. Teaching us that, denying ungodliness and worldly lusts, we should live soberly, righteously, and godly, in this present world;

Titus 2:13. Looking for that blessed hope, and the glorious appearing of the great God and our Saviour Jesus Christ.

Titus 3:1. Put them in mind to be subject to principalities and powers, to obey magistrates, to be ready to every good work.

Titus 3:14. And let ours also learn to maintain good works for necessary uses, that they be not unfruitful.

Philemon 6. That the communication of thy faith may become effectual by the acknowledging of every good thing which is in you in Christ Jesus.

Hebrews 1:14. Are they not all ministering spirits, sent forth to minister for them who shall be heirs of salvation?

Hebrews 2:11. For both he that sanctifieth and they who are sanctified are all of one: for which cause he is not ashamed to call them brethren.

Hebrews 2:15. And deliver them who through fear of death were all their lifetime subject to bondage.

Hebrews 3:1. Wherefore, holy brethren, partakers of the heavenly calling, consider the Apostle and High Priest of our profession, Christ Jesus;

Hebrews 3:7. Wherefore (as the Holy Ghost saith, To day if ye will hear his voice,

Hebrews 3:8. Harden not your hearts, as in the provocation, in the day of temptation in the wilderness:

Hebrews 3:14. For we are made partakers of Christ, if we hold the beginning of our confidence stedfast unto the end.

Hebrews 4:10. For he that is entered into his rest, he also hath ceased from his own works, as God did from his.

Hebrews 4:11. Let us labour therefore to enter into that rest, lest any man fall after the same example of unbelief.

Hebrews 4:12. For the word of God is quick, and powerful, and sharper than any twoedged sword, piercing even to the dividing asunder of soul and spirit, and of the joints and marrow, and is a discerner of the thoughts and intents of the heart.

Hebrews 4:14. Seeing then that we have a great high priest, that is passed into the heavens, Jesus the Son of God, let us hold fast our profession.

Hebrews 4:15. For we have not an high priest which cannot be touched with the feeling of our infirmities; but was in all points tempted like as we are, yet without sin.

Hebrews 4:16. Let us therefore come boldly unto the throne of grace, that we may obtain mercy, and find grace to help in time of need.

Hebrews 7:22. By so much was Jesus made a surety of a better testament.

Hebrews 9:6. Now when these things were thus ordained, the priests went always into the first tabernacle, accomplishing the service of God.

Hebrews 9:7. But into the second went the high priest alone once every year, not without blood, which he offered for himself, and for the errors of the people:

Hebrews 9:8. The Holy Ghost this signifying, that the way into the holiest of all was not yet made manifest, while as the first tabernacle was yet standing:

Hebrews 9:9. Which was a figure for the time then present, in which were offered both gifts and sacrifices, that could not make him that did the service perfect, as pertaining to the conscience;

Hebrews 9:10. Which stood only in meats and drinks, and divers washings, and carnal ordinances, imposed on them until the time of reformation.

Hebrews 9:11. But Christ being come an high priest of good things to come, by a greater and more perfect tabernacle, not made with hands, that is to say, not of this building;

Hebrews 9:12. Neither by the blood of goats and calves, but by his own blood he entered in once into the holy place, having obtained eternal redemption for us.

Hebrews 9:13. For if the blood of bulls and of goats, and the ashes of an heifer sprinkling the unclean, sanctifieth to the purifying of the flesh:

Hebrews 9:14. How much more shall the blood of Christ, who through the eternal Spirit offered himself without spot to God, purge your conscience from dead works to serve the living God?

Hebrews 10:16. This is the covenant that I will make with them after those days, saith the Lord, I will put my laws into their hearts, and in their minds will I write them.

Hebrews 10:19. Having therefore, brethren, boldness to enter into the holiest by the blood of Jesus.

Hebrews 10:23. Let us hold fast the profession of our faith without wavering; (for he is faithful that promised;)

Hebrews 10:24. And let us consider one another to provoke unto love and to good works:

Hebrews 10:25. Not forsaking the assembling of ourselves together, as the manner of some is; but exhorting one another: and so much the more, as ye see the day approaching.

Hebrews 10:35. Cast not away therefore your confidence, which hath great recompence of reward.

Hebrews 10:38. Now the just shall live by faith: but if any man draw back, my soul shall have no pleasure in him.

Hebrews 11:6. But without faith it is impossible to please him: for he that cometh to God must believe that he is, and that he is a rewarder of them that diligently seek him.

Hebrews 12:1. Wherefore seeing we also are compassed about with so great a cloud of witnesses, let us lay aside every weight, and the sin which doth so easily beset us, and let us run with patience the race that is set before us.

Hebrews 12:2. Looking unto Jesus the author and finisher of our faith; who for the joy that was set before him endured the cross, despising the shame, and is set down at the right hand of the throne of God.

Hebrews 12:3. For consider him that endured such contradiction of sinners against himself, lest ye be wearied and faint in your minds.

SCRIPTURES FOR REFERENCE

Hebrews 12:12. Wherefore lift up the hands which hang down, and the feeble knees;

Hebrews 12:13. And make straight paths for your feet, lest that which is lame be turned out of the way; but let it rather be healed.

Hebrews 12:14. Follow peace with all men, and holiness, without which no man shall see the Lord:

Hebrews 12:15. Looking diligently lest any man fail of the grace of God; lest any root of bitterness springing up trouble you, and thereby many be defiled.

Hebrews 12:24. And to Jesus the mediator of the new covenant, and to the blood of sprinkling, that speaketh better things than that of Abel.

Hebrews 13:4. Marriage is honourable in all, and the bed undefiled: but whoremongers and adulterers God will judge.

Hebrews 13:5. Let your conversation be without covetousness; and be content with such things as ye have: for he hath said, I will never leave thee, nor forsake thee.

Hebrews 13:6. So that we may boldly say, The Lord is my helper, and I will not fear what man shall do unto me.

Hebrews 13:8. Jesus Christ the same yesterday, and to day, and for ever.

Hebrews 13:15. By him therefore let us offer the sacrifice of praise to God continually, that is, the fruit of our lips giving thanks to his name.

Hebrews 13:20. Now the God of peace, that brought again from the dead our Lord Jesus, that great shepherd of the sheep, through the blood of the everlasting covenant.

James 1:2. My brethren, count it all joy when ye fall into divers temptations;

James 1:3. Knowing this, that the trying of your faith worketh patience.

James 1:4. But let patience have her perfect work, that ye may be perfect and entire, wanting nothing.

James 1:5. If any of you lack wisdom, let him ask of God, that giveth to all men liberally, and upbraideth not; and it shall be given him.

James 1:6. But let him ask in faith, nothing wavering. For he that wavereth is like a wave of the sea driven with the wind and tossed.

James 1:7. For let not that man think that he shall receive any thing of the Lord.

James 1:8. A double minded man is unstable in all his ways.

James 1:13. Let no man say when he is tempted, I am tempted of God: for God cannot be tempted with evil, neither tempteth he any man.

James 1:17. Every good gift and every perfect gift is from above, and cometh down from the Father of lights, with whom is no variableness, neither shadow of turning.

James 1:19. Wherefore, my beloved brethren, let every man be swift to hear, slow to speak, slow to wrath.

James 1:21. Wherefore lay apart all filthiness and superfluity of naughtiness, and receive with meekness the engrafted word, which is able to save your souls.

James 1:22. But be ye doers of the word, and not hearers only, deceiving your own selves.

James 1:23. For if any be a hearer of the word, and not a doer, he is like unto a man beholding his natural face in a glass:

James 1:24. For he beholdeth himself, and goeth his way, and straightway forgetteth what manner of man he was.

James 1:25. But whoso looketh into the perfect law of liberty, and continueth therein, he being not a forgetful hearer, but a doer of the work, this man shall be blessed in his deed.

James 2:1. My brethren, have not the faith of our Lord Jesus Christ, the Lord of glory, with respect of persons.

James 2:17. Even so faith, if it hath not works, is dead, being alone.

James 3:1. My brethren, be not many masters, knowing that we shall receive the greater condemnation.

James 3:2. For in many things we offend all. If any man offend not in word, the same is a perfect man, and able also to bridle the whole body.

James 3:5. Even so the tongue is a little member, and boasteth great things. Behold, how great a matter a little fire kindleth!

James 3:6. And the tongue is a fire, a world of iniquity: so is the tongue among our members, that it defileth the whole body, and setteth on fire the course of nature; and it is set on fire of hell.

James 3:17. But the wisdom that is from above is first pure, then peaceable, gentle, and easy to be intreated, full of mercy and good fruits, without partiality, and without hypocrisy.

James 3:18. And the fruit of righteousness is sown in peace of them that make peace.

James 3:9. Therewith bless we God, even the Father; and therewith curse we men, which are made after the similitude of God.

James 3:10. Out of the same mouth proceedeth blessing and cursing. My brethren, these things ought not so to be.

James 3:11. Doth a fountain send forth at the same place sweet water and bitter?

James 3:12. Can the fig tree, my brethren, bear olive berries? either a vine, figs? so can no fountain both yield salt water and fresh.

James 3:13. Who is a wise man and endued with knowledge among you? let him shew out of a good conversation his works with meekness of wisdom.

James 3:14. But if ye have bitter envying and strife in your hearts, glory not, and lie not against the truth.

James 3:15. This wisdom descendeth not from above, but is earthly, sensual, devilish.

James 3:16. For where envying and strife is, there is confusion and every evil work.

James 4:2. Ye lust, and have not: ye kill, and desire to have, and cannot obtain: ye fight and war, yet ye have not, because ye ask not.

James 4:3. Ye ask, and receive not, because ye ask amiss, that ye may consume it upon your lusts.

James 4:6. But he giveth more grace. Wherefore he saith, God resisteth the proud, but giveth grace unto the humble.

James 4:7. Submit yourselves therefore to God. Resist the devil, and he will flee from you.

James 4:8. Draw nigh to God, and he will draw nigh to you. Cleanse your hands, ye sinners; and purify your hearts, ye double minded.

James 4:10. Humble yourselves in the sight of the Lord, and he shall lift you up.

James 5:5. Ye have lived in pleasure on the earth, and been wanton; ye have nourished your hearts, as in a day of slaughter.

James 5:6. Ye have condemned and killed the just; and he cloth not resist you.

James 5:7. Be patient therefore, brethren, unto the coming of the Lord. Behold, the husbandman waiteth for the precious fruit of the earth, and hath long patience for it, until he receive the early and latter rain.

James 5:8. Be ye also patient; stablish your hearts: for the coming of the Lord draweth nigh.

James 5:15. And the prayer of faith shall save the sick, and the Lord shall raise him up; and if he have committed sins, they shall be forgiven him.

James 5:16. Confess your faults one to another, and pray one for another, that ye may be healed. The effectual fervent prayer of a righteous man availeth much.

1 Peter 1:2. Elect according to the foreknowledge of God the Father, through sanctification of the Spirit, unto obedience and sprinkling of the blood of Jesus Christ: Grace unto you, and peace, be multiplied.

1 Peter 1:6. Wherein ye greatly rejoice, though now for a season, if need be, ye are in heaviness through manifold temptations:

1 Peter 1:7. That the trial of your faith, being much more precious than of gold that perisheth, though it be tried with fire, might be found unto praise and honour and glory at the appearing of Jesus Christ.

1 Peter 1:13. Wherefore gird up the loins of your mind, be sober, and hope to the end for the grace that is to be brought unto you at the revelation of Jesus Christ.

1 Peter 1:18. Forasmuch as ye know that ye were not redeemed with corruptible things, as silver and gold, from your vain conversation received by tradition from your fathers;

1 Peter 1:19. But with the precious blood of Christ, as of a lamb without blemish and without spot.

1 Peter 1:23. Being born again, not of corruptible seed, but of incorruptible, by the word of God, which liveth and abideth for ever.

1 Peter 2:1. Wherefore laying aside all malice, and all guile, and hypocrisies, and envies, and all evil speakings,

1 Peter 2:2. As newborn babes, desire the sincere milk of the word, that ye may grow thereby.

1 Peter 2:6. Wherefore also it is contained in the scripture, Behold, I lay in Sion a chief corner stone, elect, precious: and he that believeth on him shall not be confounded.

1 Peter 2:23. Who, when he was reviled, reviled not again; when he suffered, he threatened not; but committed himself to him that judgeth righteously:

1 Peter 2:24. Who his own self bare our sins in his own body on the tree, that we, being dead to sins, should live unto righteousness: by whose stripes ye were healed.

1 Peter 3:1. Likewise, ye wives, be in subjection to your own husbands; that, if any obey not the word, they also may without the word be won by the conversation of the wives;

1 Peter 3:2. While they behold your chaste conversation coupled with fear.

1 Peter 3:3. Whose adorning let it not be that outward adorning of plaiting the hair, and of wearing of gold, or of putting on of apparel;

1 Peter 3:4. But let it be the hidden man of the heart, in that which is not corruptible, even the ornament of a meek and quiet spirit, which is in the sight of God of great price.

1 Peter 3:5. For after this manner in the old time the holy women also, who trusted in God, adorned themselves, being in subjection unto their own husbands.

1 Peter 3:7. Likewise, ye husbands, dwell with them according to knowledge, giving honour unto the wife, as unto the weaker vessel, and as being heirs together of the grace of life; that your prayers be not hindered.

1 Peter 3:8. Finally, be ye all of one mind, having compassion one of another, love as brethren, be pitiful, be courteous.

1 Peter 3:9. Not rendering evil for evil, or railing for railing: but contrariwise blessing; knowing that ye are thereunto called, that ye should inherit a blessing.

1 Peter 3:11. Let him eschew evil, and do good; let him seek peace, and ensue it.

1 Peter 3:12. For the eyes of the Lord are over the righteous, and his ears are open unto their prayers: but the face of the Lord is against them that do evil.

1 Peter 3:13. And who is he that will harm you, if ye be followers of that which is good?

1 Peter 3:14. But and if ye suffer for righteousness' sake, happy are ye: and be not afraid of their terror, neither be troubled;

1 Peter 3:15. But sanctify the Lord God in your hearts: and be ready always to give an answer to every man that asketh you a reason of the hope that is in you with meekness and fear:

1 Peter 3:16. Having a good conscience; that, whereas they speak evil of you, as of evildoers, they may be ashamed that falsely accuse your good conversation in Christ.

1 Peter 3:17. For it is better, if the will of God be so, that ye suffer for well doing, than for evil doing.

1 Peter 3:18. For Christ also hath once suffered for sins, the just for the unjust, that he might bring us to God, being put to death in the flesh, but quickened by the Spirit.

1 Peter 4:7. But the end of all things is at hand: be ye therefore sober, and watch unto prayer.

1 Peter 4:8. And above all things have fervent charity among yourselves: for charity shall cover the multitude of sins.

1 Peter 5:2. Feed the flock of God which is among you, taking the oversight thereof, not by constraint, but willingly; not for filthy lucre, but of a ready mind.

1 Peter 5:3. Neither as being lords over God's heritage, but being ensamples to the flock.

1 Peter 5:4. And when the chief Shepherd shall appear, ye shall receive a crown of glory that fadeth not away.

1 Peter 5:5. Likewise, ye younger, submit yourselves unto the elder. Yea, all of you be subject one to another, and be clothed with humility: for God resisteth the proud, and giveth grace to the humble.

1 Peter 5:6. Humble yourselves therefore under the mighty hand of God, that he may exalt you in due time:

1 Peter 5:7. Casting all your care upon him; for he careth for you.

1 Peter 5:8. Be sober, be vigilant; because your adversary the devil, as a roaring lion, walketh about, seeking whom he may devour.

1 Peter 5:9. Whom resist stedfast in the faith, knowing that the same afflictions are accomplished in your brethren that are in the world.

1 Peter 5:10. But the God of all grace, who hath called us unto his eternal glory by Christ Jesus, after that ye have suffered a while, make you perfect, stablish, strengthen, settle you.

2 Peter 1:6. And to knowledge temperance; and to temperance patience; and to patience godliness.

2 Peter 3:9. The Lord is not slack concerning his promise, as some men count slackness; but is longsuffering to us-ward, not willing that any should perish, but that all should come to repentance.

2 Peter 3:18. But grow in grace, and in the knowledge of our Lord and Saviour Jesus Christ. To him be glory both now and for ever. Amen.

1 John 1:3. That which we have seen and heard declare we unto you, that ye also may have fellowship with us: and truly our fellowship is with the Father, and with his Son Jesus Christ.

1 John 1:7. But if we walk in the light, as he is in the light, we have fellowship one with another, and the blood of Jesus Christ his Son cleanseth us from all sin.

1 John 1:9. If we confess our sins, he is faithful and just to forgive us our sins, and to cleanse us from all unrighteousness.

1 John 2:5. But whoso keepeth his word, in him verily is the love of God perfected: hereby know we that we are in him.

1 John 2:12. I write unto you, little children, because your sins are forgiven you for his name's sake.

1 John 2:13. I write unto you, fathers, because ye have known him that is from the beginning. I write unto you, young men, because ye have overcome the wicked one. I write unto you, little children, because ye have known the Father.

1 John 2:14. I have written unto you, fathers, because ye have known him that is from the beginning. I have written unto you, young men, because ye are strong, and the word of God abideth in you, and ye have overcome the wicked one.

1 John 2:15. Love not the world, neither the things that are in the world. If any man love the world, the love of the Father is not in him.

1 John 2:16. For all that is in the world, the lust of the flesh, and the lust of the eyes, and the pride of life, is not of the Father, but is of the world.

1 John 2:17. And the world passeth away, and the lust thereof: but he that doeth the will of God abideth for ever.

1 John 2:20. But ye have an unction from the Holy One, and ye know all things.

1 John 2:21. I have not written unto you because ye know not the truth, but because ye know it, and that no lie is of the truth.

1 John 2:24. Let that therefore abide in you, which ye have heard from the beginning. If that which ye have heard from the beginning shall remain in you, ye also shall continue in the Son, and in the Father.

1 John 2:27. But the anointing which ye have received of him abideth in you, and ye need not that any man teach you: but as the same anointing teacheth you of all things, and is truth, and is no lie, and even as it hath taught you, ye shall abide in him.

1 John 3:1. Behold, what manner of love the Father hath bestowed upon us, that we should be called the sons of God: therefore the world knoweth us not, because it knew him not.

1 John 3:2. Beloved, now are we the sons of God; and it Both not yet appear what we shall be: but we know that, when he shall appear, we shall be like him; for we shall see him as he is.

1 John 3:3. And every man that hath this hope in him purifieth himself, even as he is pure.

1 John 3:8. He that committeth sin is of the devil; for the devil sinneth from the beginning. For this purpose the Son of God was manifested, that he might destroy the works of the devil.

1 John 3:9. Whosoever is born of God doth not commit sin; for his seed remaineth in him: and he cannot sin, because he is born of God.

1 John 3:18. My little children, let us not love in word, neither in tongue; but in deed and in truth.

1 John 3:22. And whatsoever we ask, we receive of him, because we keep his commandments, and do those things that are pleasing in his sight.

1 John 3:23. And this is his commandment, That we should believe on the name of his Son Jesus Christ, and love one another, as he gave us commandment.

1 John 4:4. Ye are of God, little children, and have overcome them: because greater is he that is in you, than he that is in the world.

1 John 4:12. No man hath seen God at any time. If we love one another, God dwelleth in us, and his love is perfected in us.

1 John 4:16. And we have known and believed the love that God hath to us. God is love; and he that dwelleth in love dwelleth in God, and God in him.

1 John 4:17. Herein is our love made perfect, that we may have boldness in the day of judgment: because as he is, so are we in this world.

1 John 4:18. There is no fear in love; but perfect love casteth out fear: because fear hath torment. He that feareth is not made perfect in love.

1 John 4:19. We love him, because he first loved us.

1 John 5:3. For this is the love of God, that we keep his commandments: and his commandments are not grievous.

1 John 5:4. For whatsoever is born of God overcometh the world: and this is the victory that overcometh the world, even our faith.

1 John 5:5. Who is he that overcometh the world, but he that believeth that Jesus is the Son of God?

1 John 5:14. And this is the confidence that we have in him, that, if we ask any thing according to his will, he heareth us:

1 John 5:15. And if we know that he hear us, whatsoever we ask, we know that we have the petitions that we desired of him.

SCRIPTURES FOR REFERENCE

1 John 5:16. If any man see his brother sin a sin which is not unto death, he shall ask, and he shall give him life for them that sin not unto death. There is a sin unto death: I do not say that he shall pray for it.

1 John 5:18. We know that whosoever is born of God sinneth not; but he that is begotten of God keepeth himself, and that wicked one toucheth him not.

1 John 5:19. And we know that we are of God, and the whole world lieth in wickedness.

1 John 5:21. Little children, keep yourselves from idols. Amen.

3 John 2. Beloved, I wish above all things that thou mayest prosper and be in health, even as thy soul prospereth.

3 John 4. I have no greater joy than to hear that my children walk in truth.

Jude 1:20. But ye, beloved, building up yourselves on your most holy faith, praying in the Holy Ghost.

Revelation 3:8. I know thy works: behold, I have set before thee an open door, and no man can shut it: for thou hast a little strength, and hast kept my word, and hast not denied my name.

Revelation 4:11. Thou art worthy, O Lord, to receive glory and honour and power: for thou hast created all things, and for thy pleasure they are and were created.

Revelation 5:8. And when he had taken the book, the four beasts and four and twenty elders fell down before the Lamb, having every one of them harps, and golden vials full of odours, which are the prayers of saints.

Revelation 11:15. And the seventh angel sounded; and there were great voices in heaven, saying, The kingdoms of this world are become the kingdoms of our Lord, and of his Christ; and he shall reign for ever and ever.

Revelation 12:11. And they overcame him by the blood of the Lamb, and by the word of their testimony; and they loved not their lives unto the death.

Revelation 22:1. And he shewed me a pure river of water of life, clear as crystal, proceeding out of the throne of God and of the Lamb.

Revelation 22:2. In the midst of the street of it, and on either side of the river, was there the tree of life, which bare twelve manner of fruits, and yielded her fruit every month: and the leaves of the tree were for the healing of the nations.

ABOUT THE AUTHOR

Germaine Griffin Copeland, founder and president of Word Ministries, Inc., is the author of the *Prayers That Avail Much*® family of books. Her writings provide scriptural prayer instruction to help you pray effectively for those things that concern you and your family and for other prayer assignments. Her teachings on prayer, the personal growth of the intercessor, emotional healing, and related subjects have brought understanding, hope, healing, and liberty to the discouraged and emotionally wounded. She is a woman of prayer and praise whose highest form of worship is the study of God's Word. Her greatest desire is to know God.

Word Ministries, Inc. is a prayer and teaching ministry. Germaine believes that God has called her to teach the practical application of the Word of Truth for successful, victorious living. After years of searching diligently for truth and trying again and again to come out of depression, she decided that she was a mistake. Out of the depths of despair she called upon the name of the Lord, and the light of God's presence invaded the room where she was sitting.

It was in that moment that she experienced the warmth of God's love; old things passed away, and she felt brand new. She discovered a motivation for living—life had purpose. Living in the presence of God, she has found unconditional love and acceptance, healing for crippled emotions, contentment that overcomes depression, peace in the midst of adverse circumstances, and grace for developing healthy relationships. The ongoing process of transformation evolved into praying for others, and the prayer of intercession became her prayer focus.

Germaine is the daughter of the late Reverend A. H. "Buck" and Donnis Brock Griffin. She and her husband, Everette, have four children, and their prayer assignments increase as grandchildren and great-grandchildren are born into the family. Germaine and Everette reside in Roswell, a suburb of Atlanta, Georgia.

MISSION STATEMENT

Word Ministries, Inc.

Motivating individuals to pray
Encouraging them to achieve intimacy with God
Bringing emotional wholeness and spiritual growth

You may contact Word Ministries by writing:

Word Ministries, Inc.
38 Sloan Street
Roswell, Georgia 30075
or calling 770-518-1065

www.prayers.org

*Please include your testimonies
and praise reports when you write.*

OTHER BOOKS BY GERMAINE COPELAND

www.harrisonhouse.com

Fast. Easy. Convenient!

◆ New Book Information

◆ Look Inside the Book

◆ Press Releases

◆ Bestsellers

◆ Free E-News

◆ Author Biographies

◆ Upcoming Books

◆ Share Your Testimony

◆ Online Product Availability

◆ Product Specials

◆ Order Online

For the latest in book news and author information, please visit us on the Web at www.harrisonhouse.com. Get up-to-date pictures and details on all our powerful and life-changing products. Sign up for our e-mail newsletter, *Friends of the House,* and receive free monthly information on our authors and products including testimonials, author announcements, and more!

Harrison House—
Books That Bring Hope, Books That Bring Change

THE HARRISON HOUSE VISION

Proclaiming the truth and the power

Of the Gospel of Jesus Christ

With excellence;

Challenging Christians to

Live victoriously,

Grow spiritually,

Know God intimately.